The Symphony
Orchestra
and its
Instruments

——

This 1993 edition published by Crescent Books,
distributed by Outlet Book Company,
Inc., a Random House Company,
40 Engelhard Avenue, Avenel, New Jersey 07001
Random House
New York ▪Toronto ▪London ▪Sydney ▪Auckland
Printed and bound in Spain 1993
ISBN 0-517-051-757

THE SYMPHONY ORCHESTRA AND ITS INSTRUMENTS
has been originated, designed and produced
by AB Nordbok, Gothenburg, Sweden.
EDITOR: Siri Reuterstrand
GRAPHIC DESIGN: Claes Franzén/Mix Direction
ARTWORK: Ulf Söderqvist
CONSULTANT: Magnus Haglund
TRANSLATOR: Jon van Leuven

Nordbok would like to express special thanks to
the Gothenburg Symphony Orchestra and the Gothenburg Opera Orchestra
for their contributions to this book.

The Symphony
Orchestra
and its
Instruments

Sven Kruckenberg

CRESCENT BOOKS
NEW YORK · AVENEL, NEW JERSEY

Contents

Preface

*A*s a musicologist Sven Kruckenberg is well known for his many years of collaboration with the great Swedish orchestras. Like all wise men of art and science, he is modest about his proficiency; yet this makes it the more gratifying that a comprehensive, and equally detailed, book about the symphony orchestra has issued from his pen. Its value will certainly soon gain international recognition.

The work is in three movements, and these are united. Both amateurs and specialists are shown clearly, first, how the large orchestras of our time have developed, and which individuals have contributed to their form. Next, the craft of conducting is followed – from the days when dictatorial leaders stamped a rhythm on the floor, to the modern master with his or her slender baton. Finally a discussion of the orchestra's varied instruments is deepened by turning, for instance, to Berlioz' theory of instrumentation – which was later revised and, with a twinkle in his eye, revitalized by Richard Strauss.

Attractive, too, are the humorous episodes from musical history with which the author spices his narrative. Levity has always had its place in the musician's profession.

OTMAR SUITNER

PROFESSOR, VIENNA COLLEGE OF MUSIC

(FORMERLY MUSICAL DIRECTOR OF THE GERMAN NATIONAL OPERA IN BERLIN)

Introduction

The fascinating world of the symphony orchestra well deserves a glimpse into its workings, which this book tries to provide in an easily accessible form. As one of the most refined artistic expressions of Western civilization, the symphony orchestra is central to musical life in many countries. Its sounds are an endless source of emotional experience for millions of people. They find in it everything from a moment of comfort, or escape from the daily routine, to great inspiration and enrichment of other activities. Human beings, whether at times of crisis or of creativity, draw strength from the pure energy of orchestral music.

There may be more than symbolic significance in the fact that, since the recent political changes in Eastern Europe began, those who were chosen to lead their nations are not seldom members of artistic professions – including musical ones. That  they were taken seriously enough to be given positions of power is a cause for hope. Naturally, artists are not infallible; but in general they have something which is lacking in ordinary bureaucrats and bigwigs, regardless of their party affiliations. They possess a feeling for other dimensions of existence than what is normally measured by opinion polls or superficial achievements. Artists are devoted to liberating and stimulating the inner life of the individual. They are humanists defending human values.

For symphony orchestras, too, optimism is justified in an age when many of them are struggling with economic problems, and when they are sometimes viewed as cost-ineffective museum-fossils by populistic politicians, who occasionally even want to close them down. The vast treasure of orchestral works of art in our civilization is a priceless cultural heritage, which should under no circumstances be sacrificed to short-sighted political objectives.

While this book directly concerns the symphony orchestra, nearly all of its contents are equally applicable to, for example, theatre and chamber orchestras. These use identical instruments, are conducted in the same way, and have a very similar history. Yet the early developments occurred mainly in the art of the opera, which therefore dominates the tale at the beginning.

The history of orchestras is closely related to the composers who wrote for them in the past. Changes in their composition, size and organization have almost always been introduced by originators of music, with visions of new means of expression. The instruments have been improved through dynamic interplay among composers, players and instrument-designers. When musical performers belonged to the servant-staff of royalty and aristocracy, so did musical creators (who were

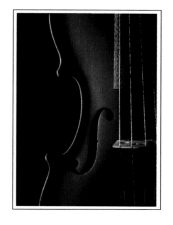

often the performers themselves); but once independent concert orchestras arose, the composer also began to evolve from a lowly artisan into a free artist. It would thus be meaningless to describe the symphony orchestra's progress without focussing on the composers of special importance for it.

Four hundred years of elaboration in orchestras have, of course, taken place on several levels. Like most historical processes, this one is due to a whole network of contributions, stretching far beyond the figures whose names remain famous. Rather than attempting to mention as many of them as possible in a few words, I have concentrated on events and participants that were typical of their times or decisive for the future.

As these pages are addressed to a worldwide audience, the need for universal validity is obvious, but it has not been entirely fulfillable. Historical developments may look different from each geographical and cultural perspective, just as distinctive variants of an instrument are favoured in separate parts of the world. An author in Italy, England or America, for example, will not necessarily have the same priorities as a Swede.

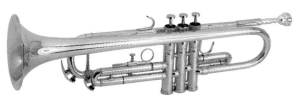

Finally I would like to thank the orchestra players who have made helpful comments on the chapter about instruments. It is extremely useful to see that the description of musical devices, particularly their construction and playing technique, is approved by practising professionals who encounter their problems and requirements every day. The text has been supplemented with a variety of viewpoints from members of the Gothenburg Symphony Orchestra, the Malmö Symphony Orchestra, and the Royal Stockholm Philharmonic Orchestra. My gratitude goes to Björn Bohlin, Anders Engström, Gérard Schaub and Olle Schill (woodwind instruments), Rolf Bengtsson, Jonas Bylund, Mats Engström, Michael Lind, John Petersen and Claes Strömblad (brass instruments), Bo Holmstrand and Karl-Axel Lahger (percussion), Lena Ader (harp), Gunnar Jansson, Chrichan Larson, Anna Lindal and Kristina Mårtensson (string instruments).

HERE'S TO A DEEPER APPRECIATION OF MUSIC BY US ALL!

SVEN KRUCKENBERG

1
The History of the Symphony Orchestra

What are the characteristics
of a symphony orchestra?
Has it always sounded
as it does today?
The orchestral form has a long
and colourful history, including
other musical ideals than our own.

THE ORCHESTRA

What is an orchestra?

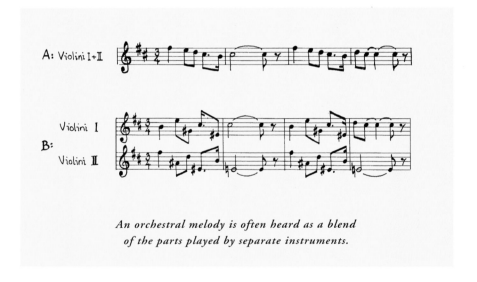

An orchestral melody is often heard as a blend
of the parts played by separate instruments.

THE TERM "ORCHESTRA" HAS MANY meanings and can evoke a variety of associations. Even a traditional symphony orchestra is regarded by some people as a collection of instruments and players, while others consider the orchestra to be an instrument in itself. There are good arguments for both viewpoints. On the one hand, a great number of musicians and diverse types of instruments are involved. On the other hand, what primarily impresses the composer and the concert audience may not be the individuals and their parts of the music, but rather how they unite as a tonal, harmonious, melodic whole.

If we ask a member of the orchestra to play his part alone for half a minute, the music is often unrecognizable. The fragment might be taken from one of our favourite symphonies, yet it can sound odd and vague. In much music, only one or two parts at a time produce the melodies we remember; the other parts are busy building up harmonies, accentuating rhythms, and filling out the tonal palette. Hearing them separately makes it hard to understand their context.

A detached melody part, too, occasionally sounds strange. Most music-lovers are familiar with the beginning of the finale in Tchaikovsky's *Pathétique* symphony (Ex. A). But actually the violins play quite different melodies (Ex. B). Only when they are heard together do we realize that the combination is the well-known, continuous melody line.

Thus, we have strong reasons for thinking of the orchestra as a single instrument. An obvious parallel is a large organ, whose distinctive stops – the

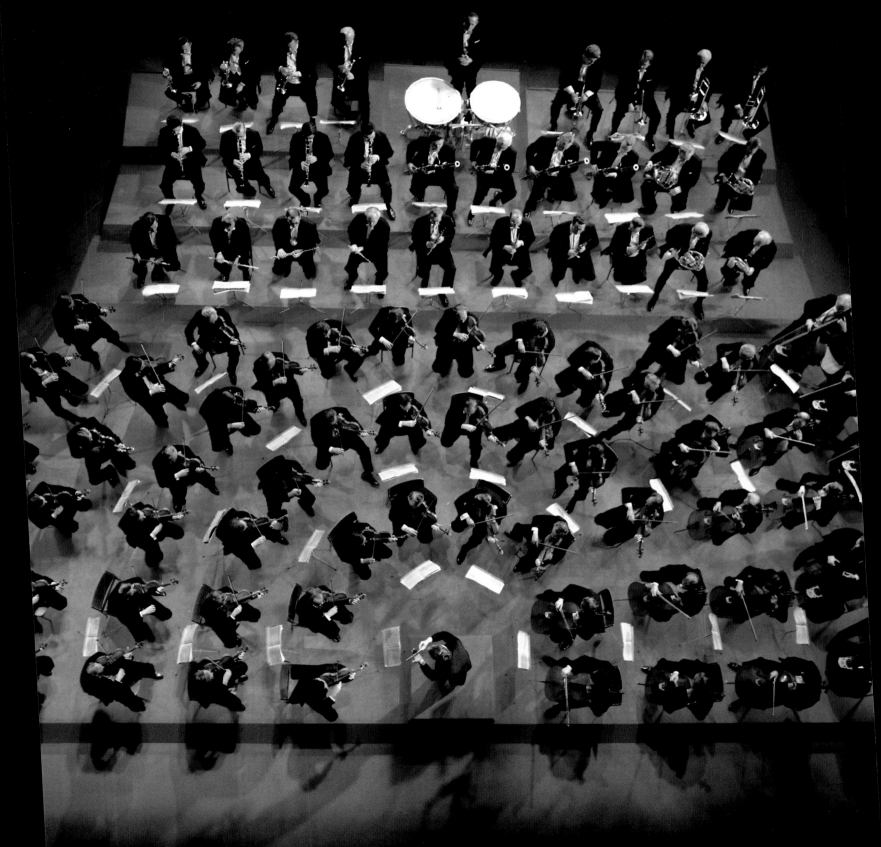

registers – nobody would call separate instruments. Strictly speaking, every pipe in the organ is its own instrument!

The organ, of course, is played by one person. Some of us may want to speak of an orchestra only when several musicians participate. As an extreme case, take the street-busker with a harmonica strapped in front of his mouth, a guitar in his hand, cymbals between his elbow and body, and a bass drum on his back with a cord to his foot. Is this an orchestra? We might insist that four different musicians would have to be playing the instruments. Nonetheless, it has been termed a "one-man orchestra". Whatever our attitude, the above examples illustrate the difficulty of finding clear definitions.

The restaurant trio

Things become even more complicated if we compare orchestras for "serious" music with those for entertainment, dance and jazz. To call a string quartet, quintet or sextet an orchestra would probably never occur to us. Such groups are known as *chamber ensembles*. Yet in the genres of "light" music, an orchestra is simply a group – large or small – of musicians who play together. Even the restaurant trios of yesteryear could be commanded as follows: "Headwaiter, tell the orchestra to play Schubert's military march!"

The question of size

Fifteen musicians seem a lot for a jazz or dance orchestra. Here, the common term is a "big band". But if a classical orchestra includes the same number of players, it is called a *chamber orchestra*, for the opposite purpose of emphasizing its small format. Indeed, a chamber orchestra with fifteen musicians is almost tiny!

So where does the border run between symphony and chamber orchestras? Once again, no strict rule exists. At times, it even depends on the kind of music being played. Many of Haydn's symphonies are written for a group of bowed instruments along with two oboes, two horns, and occasionally a couple of kettledrums. This is certainly a symphony orchestra, in fact the very prototype of one. Its 20-25 musicians, though, amount to a chamber orchestra by modern standards.

The ensemble

A chamber orchestra can be more easily distinguished from a chamber ensemble. Frequently an ensemble is defined as a group in which every musician performs an individual part, whereas some parts in an orchestra are *choral*: the same part is played by several musicians, like the singers in a choir. For example, Schubert's Octet gives separate music to each player, but his symphonies – which may themselves resemble chamber music – present the string parts chorally to balance the wind instruments.

A title with traditions

In sum, it is impossible to unambiguously state what an orchestra is, or distinguish it from other musical groups. The concept of an orchestra is elusive, and we should instead focus upon the word. Originally this had nothing to do with musicians or their instruments. In ancient Greece, an *orkhéstra* meant the forepart of an amphitheatre's stage, or the area between the public and the rounded front edge of the stage. It was there that the chorus acted and danced. The Greek word *khorós* also meant a

Is this an ensemble or an orchestra?

place for dancing. Hence, the words "chorus" and "orchestra" have a common background.

Did the Greeks organize musical groups that were similar to later ensembles or orchestras? Presumably not. Their main stringed instrument, the soft *kithara*, and their sharp oboe-like *aulos* were too different to sound well together. Still more importantly, the two kinds of instruments contrasted in symbolic and religious significance. To combine them was, therefore, hardly desirable.

As late as the seventeenth century, an orchestra was the place in front of the scene where musicians sat to accompany operas. Not before some way into the 1700s did musical groups begin to be termed orchestras, both in the theatre and elsewhere.

How old is the

The constitution of orchestras varied widely until the end of the Baroque period. Far from being standardized, almost any mixture of instruments was allowed. Good examples are Bach's six *Brandenburg Concertos*, with their ever-shifting combinations). A fairly constant pattern first emerged in the mid-eighteenth century, and only slight departures were made from it.

Reasonable consistency in the orchestra's form, then, can be said to have existed for about 250 years, as long as symphonic music itself. This period is a plausible framework for the history of the symphony orchestra. Older composers did not always distinguish between orchestras and ensembles, but their music was often performed by orchestra-like groups, with chorally arranged string sections and, sometimes, even with choral playing of the wind instruments. Consequently, we must go much farther back to discover the orchestra's roots, and to see how it gradually acquired a firmer shape.

The year 1600

When did the idea arise of assembling instrumental groups and composing music for them? Many events suggest that it happened around the beginning of the seventeenth century. New stylistic tendencies appeared, leading to the concept of Baroque music. The thorough-bass system, and the musical adventure of *opera*, were introduced. Violin instruments, developed a generation or two earlier, had revealed their versatility. Composers started to specify instruments in their scores. The notation had become precise enough to describe more complex music.

We thus have strong grounds for dating the birth of the orchestra about 400 years ago. Admittedly, this was not an abrupt phenomenon: successive steps occurred on many levels, aesthetic and practical as well as social. The motley crowd of instrumental groupings in the sixteenth century already included some that were nearly orchestral in terms of tonic density. Likewise, a few types of Renaissance ensembles survived long into the Baroque era, even until the early 1700s.

The thorough-bass period

Throughout the Baroque, roughly between 1600 and 1750, a "figured" bass prevailed everywhere in Europe, the so-called thorough bass or *basso continuo*. The music's construction was often scanty: a violin sonata consisted of just two parts, one for the violin and one for, say, a cello. Solo numbers in opera also often had only a song part and a bass part.

When a complete string orchestra was used, the possibilities increased, at least in theory. Its early constitution was identical to the modern standard: first and second violin, viola, cello (*viola da gamba*) and double bass (*violone*). Yet the possibilities were rarely exploited. Cellos and basses almost always played the same part, and viola players – where

orchestra?

During the seventeenth century, public concerts were still unusual and most music was played at private gatherings.

François Couperin (1668-1733) was among the leading musicians at the court of Louis XIV. He wrote, for instance, many excellent works for the harpsichord, as well as ensemble music for different groups of instruments.

they existed – frequently had to be satisfied with doubling the second violins or the upper register of the cellos. So the orchestra effectively had no more than three parts, and was utilized as in the period's trio sonata for two melody instruments with bass.

To clarify the harmonic sequence in the music, composers began to provide its bass melody with chord indications, written as combinations of figures and some extra symbols. With this help, a harpsichordist or organist, and sometimes a lute-player or harpist, could "fill in" the harmonic costume that was lacking. The system was a kind of musical shorthand, based on the numbers of the notes as counted upward from every indicated bass note. The execution might be limited to such chords, but many players developed great imagination and improvised a polyphonic texture with various ornamentations. Some of them could do so even without any figured notation.

Expert thorough-bass players were highly valued, earning a central role in ensembles and orchestras. They often served simultaneously as the groups' leaders. We shall return to their functions in the chapter on conductors.

Gabrieli and stereophony

The honour of having laid the foundations for the first orchestras can be partly attributed to a certain person: Giovanni Gabrieli, organist at St. Mark's Cathedral in Venice. An important point of departure was the peculiar form of this hall of worship – with two seating galleries on opposite sides, each of them with an organ, as well as several smaller spaces. Some of Gabrieli's predecessors had used these areas for contrasting choral groups. The idea of a multiple choir was not limited to Venice; similar churches existed in other places.

Gabrieli seems to have had a keen sense of stereophony, or three-dimensional sound. He played not only two, but up to five, groups against each other. At first it was in vocal compositions that, following contemporary custom, he strengthened the vocal parts with instruments. In 1597, he applied the technique to entirely instrumental groups, giving them contrasts in timbre and different dynamic registers.

St. Mark's was one of the country's principal cathedrals and enjoyed a flourishing musical life. Gabrieli had access to many musicians, often of high calibre. At plain masses, they might number around a dozen, playing trombones and violin instruments. For greater celebrations, it was not unusual to gather twenty-five bowed and ten wind instruments, quite a lot at the time. Gabrieli particularly cherished the trombone, which experienced its initial golden age with him.

Specifying the instruments

Giovanni Gabrieli was among the first composers to care about indicating the desired instruments in notation. Until then, music had almost always been tonally unspecified. It was performed with the instruments, or voices, which happened to be at hand. No doubt it was occasionally played by large groups, but this is mostly unknown to us, since nobody bothered to write it down. The composer was also a performer, these professions being two sides of the same coin. Because it was often he who would perform the music, there was no need for detailed guidelines.

One of the main reasons for dating the orchestra's emergence to around 1600 is that, from then onward, we have clear proof of the instruments demanded by individual composers. This does not, however, mean that everything is clear. Specifying the instruments stopped short of writing detailed scores. Frequently it was enough to summarize the relevant instruments on the first page. The musicians themselves had to decide who would play what.

A harpsichord's strings are plucked with plectra, instead of being struck by hammers like those of a grand piano.

Theatrical beginnings

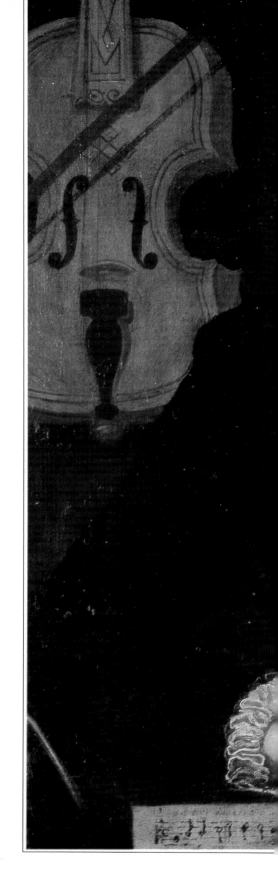

Outside the churches, though, a related revolution was going on. In the next pages we may be surprised to find that a primary element in this historical drama was the art of the opera. But many innovations have occurred on the stages of theatres. Opera, born in Italy just before 1600, was to be the most advanced form of early Baroque music. It continually sought new ways of portraying every emotion from sweet love to bitter separation, every perception from bird-song in spring to storms in autumn. The stage swarmed with shepherds and damsels, warriors and villains, deities and monsters. Musicians had to keep in smooth step with these novelties of theatrical imagination.

Monteverdi goes underground

An interesting example of how soon the resources of orchestras were exploited, namely in 1607, is Claudio Monteverdi's opera *Orfeo*. Monteverdi was a pioneer in the conscious use of varying tonal characteristics for enlivening different states of emotion. The opera's brighter parts are dominated by "pastoral" instruments such as recorders and high-sounding strings. Once Orpheus reaches the underworld, its atmosphere is darkened with trombones, organ and low gambas (although trombones in this context were not his own idea).

Monteverdi's orchestra consisted of no fewer than thirty bowed and wind instruments – about the same number of each, but including several types. In addition, there were a harp, lutes, organs and harpsichords, so as to vary the important thorough bass. It would, however, be misleading to consider this group of more than forty instruments as an orchestra in the later sense. Monteverdi used them not collectively but as a "pool" from which he chose combinations for different purposes. Possibly, too, the musicians were fewer in number and switched between instruments that were not needed simultaneously.

Emotional music

Orfeo stands at the frontier between the Renaissance's colourful ensembles and the Baroque's more sharply contoured orchestras. Until his death in 1643, Monteverdi remained the central figure of the opera, producing a series of pivotal works. He experimented ceaselessly with means of transferring the expressions in a text to music, and of streng-

troduce new instruments. He employed those available, both new and old. Yet he did so with an unusual awareness of tonality – and with unprecedented ways of handling the strings, utilizing devices such as *tremolo* and *pizzicato*. He was far ahead of his contemporaries in the use of tonal colouring to strengthen expression. His manner of composition and his imaginative command of the orchestra were influential for 150 years, until the age of Mozart.

Opera for the masses

During its first few decades, opera was intended for the inner circles of royalty. But already in the 1630s, while Monteverdi was still active, the first musical theatres for a paying public were opened in Rome and Venice. They were no small affair: the one in Rome is said to have seated 3,000! Their stage equipment was a mechanical marvel, able to achieve dramatic miracles and change scenery before the amazed eyes of audiences. Spectacular visual ingredients became fashionable. The scenery often had an extreme central perspective, giving the stage an impression of vast depth.

Success was so great that Venice, towards the end of that century, had fifteen opera houses. The enthusiasts came increasingly from the middle class, so that creators of opera began to cultivate more earthy subjects, preferably including comedy and burlesque. These provided enjoyable alternatives to the formal, often tragic tales of kings, prophets, generals and other distant figures, as well as to the lyrical pastorals with their themes taken from ancient mythology.

thening them by the power of sound to communicate emotions. His harmony was, for its time, rich in dissonances and he complemented it with a personal *stile concitato* in order to evoke unrest and drama.

Monteverdi's role in the history of the orchestra was not to develop or in-

The orchestra finds its forms

Due to this broader support and social background, the art of opera became popular entertainment and spread across Europe during the late seventeenth century. The royal courts had already imitated the Italian prototypes; now it was the bourgeoisie's turn. Paris and London acquired public opera theatres in 1671, Hamburg in 1678, and Dresden in 1686.

Both national works and a variety of imported Italian products were performed everywhere. International exchange contributed to a growing need for common features in the orchestra's constitution. With Monteverdi, orchestras were put together almost haphazardly, in particular at the beginning when they still smacked of the Renaissance. But when an opera was to be performed beyond its place of origin, the creator could no longer easily supervise or participate in its performance.

There were no agreements about copyright in those days. A work of art was treated as public property. Anyone could alter the action, music, or orchestral arrangement to suit a new stage or

The viola da gamba

an audience with different tastes. Large opera houses had many kinds of instruments, but not even their selections were always identical. From the fifteen musical theatres in Venice alone, we can understand that minor cities possessed plenty of them, yet with far smaller resources. The composers were forced to accept adaptations which, in our view, wreck the music – such as cellos instead of trombones, or violins substituting for trumpets.

Until the end of the eighteenth century, what primarily counted was the musical material, not the tonal clothing. Music was regarded not as art, but as handicraft. Nor did anyone think that it would last forever. Spoons and wooden shoes were judged by their utility, and music was similarly expected to

Public opera theatres arose during the late seventeenth century, as in Paris, Dresden and London. Covent Garden was inaugurated in 1732 in London. Burned and rebuilt several times (most recently in 1858), it still serves as a national opera stage.

function well in a given situation. Its creators must have realized, at all events, that their works were more fortunate to be performed "wrongly" in many places than "rightly" in one.

Violins in the centre

The string section had been prominent in orchestras since the beginning of the Baroque. At first the *viol* instruments alternated with newer violin instruments – violins, violas, cellos – and sometimes played together with them, as in Monteverdi's *Orfeo*. Gradually the violin instruments became better and more widespread, and were fully adopted by most orchestras. Their high quality and flexibility earned enormous appeal, strengthening their status as the core of the orchestra.

Practical factors were also important. Adaptation of works, mentioned above, was never entirely avoidable, but it could be limited. By using only the instruments to which everyone had access, far-reaching changes became less necessary when an opera appeared on a new stage. Thus, much of the period's theatre music was designed solely for

string orchestras with thorough bass.

Lully – an Italian at the French court

One of the foremost musicians and composers in Europe during the later seventeenth century was Jean-Baptiste Lully. Although by no means unique in contemporary France, he was many-sided and single-minded, and gained exceptional influence. Lully came from Italy and, already as a child, joined the servant-staff at the French court. When aged 21, he was made a court composer of Louis XIV (then just 15 years old), for whom he would continue to work throughout his life.

In 1661, Louis turned 23 and took over the government after his minister Mazarin died. He promoted Lully to the position of director, and soon to *maitre de la musique.* Such favour by the "Sun King" certainly owed, in part, to the fact that Lully was a fine dancer and loved the royal ballet, where they often danced together. With time, Lully climbed to virtual omnipotence as leader of the country's musical life. He was a power-hungry and not very likable person, but also a great Baroque innovator.

As early as 1626, Louis XIII had founded a string orchestra that paved the way for other courts. Entitled *Les vingt-quatre violons du Roi,* it included violas and cellos as well as violins. Lully organized a second group, *Les petits violons du Roi* (meaning "few" rather than "small"), which he developed to a truly elite level. Eventually the two en-sembles were merged to form a sizable string orchestra.

Further, a wind ensemble existed for outdoor use: *La grande écurie* (referring to a large stable, as the musicians were quartered near the cavalry). It played march music and at various ceremonies

Jean-Baptiste Lully (1632-87), a dominant figure in the musical life of his age, is regarded as the founder of French opera.

Lully introduced the kettle-drum to the orchestra. This military instrument even began to be played indoors.

or festivities, which abounded at the court of Versailles.

A versatile pioneer

Lully's influence was pervasive. His very demanding rehearsals, first with *Les petits violons* and later with all available musicians, resulted in a degree of perfection that had no equal at the time. He gave relatively precise instructions as to which instruments should be used. Moreover, he often required that the music be played as it was written, without the usual ornamentations according to a player's own taste and ability. He used the most modern instruments – often, for example, transverse flutes instead of recorders – and he promoted the invention of new ones.

Reviving instruments from earlier periods (something which Bach, fifty years younger, would do frequently) was, for Lully, an obsolete and boring way to make music. Since the French enjoyed dancing and easy entertainment, however, he had no reason to make his music very difficult to play.

Louis XIV, the "Sun King", whose court included many important players and composers.

Greater technical innovators could be found elsewhere.

The winds move indoors

When Louis XIV became king, the wind musicians increasingly blew gaiety into the palace halls. They urgently needed instruments that were not so loud and shrill. Most revolutionary was the *oboe*, built by Jean Hotteterre and developed in cooperation with Lully's musicians (see page 134). The violin's near-supremacy as a solo instrument was thereby broken. During the rest of the Baroque period, the oboe would occupy an almost equivalent throne. Hotteterre also improved the bassoon, two of which were combined with a group of oboes to form *Les douze grands hautbois du Roi* (the king's twelve leading oboists). This ensemble, too, won fame for its high standards of playing.

Dialogue and contrast

Lully refined a technique of exploiting tonal resources that was to predominate until the mid-eighteenth century. Bowed instruments with figured bass were its foundation. To these Lully added, as Monteverdi had done, other instruments when they were needed to illustrate the stage action or to evoke contrast. The novelty was that he used them in a calculated dialogue, letting the music wander between the woodwinds, the strings, and sometimes the brass instruments.

What was more, he introduced military instruments, the kettledrums, to the orchestra – even for indoor performances. Other percussion instruments such as tambourines, castanets and cymbals were not seldom heard. Lully's music is colourful and sounds remarkably modern to our own ears. But there was no question of orchestration as we know it. A coordinated use of all resources occurred only in special climaxes. Lully was more interested in the contrasts, and in altering or shifting the timbre.

Dance liberates the orchestra

Before Lully, theatre orchestras had mainly filled a supportive role. They rarely played distinctive music, except short preludes and the like. In Italy, the obvious stars of opera were the singers, around whom everything else revolved. But the French penchant for dance created a need for more independent music, not tied to the singing. Lully and his contemporaries responded by composing many stylized dances such as the *allemande, courante, bourrée, sarabande, menuet* and *gavotte*. Paradoxically, therefore, we have the ballet to thank for the rise of French orchestra music!

Another important form of music that came to be widely cultivated was the *French overture*. Probably it was not due to Lully, but he brought it to perfection. It was normally divided into three parts on the pattern slow-fast-slow and begun with a solemnly dotted rhythm, originally as entry music for the king. A century later, its echoes could still be felt in, for example, the introduction to Mozart's *Linz Symphony*.

Conducted to death

Lully's life met a sorry end, to the undoubted glee of all the enemies he had acquired through his megalomania. It can well be said that he crushed himself by mistake. In 1687, he presented his great *Te Deum*, a high point of French church music. The baton he was using, far from being light and thin like a mo-

dern one, was a wooden staff to be knocked against the floor. It hit his foot, whereupon the injury was mistreated. Gangrene set in, and did away with a superb musician.

The concerto grosso

At the same time, Italy gave birth to a further medium of independent orches-

tral music. In the *concerto grosso* (grand concerto), the instruments were divided into two contrasting groups. The larger was called *tutti* (all), *ripieno* (full), or simply *concerto grosso*, while the smaller was termed *concertino* (small concerto). Often the former group was chorally arranged, with several musicians for each part. The latter had individual parts, usually for two or three instruments.

This technique built upon the polyphonic vocal style of the 1500s, as well as on the solo and trio sonatas of seventeenth-century chamber music. One type, the *sonata da chiesa* (church sonata), contained four movements in a sequence: slow, fast, slow, fast. Another was the *sonata da camera* (chamber sonata), with a varying number of movements. It resembled the French and German *suite* of stylized dances.

All of these types flowed together in the *concerto grosso*. Normally, all players participated at the beginning and end of a composition. In between, the music was "bounced" back and forth between the instrumental groups. The *concertino* usually had two violins and a cello (with thorough bass), appropriate to a trio sonata. At first, the orchestra consisted only of strings; soon it became common to add wind instruments as required, especially when playing in a large hall.

Corelli's singing violins

The *concerto grosso* was named by Alessandro Stradella, but its most famous practitioner was to be Arcangelo Corelli. Among the foremost violinists of his day, he had considerable significance for the development of violin playing . In contrast to other virtuosi, he did not emphasize techniques such as double stopping. What concerned him most were the instrument's "singing" possibilities. Corelli was also extraordinary in devoting himself solely to instrumental music. Yet he benefitted from the Italian song tradition, not least the expressiveness of opera.

The *concerto grosso* idea soon spread to Germany, England and other countries, though hardly at all to France. Corelli's twelve *concerti grossi* Op. 6, composed since the 1680s and published in 1714, established a style for several generations to come. Such composers as Albinoni, Vivaldi, Telemann, Bach and Handel learned from them.

Antonio Vivaldi limited the movements to three in a sequence, fast-slow-fast, which was the same formula used by the contemporary *opera sinfonia*, or *Italian overture*. This and the French overture were gradually expanded and, towards the mid-eighteenth century, became the first true *symphonies*. For solo concertos, Vivaldi's tripartite form has remained standard long into modern times.

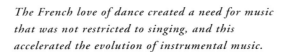

The French love of dance created a need for music that was not restricted to singing, and this accelerated the evolution of instrumental music.

Archangelo Corelli (1653-1713) developed the violin's possibilities. He devoted himself exclusively to instrumental music, although he was inspired by the Italian song tradition.

Public concerts

Georg Friedrich Händel (1685-1759) was one of the great masters of the High Baroque period, and among the first to compose specifically for amateur orchestras.

Corelli was employed during his later years by the music-loving Cardinal Ottoboni in Rome. There he gave a much-appreciated series of concerts that set the fashion in Italy. But how were concert activities progressing in the rest of Europe? Next to the theatre, it was mainly the church that presented public music in the seventeenth century. Naturally, only religious music was involved, normally of small format and shaped for specific purposes in the services.

One of those who widened the function of such music was a Danish cantor and organist, Dietrich Buxtehude, at St. Mary's Church in Lübeck. For decades he performed "evening music" on five Sundays before Christmas. His 25 stringed instruments, with winds and thorough bass, occupied at least 35 players in sizable works for choir and orchestra. Buxtehude's contributions inspired musicians in other German cities to expand their church repertoire. Bach, for example, visited Lübeck in his youth and acquired impressions that would last for many years.

The secular scene

By then, public musical theatres had been open for half a century. Secular concerts for the public began to take place, probably first around 1670 in London, where numerous organizers were soon competing to attract audiences. Initially the concerts occurred in small halls with few players, but enthusiasm grew so rapidly that they moved to ample premises and engaged more musicians. Occasionally a small orchestra convened, although not for purely orchestral concerts but in order to accompany excerpts from operas or other vocal works.

Court musicians and pipers

Orchestras with a fixed organization were seldom seen. Until the mid-eighteenth century, they appeared only at the courts, musical theatres and some large churches. The general rule was to gather a temporary orchestra according to need and availability. Players were often recruited from the court and theatre groups, or with the help of *city musicians* in Central Europe.

Today we tend to think of courts as kingly institutions. Once, however, when Europe was a patchwork of rather independent princedoms and ecclesiastical states, courts existed just about everywhere. In addition, the population centres were guarded by forces that included city musicians, who served as night watchmen and tower buglers to warn of intruders, sound fire alarms, and join in secular or religious festivals. Most of them played wind instruments, but many were versatile and could play

bowed instruments as well. The trumpeters of courts and cities belonged to a privileged guild.

Significant amateur orchestras

In many places, too, orchestral music was performed at an amateur or apprentice level, sometimes aided by a professional player or leader. This activity was chiefly meant to please the participants themselves. But in an age when musical events were far and few between, even amateur concerts made a valuable contribution to public cultural life. In England, Handel composed his famous *concerti grossi* Op. 6 specifically for the plentiful amateur orchestras.

Various cities had a music society, which the Germans called a *collegium musicum* and the Italians an *accademia.* In both countries, it was usually associated with the university or a school of music. While such societies were not run professionally, we should not underestimate their importance for the development of public music outside the courts, theatres and churches.

The Italian academies also provided comprehensive training of musicians and singers. In Venice, for instance, there were some lively homes for orphaned girls. At one of these convent-like schools, the *Conservatorio* (or *Seminario Musicale*) *dell'Ospedale della Pietà*, a teaching post was held for thirty years by Antonio Vivaldi. Here he composed much of his chamber music, and his several hundred concertos for one or more solo instruments with a string orchestra. The pupils learned them for performance at public concerts which the school regularly arranged.

Consummator of the Baroque

As noted previously, Johann Sebastian Bach took a view of the orchestra and its instruments that was traditional in his time. The great expressiveness we often hear from him, as in the *Passions*, is due more to his treatment of the musical material than to his tonal methods. Usually he exploited the instruments for variety and contrast, not to strengthen expression. Nevertheless, he is important in the history of the orchestra because, by summing up and perfecting the expressive means of the Baroque period, he left an enduring key to the orchestra's early evolution.

Bach's main contributions to this field came fairly soon in his career, due to the circumstances under which he worked. From 1717 until 1723, he was employed as musical director by Prince Leopold in Köthen, a small town southwest of Berlin, with a small but professional orchestra at his disposal. These years enabled him to compose most of his orchestral and other instrumental masterpieces: the *Brandenburg* and violin concertos, two of the four orchestral suites, and a great deal of chamber music.

Thanks to his excellent players, Bach could experiment with very difficult music. His six sonatas and partitas for solo violin, and six suites for solo cello, had a crucial impact on the use of these instruments and, therefore, on orchestral technique.

The Brandenburg Concertos

Bach came perhaps farthest in the six concertos which he dedicated to the Margrave of Brandenburg (but probably composed earlier for Köthen). Most of them were based on the *concerto grosso* idea of Stradella and Corelli, with a *concertino* group contrasting against the or-

chestra's other instruments.

While Corelli and Handel, for instance, used a fixed *concertino* in work after work, Bach continually changed his combinations of instruments, both between concerts and between individual movements. In the second concerto, the solo instruments are a trumpet in the high clarino register, recorder, oboe and violin. The *tutti* group and the trumpet fall silent in the middle movement, which instead functions as in a *sonata a quattro*. The fourth concerto has a virtuoso violin and two recorders; the fifth a transverse flute, violin and harpsichord. In the latter, its first movement contains a comprehensive solo cadenza for the harpsichord, yet the second returns to pure chamber music.

The third and sixth concertos, lacking a *concertino* group, were written for bowed instruments alone – but in quite different ways. In the third, Bach used three each of violins, violas and cellos, as well as a double bass. In the sixth, we find two violas as the highest instruments, two *viole da gamba*, a cello and a double bass: in other words, a mixture of violin and viol instruments. Finally, the first concerto built a bridge between the *concerto grosso* and the orchestral concerto. It calls for a small *violino piccolo*, three oboes, a bassoon, two horns and a string group. The instruments contrast in shifting combinations, forming and dissolving momentary *concertino* groups.

These concertos show how a genius could exploit and vary resources that were few in number but fine in quality. The individual potential of instruments emerged, their capacities were some-

Johann Sebastian Bach (1685-1750) had a small professional orchestra at his disposal, which enabled him to experiment with and improve the orchestral technique.

times stretched to the utmost, and many tonal mixtures were attempted. Bach made an unusual display of the Baroque orchestra's versatility.

In spite of this, Bach was most fascinated with the sounds of individual instruments and their interplay. He did not blend colours into new nuances: such an approach would arise only long after his death and, properly speaking, not until the nineteenth century.

A shortage of musicians

Bach's service from 1723 onward, as cantor of St. Thomas' Church in Leipzig, took him back a step. He no longer had access to an elite orchestra; actually no fixed group existed there at all. Now and then, some professional players could be joined by students and amateurs, but their numbers were small and the quality was uneven.

Although Bach was formally bound to the city's main church, his duties included providing other churches with instrumentalists, singers and music. When the players did not suffice, the boys of St. Thomas' School, associated with the church, had to fill the missing parts. As they were also singers, the result was a thinner choir.

Likewise, some of the city musicians commanded more than one instrument. Bach wrote at times for both horns and trumpets, but could not call on them simultaneously, as they were played by the same persons. Others were also adept at bowed instruments, and came in handy when not enough players could be found for these, even though it meant thinning out the rest of his little orchestra.

Thus, much of Bach's work from his 27 years at Leipzig was performed by unspecialized musicians, and often required the help of nonprofessionals. One hardly dares to imagine how it

*Drinking coffee was all the rage in Bach's society,
and he praised it in the "Coffee Cantata" (1732).*

sounded, particularly with Bach's contrapuntally transparent way of writing, which demands expert playing in most parts and, not seldom, true virtuosi.

In his letters to the heads of church and city, Bach complained repeatedly about the minimal resources. On the whole, his prayers went unanswered. Leipzig's churches traditionally needed a large-scale musical life, but nobody was willing to pay what it would cost.

Odd instruments

One may wonder why Bach often called for instruments which were unusual or considered obsolete. Especially in the church cantatas, we find many older forms alongside the violin and new woodwind instruments that were then typical. The *viola da gamba* was still current, and the *viola d'amore* enjoyed brief popularity – but the *violino piccolo, viola pomposa, violetta* and others were peculiar. The recorder was about to be superseded by the stronger, more expressive transverse flute, while the *oboe d'amore* and *oboe da caccia* were less common than the oboe.

Yet Bach regularly employed such oddities. In musical terms, the most plausible reason is that he needed many colour nuances to enliven the religious texts, and he was known for depicting

the texts in a lucid manner.

Moreover, competent specialists on all these instruments were not always lacking. Why else did Bach, in the face of a chronic scarcity of players, indulge in extravagances which had already been rare at the musical court in Köthen? An explanation is that the supply varied with time, and Bach did not hesitate to engage musicians who were only visiting Leipzig. The more unusual instruments seldom occurred in his basic orchestra, but performed conspicuous solo roles.

Composing for coffeehouses

Evidently much of Bach's later production was devoted to the needs of the Church. Notwithstanding his difficult circumstances, he carried out this duty with zeal. Undoubtedly, though, he sometimes missed the artistic freedom which he had enjoyed at Köthen. Beginning in 1729, he obtained a kind of breathing-hole as leader of the student *collegium musicum*. It had been founded at the outset of the century by Georg Philipp Telemann as a student at Leipzig University. For at least a decade, Bach and its musicians gave concerts for the citizens. This orchestra, too, was

small and often consisted solely of bowed instruments.

The group usually played at "Zimmermann's Coffeehouse" or in the gardens near other such establishments. Coffee was the fashionable drink, and Bach even composed a cantata in its honour! His repertoire included both old and recent music. Since he had heavy responsibilities at church and as a teacher of music and Latin, Bach occasionally saved time by rearranging compositions from his years before Leipzig. Thus arose most of his concertos for one or more harpsichords with a string orchestra. Still, we may imagine that these projects gave him a welcome break from the ecclesiastical routine.

Handel at the heights

It is obvious that the conditions of musical life in a huge city like London, with half a million inhabitants, were quite different from those in Leipzig with its 25,000 people. Georg Friedrich Händel, as he was known in his native Germany, worked in the English capital for almost half a century. He frequently had his own troubles in scraping together an orchestra, but the reason was his lack of finances, seldom a shortage of professional musicians.

Bach continually varied the instruments in the "Brandenburg Concertos" to get the most out of his small orchestra.

These giants of equal age, Bach and Handel, are commonly regarded as a pair. Yet many factors separated them in terms of art. Bach, when young, had received strong influence from North Germany. His music is mainly polyphonic, giving comparable importance to its parts and uniting them in a texture of counterpoint. He thought instrumentally even when writing for voices. By contrast, much of Handel's music is homophonically designed for one or two dominant parts, with support from the others. The distinction is easy to understand if one considers that the young Handel studied in Italy. Ever since then, he based everything on song, viewing himself essentially as an opera composer.

Handel was in fact also a great contrapuntalist, as is often heard in his instrumental music and in the choral parts of his oratorios, though less in the operas. With hindsight, we can recognize that Handel's singable, melodic style was more in tune with the times than Bach's approach. However, this did not prevent him, too, from eventually being considered outdated.

In the present context, it is interesting that this "pair" used the orchestra in different ways as well. We might expect that Handel, in his operas, had as much need as Monteverdi of expressing variations in atmosphere. But he did so primarily through the music itself, rather than through choice of instruments – a tendency he shared with Bach. His orchestral style is transparent and easily listened to. In particular, it was not supposed to attract excessive attention away from the important song parts.

In isolated cases, Handel called for a harp; and he was among the first to exploit the clarinet, long before it was widely accepted. But on the whole, he felt content with the Baroque's standard orchestra of modern instruments: strings with thorough bass, and whatever else was required (or could be paid for) in flutes, oboes, bassoons, horns, trumpets and kettledrums. Handel's tonal thinking was unified, especially as compared to Bach's many excursions among the instruments.

Water Music

At theatres, churches, and other indoor places, the emphasis was on the strings. For outdoor performances, greater tonal strength was demanded, so woodwinds and brass instruments were used in larger numbers. A nearby audience could still hear the string instruments, at least as a group. In his famous *Water Music*, Handel let the orchestra's constitution vary. This work was composed for boat trips on the River Thames, which George I – the king since 1714 – enjoyed with his retinue. One of the accompanying vessels carried Handel and the orchestra, who provided the nobles with background music for their conversation.

The *Water Music* was probably written in pieces, at intervals of a few years. This may explain why some movements have lighter instrumentation, with strings and occasional woodwinds, while a second portion (about half of the work) also demands horns, and a third calls for both horns and trumpets. Furthermore, each of the three portions has a different tonic key, because of how the dominant instruments were tuned.

Royal Fireworks

Sometimes the amusements were more

spectacular. A famous event took place in 1749, to celebrate the Treaty of Aachen (Aix-la-Chapelle) which had ended the War of the Austrian Succession in the preceding year. Handel received an order for festive music that, in King George II's words, should use "as many military instruments as possible – and absolutely no violins". The outcome was a suite with powerful components: 24 oboes, 12 bassoons, 9 horns, 9 trumpets, serpents and three pairs of kettledrums. Besides these, Handel added a double bassoon and a snare drum, both of them extremely unusual in contemporary musical art.

Handel was asked to rehearse the music in Vauxhall Gardens the week before the festival. He did so unwillingly, yet noticed that the interest in his large wind orchestra was spreading wildly. Several thousand enthusiasts assembled, and newspapers reported that the event had caused traffic chaos!

Outdoor concerts are always a risk, and the great day of April 27 in Green Park did not turn out as the King had hoped. Handel's music made a hit again, but it began to rain. The enormous fireworks show went wrong, and some pieces simply fizzled out. Suddenly they set the launching ramp ablaze, and the flames engulfed a "peace pavilion" that had been built for the occasion, burning it to the ground.

Handel had wanted all along to include string instruments, but was prevented by the royal decree. A month later, he played his *Fireworks Music* at a benefit concert, with fewer winds and a doubling string orchestra. This is how the music has usually been played since then. The extraordinary original composition of the orchestra was, of course, exceptional – the extreme opposite of Bach's miniature groups. Twenty-five years after Handel's death, the English would begin to honour him with musical festivals using far larger orchestras; but that is another story.

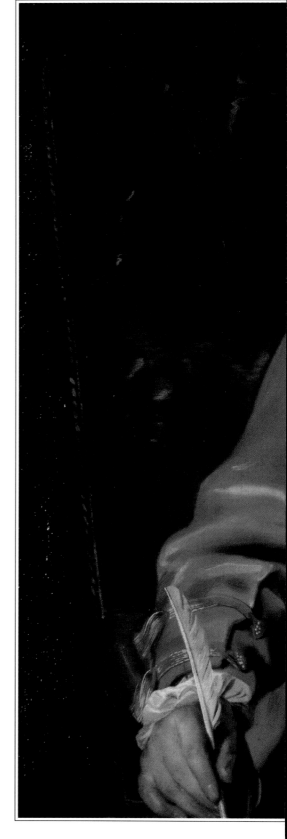

Handel's "Music for the Royal Fireworks" (1749) was ordered for "as many military instruments as possible – no violins".
But he wanted to use string instruments, and performed the music with a new orchestra one month after its première.

From rococo to classicism

The transition from Baroque, through the "gallant" style of rococo, to full-fledged Classicism was a long process, starting already in the 1720s. To some degree it had been anticipated even fifty years earlier by Lully's *divertissements*. But now a spirit of renewal arose for many reasons, chiefly a reaction against what was considered too heavy and artificial.

A good example is how *The Beggar's Opera*, a popular ballad opera of 1728, made fun of Handel's ceremonial opera style with its antique subjects and virtuoso song parts. At the same time, Giovanni Bononcini, an Italian who had moved to London, presented entertaining operas that contributed to the declining interest in Handel. Thus he was forced to give up opera for the better-appreciated oratorio.

Enlightened ideals

The change in musical taste was certainly no isolated phenomenon. The eighteenth century saw great transformations in society as well as philosophy and lifestyles. The darkness of the preceding century was followed by an era of bright faith in progress. Even if it took awhile before the new climate spread to the common man, the Enlightenment involved a real revolution of ideas.

For the first time, monarchy and church power could be questioned, if only in disguised terms. The upper classes lost strength and the bourgeoisie gained it, especially as a promoter of culture. Rousseau introduced concepts of human value and of nature's supremacy. Towards the end of the century, the principle of subjective expression began to challenge the old view of artists as handicrafters.

The emergence of the sonata

Music also experienced fifty years of innovation. In the instrumental realm, loosely composed suites and partitas, overtures and so forth (the names being many and, to a large extent, equivalent) were gradually replaced by the *sonata*. This comparatively fixed form soon became predominant, and has remained in use down to our time. Normally a sonata had three or four movements, at least one of which built on a contrast between several themes and on their elaboration. The whole complex of movements was called a sonata, although the actual sonata form was used primarily in the first movement.

Symphonies by the thousand

A sonata composed for orchestra was known as a *sinfonia* (after the Italian

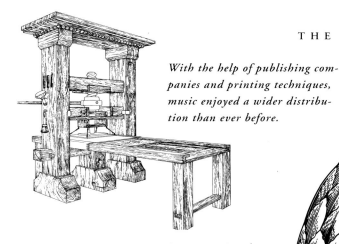

With the help of publishing companies and printing techniques, music enjoyed a wider distribution than ever before.

Johann Stamitz (1717-57)

opera overture), or a symphony. In the eighteenth century, this new genre was a bigger success than we may imagine. To be sure, Joseph Haydn created more than a hundred symphonies, and his endless inventiveness amazes us. But Haydn was just one of the many who devoted such energy to the symphony. A number of his contemporaries were even more productive, and some others wrote at least fifty such works. For instance, the symphonies of his brother Michael Haydn are among the best from that period.

Another incentive to the spread of new music was an extensive publishing business, particularly in Paris and London. Research has proved that, until the end of Classicism in the early 1800s, over one and a half thousand symphonies and similar works were printed. A further five thousand or so are preserved in manuscript, apart from the many which must have been lost.

The symphonies of Vienna Classicism which we hear today are, therefore, a mere fraction of all that were composed. Their artistic quality was indeed inconsistent, but clearly a great deal is still worth awakening from its "beauty sleep".

The Mannheim orchestra

That a small city like Mannheim could compete with such metropoli as London, Paris and Vienna may seem astonishing. Yet during the mid-eighteenth century, it was the home of the "palatine counts". Deeply interested in

the fine arts, they maintained their own orchestra, led by a truly adept and versatile musician: Johann Stamitz, a Bohemian. He had acquired fame as a violinist before becoming the concertmaster for Prince Karl Theodor. In a few years he developed the orchestra into one of Europe's best. Through guest performances in Paris and other centres, it secured an international reputation and continued to set the pace long after Stamitz' death in 1757.

Uniform style

We have seen how the royal orchestra of Louis XIV attained high quality because of its many excellent musicians, and primarily due to the ambitious, clear-sighted guidance of its conductor Lully. In the same way, the Mannheim orchestra's success owed to a combination of its members and the discerning work of Stamitz as an inspiring teacher.

Several of Stamitz' violin students

decided to stay at Mannheim and occupy important posts in the orchestra. Their common schooling promoted a homogeneous style of playing, with a uniform bowing technique and phrasing. Conscientious rehearsal (which recalls Lully!) gave them unusual precision – and the wind groups were no worse. The English musical author Charles Burney wrote that, in this city, one could probably find more soloists and superb composers than in any other European orchestra.

A river of crystal

The orchestra at Mannheim, with about 50 musicians, was strong for its time. It was therefore able to create an extraordinarily large and differentiated dynamic register. Another observer, Daniel Schubart, concluded: "No orchestra has excelled that at Mannheim. Its forte is like a thunderstorm, its piano like a spring breeze. Its crescendo

Carl Stamitz (1746-1801) established a style with his pioneering way of using the clarinet. It was also improved technically at this time, with more keys and an outcurved bell.

resembles a waterfall, its diminuendo a river of crystal that disappears murmuring into the distance..." With such picturesque language, it is not surprising that Schubart became one of the founders of Romanticism!

A dozen composers

Burney's remark about superb composers might sound strange, but in those days no sharp line was drawn between creating and performing. Most of the music played was contemporary, and the bulk of it was inevitably produced by the players themselves – so much that they campaigned for a new aesthetic view of music. Players who are fairly unknown to us wrote works in all manner of genres: the violinist Christian Cannabich (who succeeded Stamitz as concert-master), the cellist Anton Filtz, the conductor Ignaz Holzbauer, the oboist Ludwig Lebrun, the singer Franz Xaver Richter, and others. In total, there were at least a dozen of them.

Johann Stamitz kept his preeminence for a long time. He introduced many features that his colleagues would carry onward. His writing showed a new, expressive, dynamic and contrastive style, which was to have wide influence, as on Mozart. Among the students were his sons Carl and Anton, of whom the first became even more famous as a composer, exploiting numerous such features: a love of crescendo and diminuendo effects, sharp contrasts, surprising accents and pauses.

The Mannheim group was expected to produce new music continually. However, the ability to vary and renew oneself is not universal. Like Vivaldi and other mass-producers, the Mannheimers handled their forms rather stereotypically. Sighing, syncopation, and surprises

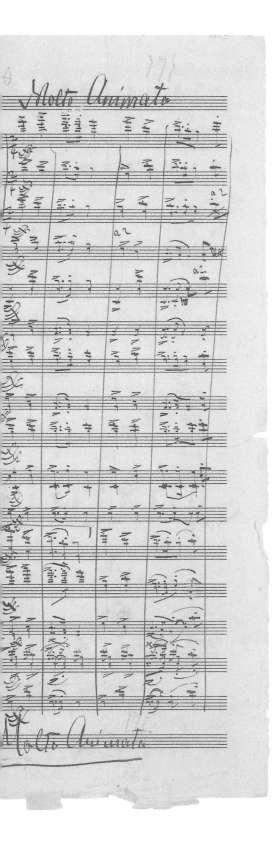

were exploited to excess. But despite its lack of originality, this music often has a natural melodic flow, which can be notably expressive in slow passages. Seldom profound, it is spontaneous and playful, sometimes approaching the passion of *Sturm und Drang*.

Orchestration begins

Carl Stamitz emphasized the role of wind instruments more clearly than was yet the rule. In particular, his use of the clarinet established a precedent. Johann had included it in symphonies since the 1750s, several decades before it became common in other orchestras. The Stamitz family also started to mix the orchestral timbres in a calculated manner. They were not satisfied with playing the strings and winds against each other, but worked with variable combinations of instruments and groups. It can be said that the foundation was then laid for what we call orchestration.

The figured bass survives itself

Baroque chord play according to a figured bass had been invented to clarify the harmony in "thin" orchestral or instrumental music. At the outset of Classicism, instruments like the harpsichord which filled out harmonies became ever more superfluous. In a violin sonata, everything was written in the keyboard part, instead of merely being suggested with figures. The four parts of the new string quartet genre were sufficient in themselves for a clear harmonic progression. In the orchestra, this function was often taken over by the wind instruments, especially horns and trumpets. These consequently did not acquire independent, or melodically interesting, parts – a deficiency that

sent them into decline after their leading role in the Baroque.

Yet the history of the thorough bass did not end there. Reminiscences of it endured for generations. The orchestra was still normally led, not by a conductor, but by a harpsichordist or the principal violinist. One of them was often the composer himself; and if he played on a keyboard, it was quite appropriate that he, who knew the music inside out, should improvise a suitable accompaniment.

Although symphonies from Mozart's time usually indicate no thorough-bass figuring, the harpsichord was frequently used in the traditional manner. It was no longer needed for fullness, but the power of habit was strong. As late as 1792, in his symphony No. 98, Haydn even wrote a solo cadenza for the instrument!

Haydn the hermit

A musician has many ways of developing originality. He or she can travel, or linger in a place that conveys impressions from foreign artists – as is illustrated by Mozart's early trips around Europe. Alternatively, he may live apart from the world, cultivating his own inner cosmos. Joseph Haydn long thought that he embodied the latter approach. For three decades, from 1761 until 1790, he worked as a conductor and resident composer for the Esterházy princes at their court in Eisenstadt, a little town southeast of Vienna.

Some miles farther into Hungary, Prince Nikolaus Esterházy, known as "the Splendid", built a magnificent castle for summer residence, modelled on the palace of Versailles and containing a theatre. His family's importance is obvious from the fact that Empress Maria Theresa was among the lofty guests. There she heard Haydn's music and fell in love with it.

Haydn stayed for thirty years at the castle of Esterházy. He admitted that his inventiveness had been fostered by isolation in the Hungarian countryside.

liked. In his words: "I was totally shut off from the world. Nobody could restrict or confuse me. I was simply compelled to become original."

We must keep in mind that a certain amount of Haydn's music was soon spread in print, and attracted notice all over Europe. He also received assignments to compose for an international public. Yet the man himself remained for a long time in the Hungarian countryside.

A modest, masterly orchestra

Haydn's group initially comprised about 15 members, but it grew slowly. According to a record of 1783, it had 23 instrumentalists. In any case, its quality was more important. Employment with the Esterházys meant better conditions than elsewhere, so a series of excellent musicians could be engaged. Presumably Haydn's conditions in this respect were rather like those of Bach at the court in Köthen.

In Haydn's early orchestral music, the limited number of instruments reflects the modest resources at his disposal. Like many symphonies of that day, his own usually contained eight parts: four for the string instruments (cellos and double basses sharing one part) as well as two each for the oboes and horns. Often a bassoon was added, occasionally for its own tasks but normally in order to strengthen the string bass.

This was the standard which long governed the Italian opera overture, or *sinfonia*. And it was more or less the same constitution that Lully had used a century earlier. The enormously influential court at Versailles was still casting light over Europe's princely houses! Nonetheless, such unchanging resources did not make Haydn's music sound like Lully's.

Haydn's service as leader of the family orchestra was comprehensive, and he composed plenty of music in every conceivable genre. It did happen that he went to Vienna, where the Esterházys maintained another castle for occasional visits; but he stayed mostly in Eisenstadt. While such employment had its disadvantages, a benefit was that he enjoyed great trust and could experiment as he

Joseph Haydn (1732-1809) experimented with symphonic form and excelled at exploiting the potential of a small orchestra.

Like Bach before him, Haydn showed how even a small orchestra could be used to maximum effect. Solo passages, variations in the manner of playing, and other devices contributed to the creation of diversity.

Haydn's symphonies are a virtual chart of the phases in development which the genre, and the orchestra itself, underwent during the later eighteenth century. As the Esterházys' stock of instruments gradually widened, and Haydn went on concert tours that introduced him to fine orchestras such as those in Mannheim, Paris and finally London, he immediately translated the new experiences into still more artfully composed music. His complement expanded to the point where, in later works, it became typical of large orchestras at the end of the century: two each of flutes, oboes, clarinets, bassoons, horns, trumpets and kettledrums, accompanied by a string group.

Experiments

Haydn's work with the symphony is all the more interesting because it stretches over such a considerable and, for this genre, decisive period – from the late 1750s until some way into the 1790s.

He experimented vigorously with the number, character, construction and key relationships of the movements. In particular, he worked on the sonata form and its *development technique*, which means the manner of elaborating and exploiting the thematic material.

Music for everyone

As the paying public broadened its social origins, concerts addressed to it multiplied ever more rapidly. Yet it still heard operatic and royal companies, or groups that were temporarily convened, not independent symphony orchestras. The subscription system was familiar and, in regard to other features as well, the performances were rather like those of today.

A significant difference, though, lay in the contents of the programs. Often they included many pieces of extremely diverse nature, brought together with no detectable plan: operatic arias, a solo concerto, some virtuoso pieces accompanied on the harpsichord, a choral piece, a symphony or an overture. The most comprehensive work could be played first, and the program usually ended with something short and sweet – a tradition which would endure into the early twentieth century. Emphasis was commonly placed on a soloist. Already at that time, admiration for virtuosi and musical circuses was deep.

Spiritual concerts

The centres for orchestral concerts were Paris, London, Vienna, Mannheim, and periodically the courts of Berlin and Dresden. All of these places, too, enjoyed a concentration of composers. In Paris the flautist Anne Philidor had launched a series of *Concerts Spirituels* in 1725, and it grew steadily. The original idea was to present religious works during the holy days, when other public music and theatre activity were forbidden. But the repertoire became more diverse in due course. The concerts were held in a large hall at the Tuileries, and the players came primarily from the orchestra at the Opera.

For a long time, *Concerts Spirituels* provided the ideal forum in which a composer might hear his music performed. During the 1780s, several alternative series of concerts went on in the French capital. One of them was called *Concerts de la Loge Olympique*, and Haydn wrote his six *Paris Symphonies* for it. However, the *Concerts Spirituels* became the only such enterprise which survived the French Revolution. After an interruption, its sessions resumed and continued until the mid-nineteenth century.

The French example inspired simi-

The French Revolution brought changes in many areas of culture, not least orchestral music. No longer did the audiences come only from the upper classes, and concerts for paying listeners became increasingly common.

45

Wolfgang Amadeus Mozart (1756-91) was himself an experienced orchestra musician. He wrote works that demanded strict rehearsal and adept players.

lar arrangements in other countries. Even Leipzig, where Bach's resources had been so small, acquired its *Liebhaber* Concerts. In 1781, these turned into the *Gewandhauskonzerte* (originally referring to the textile merchants' exhibition hall), which are so famous today. But by then, Bach had been dead for thirty years.

More room for music

The concert activities mentioned above are only a selection from what the age had to offer. From the closing decades of the 1700s onward, orchestral events spread widely. It became more customary to build concert halls specially for orchestras. Their size varied, but many had room for at least a thousand listeners. On the other hand, they were not as big as the greatest opera houses with over 3,000 seats. This development was to expand continually during the nineteenth century, although rooted in the western and central lands of Europe. Italy produced very little symphonic music, her orchestras being almost exclusively devoted to opera.

As a well-known instance, large halls were erected in London during the eighteenth century. Among them were the Hanover Square Rooms, opened in 1775 and seating more than 1,000. Into this arena moved a concert series which was already being presented by Johann Christian Bach and Carl Friedrich Abel (a gamba virtuoso who studied under Bach's father, Johann Sebastian). The same hall later passed to other organizers, such as Johann Peter Salomon,

under whom Haydn's successful guest performances in the 1790s took place. It saw regular use for orchestral concerts until !874.

Wolfgang Amadeus Mozart

Haydn's orchestral music is not always easy to play, but he seldom asked for

The original score of Mozart's "Don Giovanni".

more than he expected a particular orchestra to manage. This is an important reason why his music was immediately heard throughout Europe, and was printed by many publishers in large editions. Like most of his contemporaries, he adapted to reality as far as he could, without denying his artistic ambition. Haydn was a musician of the old school, a craftsman devoted to manufacturing products that met a demand.

Mozart was quite different in this respect. Certainly he sometimes used ef-

Mozart's music was performed less often than, for example, Haydn's – one reason being that it was difficult to play – and his finances naturally suffered as a result. Yet his uncompromising manner of composing has vastly benefitted the technical skills of orchestral musicians.

fects that he knew the audience would enjoy. Yet he possessed great artistic integrity and disliked lowering his aim in order to hit a target of "simple" taste. Nor did he try to make things easier for the players than his musical intentions dictated. On the other hand, neither did he complicate the music any more than necessary. Virtuosity for its own sake is absent from his works.

High standards

If an orchestra could not play what he wrote, Mozart blamed the instrumentalists or conductor, or else a shortage of rehearsal time. As an experienced orchestra player, he knew exactly what could be achieved by scrupulous preparation. Some of his music was probably playable only by the best orchestras, but it was not presented even by them as often as the works of Haydn and many lesser-known composers. Consequently, it was not as profitable to publish or copy.

A proof of the limited international interest in Mozart is the information that, in the *Concerts Spirituels* which had one of the best contemporary orchestras, Mozart was performed on fifteen occasions. This may sound rather good to us, but we must compare it with the appearance of Haydn's works on more than 250 programs.

Precise practice

Such difficulties might be imagined to show that the orchestra's members were not such virtuosi as in our day (which, in general, is doubtless correct). However, modern players also hold Mozart's music in high regard – for its *combination* of musical and technical challenges. Many

consider it to be the most demanding of all music. If it is to function convincingly, everything must be done with precision; but at the same time it has to sound relaxed and natural.

Attaining these goals, of course, calls for individual adeptness, and in addition for an orchestra that carries out thorough preparations. Mozart's music has thus contributed greatly to a rise in general playing standards. The composer's artistic pride was perhaps a disaster for himself, but posterity has all the more cause to be grateful for his uncompromising character.

Sensitive instrumentation

Mozart experimented, as did Haydn, with ways of exploiting the orchestra and its separate instruments. He did not need to be as slavish, though, about keeping a fixed wind group in work after work. The supply of players was limted in Salzburg, too, but it was less static than in Eisenstadt. Through his travels, Mozart had seen places with different traditions and larger resources, which inspired him to introduce variations at home.

Mozart's use of the clarinet, influenced by the Mannheimers, set an example that endured even after Weber expanded it. The clear, transparent orchestration with sensitive treatment of each instrument became an ideal that many others tried to match. During the nineteenth century it was carried on especially by Mendelssohn.

What is a proper classical orchestra?

Present-day efforts to perform older music as authentically as possible have led, among other things, to playing with smaller string groups than was normal a few decades ago. But we should not assume that fewer such instruments automatically mean greater fidelity to style. A host of factors merge here, including the whole science of how the written music of former times should be interpreted. Eighteenth-century instruments also sounded unlike ours. Even if we reduce a symphony orchestra to 23 musicians, it gives a different impression from what Haydn's Esterházy orchestra may have done. The audibility of individual instruments has changed and, therefore, so have features such as the balance and blend of their timbres.

Using original instruments or copies of them is a definite aid, yet neither is this a guarantee of "authentic" performances (a fact which often contrasts with the claims of recording companies). However, these instruments have the value of giving players an insight into what was once possible and practical.

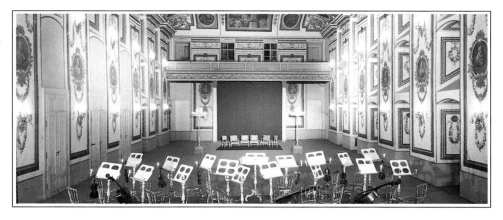

The concert salon in the Esterházy castle at Eisenstadt.

Numerous questions about phrasing, manner of playing, tempo and so forth, find immediate answers. Such knowledge can then be used when playing old music on modern instruments. All members of orchestras should have the chance to work for some time with original instruments.

There is more that distinguishes us from the eighteenth century. As a rule, contemporary concert halls are hardly reminiscent of a small theatre or festival hall in a castle. And in particular, as listeners to music, we are quite different from our ancestors who had never heard anything by Berlioz, Wagner, Mahler, Bartók or Messiaen. It is obviously worth attempting to experience the past, but human beings cannot be transported centuries back in time.

How large were early orchestras?

Symphony orchestras today are fairly similar all over the world. Their size varies considerably, but their component groups are related in established ways. It was otherwise in the eighteenth century. While the orchestra's essential structure had become unified, the number of musicians and the balance of their strengths were very diverse.

As we have seen, the Mannheim orchestra had around 50 members, whereas most court orchestras tended to be no more than half as large. The *Concerts Spirituels* employed about 40 players during the 1750s, and over 60 a few decades later. During the same period, the Paris Opera orchestra grew from just over 40 to beyond 70. In Italy, opera houses such as the San Carlo in Naples had at most 70 musicians.

Mozart tells of orchestras in Vienna that ranged from chamber ensembles to more than 80. Haydn's concerts in London during the 1790s were among his lifelong triumphs, yet he conducted an orchestra with barely 40 instrumentalists. In view of his fame, this is surprising in a city which had arranged Handel festivals with orchestral groups of several hundred players. Besides, London had an unusual wealth of musicians, due to the many Frenchmen who fled the Revolution.

Balancing the act

In the string group, cellos and double basses were normally fewer in relation to the violins than is the custom today. This was because they played the same part (separated by an octave) and should be seen as a unit. Sometimes they were strengthened by bassoons. The violas were often much fewer than the bass instruments, a practice we find unnatural, but which continued even after Haydn and Mozart began to give them more independent parts.

Balanced against a dozen wind instruments was a string group that might be of only slightly greater size, or up to four times as large. In some places, the wind players were as numerous as in modern big-city orchestras (four of each), although the strings were just a half or a third as many. To be sure, the music did not have such a quantity of individual wind parts – but since the instruments were limited in power, they could more easily fill large halls by playing *unisono* in pairs. The French taught a custom of using four bassoons even when there were only two of each other woodwind. Thus did Berlioz and many after him.

No orchestra is typical

We may conclude from these illustrations that no uniform orchestra has ever existed for the music of Vienna Classicism. Symphonies themselves were long similar in construction, but it is difficult to consider any particular orchestra as more proper in style than others; the variations were too great. There is always a point in striving to imitate the conditions of a given place or period, or of music written for a certain orchestra. Yet it would be risky to generalize on that basis. History also shows that composers have often been more broad-minded, as regards the performance of their music, than latter-day purists are!

Ludwig van Beethoven (1770-1827)

The

Vienna's classical style was introduced by a series of composers who are little known to us. Among those who perfected it were Haydn, Mozart and Gluck. The next transformation, and the accompanying change in the orchestra's role, can be largely attributed to a single musician: Ludwig van Beethoven. Not that a transition from Classicism to Romanticism was his own idea: it resulted from long, complex developments. Pre-Romantic traits occurred already in Gluck and Mozart. Conversely, half a century after them, Mendelssohn still adhered to the classical values – clarity and balance.

Beethoven's expressionism

We need not delve into the many sources of this stylistic transition. What chiefly distinguished a Romantic artist from his predecessors was an urge to express himself: this stood in the foreground, at the expense of more objective matters such as form, clarity and accessibility. Previously, a musician's private moods were rarely reflected in his work. Mozart and Haydn wrote bright, seemingly happy music even in their darkest hours. With Beethoven and Schubert, we can more directly feel the connection between creating and living.

That is just what made Beethoven a typical Romantic artist: his markedly individualistic, self-radiant personality. He allowed his circumstances – and his convictions on political and moral issues – to have an effect on his music.

Romantic adventure

Felix Mendelssohn (1809-47)

Standing with one leg in the moderate eighteenth century, and the other in the expansive nineteenth, he was the very embodiment of a transition.

In his youth, Beethoven had adopted much of the classical style and written open, uncomplicated music in tune with the times. A couple of years into the new century, when just over thirty, he began to reveal darker undertones, which eventually would characterize his music. The mature Beethoven expressed himself with less personal restriction than anyone earlier had dared to do. Gone were the merely diverting, facile and entertaining qualities that typified many of his forerunners, even in their best works.

Beethoven's revolt doubtless had to do with his reaction to increasing deafness. At least as important, though, was his awareness of contemporary life. By nature reflective, he absorbed and responded to current philosophy and subversive events. Social upheaval, to which Mozart had only alluded in *The*

Marriage of Figaro, emerged full-blown in Beethoven after the French Revolution. His longing for liberation, and his mistrust of power and traditional authority, coloured both his life and his music. The *Eroica* and ninth symphony belong, with the opera *Fidelio*, to his key works in this respect.

A free artist

The customary combination, creating one's own works and performing them, suited Beethoven as well. He won early recognition as a virtuoso pianist, but he was among the first to succeed in establishing an independent artistic career. Almost everyone had previously been forced to depend on assignments from kings, princes, theatres or the Church. Mozart served the Archbishop of Salzburg for many years, then set forth on his own in Vienna, and failed.

Beethoven's life was far from luxurious. He got by on orders, subscription editions, his piano playing and some teaching. At times he obtained support from patrons. Once his deafness ruled out public piano playing, he had little money to spare – yet until the end he preserved his artistic freedom.

It is hardly strange that such a headstrong, independent person as Beethoven was able to transform music and influence the orchestra's status. In his first four symphonies, he kept the classical group of paired woodwinds, horns and trumpets. A third horn in the *Eroica* is all that differs from Haydn's and Mozart's symphonies (although they had

occasionally used more than two horns to produce alternative tunings). However, from the finale of his second symphony onward, Beethoven's music is much more advanced in character.

Intense statements

A wider choice of instruments appears in the fifth symphony. Perhaps surprisingly, it does not occur in the dramatic first movement, where it would have been fitting. The theatrical finesse is that Beethoven saved his ammunition until the last movement. Only then do three trombones arise to add extra power and festivity, while a piccolo punctuates them with sparkling cascades of tones. To our blunted senses, a few instruments more or less may make little difference – but for those who were used to softer colours, Beethoven's radiant conclusion must have come as a shock.

The piccolo, double bassoon, and especially trombones had been employed earlier in opera, and trombones in church music as well. Well-known examples with trombones are Mozart's overture to *The Magic Flute* and his *Requiem*. Both trombones and double bassoons occur in Gluck's overture to *Alceste*, and in Haydn's oratorios *The Creation* and *The Seasons* – yet not in a single one of their symphonies.

What was revolutionary about the fifth symphony, though, was how these instruments were used: as strong colour to heighten the intensity of expression. Some years earlier, Haydn's *The Seasons* had called for exactly the same combination, but with nothing like the same explosive power. One might say, with scant exaggeration, that the fifth symphony introduced *violence* to music, releasing its feelings until it bordered on unbeautiful sound.

In the *Pastoral Symphony* from this period, Beethoven again included the piccolo and a couple of trombones. Here, too, we find violence in the fourth movement's depiction of a thunderstorm. A return to the lighter eighteenth-century orchestra occurred in his seventh and eighth symphonies. But in spite of that, the latter's orgiastic finale is more forceful and voluminous than anything in Haydn or Mozart.

The Choral Symphony

Beethoven's grandiose ninth symphony makes use of a piccolo, double bassoon, four horns, three trombones, and "Turkish music" played on a triangle, cymbals and bass drum. Its first three movements exploit all the horns, and its scherzo the trombones as well. Only in the last movement do other instrumental resources enter. These are supplemented by a chorus and four solo singers. The finale contains the largest orchestral complement ever employed by Beethoven (apart from a group of extra trumpets in his stereophonically

inclined *Battle Symphony*).

Despite such enormous forces, Beethoven did not give up the classicistic orchestra as a foundation. His additions to it generally came at selected moments, for relatively brief interventions. But so psychologically effective an application made their impact all the greater. In terms of orchestral technique, Beethoven's significance lay more in how and when he used the instruments than in which ones he used.

Mounting demands

Individual parts often stand out against the others, whether solistically (as with the oboe in the Pastoral Symphony) or grouped (such as the three horns in the *Eroica* scherzo). As the scale of expression gradually widened, the technical demands on the players increased. Certain difficulties must have seemed almost insuperable to Beethoven's contemporaries. Even today, a bassoonist prepares exhaustively for a passage like the short, but conspicuous, run in the finale of the fourth symphony. Virtuoso parts of this kind almost never occur in Mozart, but they were natural for Beethoven.

Haydn and others with access to a permanent orchestra had been able to add specific complexities for a notably

skilful player. Beethoven, though, frequently did not know who would do the playing; so the technical requirements must have been chiefly due to his own need for expression. How fundamental this music still is for an orchestra's quality may be illuminated by a statement of Herbert von Karajan: "An orchestra that plays Beethoven's symphonies in a first-class manner can play anything at all just as well."

Deeper feeling

Beethoven was one of the most influential composers of the early nineteenth century. Through him, the intensity and depth of musical expression grew rapidly, as did the development of form. He experimented with the music's ability to depict exterior phenomena (such as nature in the Pastoral Symphony) and to penetrate far into the human soul (as in the late string quartets).

On the other hand, Beethoven was less of a pioneer in regard to creating the ideal of sound for the Romantic orchestra. Usually he seems to have chosen instruments for their individual potential rather than their collective effect. They are relatively seldom exploited jointly to evoke a tender atmosphere. Beethoven lived at a time of transition, when even a revolutionary was bound to the past.

The same may be said in principle of Franz Schubert, although he treated the orchestra differently. Soft and sensitive in personality, he favoured the poetic and intimate spirit in music. Power and acuity were not his gifts. He painted with milder pastel colours in the frame of the late Haydn's orchestral constitution. Only in his last two symphonies did he use trombones, and in the fourth, two pairs of horns. They all lack the piccolo, the double bassoon, and percussion (apart from kettledrums).

Franz Schubert (1797-1828) belonged to the leading Romantics – and to the first free artists, though he did not succeed in economic terms.

E. T. A. Hoffmann (1776-1822)

Sources of Romantic inspiration

Events outside the field of music were closely associated with the evolution of the Romantic orchestra's sound. Central European opera composers frequently preferred themes taken from new trends in literature. The Enlightenment's enthusiasm for nature had given way to more profound descriptions of it, including real animals as well as fairies and goblins. At the same time, during the first two decades of the nineteenth century, famous works of folk poetry appeared: Arnim and Brentano's *Des Knaben Wunderhorn*, and the Grimm brothers' collection of tales. They were read by children and adults alike, throughout much of the Western world, and influenced artists of all kinds.

Many people were greatly inspired by the forest – a place of majesty and mystery, often frightful, sometimes warm and cosy. To evoke these aspects, the French horn was found very suitable. Its hunting origins, and its wide register of expression, made it ideal for bringing the forest's moods to life. In particular, a whole group of horns in soft nuances could produce the mysterious character that Romanticism craved.

The normal procedure was to use a quartet of horns for playing chords with a uniform timbre. This group, which had arisen in the eighteenth century for practical reasons (alternating between two pairs with different tunings), has remained standard in much music ever since the early Romantic period.

Present-day orchestras often have more horns, but the quartet is still basic. The clarinet was popular due to similar tonal factors, but more for its soloistic possibilities than as a group.

Nature and supernature

A personality of rich significance for Romanticism was at once an author, composer and conductor: Ernst Theodor Amadeus Hoffmann. He is perhaps best known to us as the creator of the plot, and principal character, of Offenbach's opera *The Tales of Hoffmann*. Also based upon one of his stories is *The Nutcracker* by Tchaikovsky.

Hoffmann broke new ground for the Romantics on several levels. His ope-

ras developed from Gluck's and Mozart's classicism and became emphatically imaginative in, for example, their depiction of nature. Especially important was *Undine* (1816). As a composer and particularly as a poet, Hoffmann had a love of visionary delusions that laid the foundation for German ideas of Romantic ope-

ra, which often combined themes from fairy-tale and myth with supernatural elements. The illustrations range from Weber's *Der Freischütz* and Wagner's *Der Ring des Nibelungen* until the end of the century with Dvorák's *Rusalka* and Humperdinck's *Hänsel und Gretel.*

Weber's universal art

As the main sources of Romantic music, poetry and nature were prominent in the work of Carl Maria von Weber. Born sixteen years after Beethoven, and dead one year earlier, Weber was among the composers who shaped the new

Nature, myth and saga were the great sources of inspiration during the Romantic period. This scenery was created by Max Bruckner for Wagner's operatic cycle "Der Ring des Nibelungen".

Mahler, as well as Herbert von Karajan in our time, he was not satisfied with conducting, but took an active role at all stages of the work: scenery, direction, lighting and so forth. Weber was one of the first to view opera as a *Gesamtkunstwerk*, and thus inspired Wagner in particular. As a skilful musical journalist, he also regularly wrote on the subject in the daily press. His articles tell a great deal about contemporary musical theatre; so this side of his talent, too, was valuable for subsequent generations.

Der Freischütz

Aptitude for instrumentation emerged early in Weber's career. At the age of sixteen, using a theme from the French Revolution thirteen years earlier, he composed the opera *Peter Schmoll und seine Nachbarn* in an almost Mozartian style. Here we find plenty of solo woodwind contributions in imaginative combinations, mysterious string passages, and other features that were to characterize his mature music, and the Romanticism to come.

He focussed increasingly on the two instruments that would become most typical of Romantic orchestras – the French horn and the clarinet. For the latter, he wrote two excellent solo con-

world of Romantic sound. He conducted successfully in Prague and Dresden, presenting most of the contemporary French, Italian and German operas. He was especially fascinated by French music, which was often colourful and made frequent use of solo winds and new instrumental effects. The period

after the French Revolution had promoted an exciting, and socially minded, musical theatre that called for fresh approaches. A home for much experimentation was the Paris Opera with its large resources and high quality.

Weber grew up with opera and devoted much of his life to it. Like

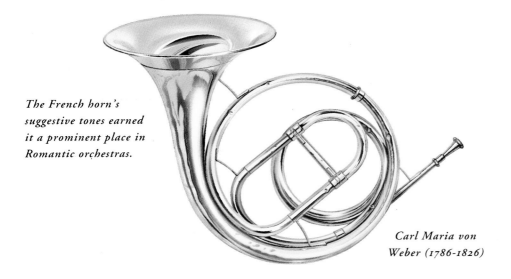

The French horn's suggestive tones earned it a prominent place in Romantic orchestras.

Carl Maria von Weber (1786-1826)

certos. Horns celebrate in the famous Huntsmen's Chorus of *Der Freischütz* (1821), which was Germany's first really important Romantic opera. This work belongs to the greatest triumphs in operatic history, and was to lead the way for many successors, notably Wagner and Bruckner.

Among Weber's other specialties was the use of treble and bass instruments, such as the piccolo and bassoon. He had a fine feeling for their potential, and sometimes let them switch roles: the high ones played in their lowest register, and the low ones in their high register.

Spotlights on the forest

Psychological characterization is not as deep in *Der Freischütz* as in Mozart's mature operas, but greater space is given to depicting the environments in which the action occurs. As a result, the forest itself is as prominent a "personage" as the figures in the drama.

After this work, Weber composed two more operas: *Euryanthe* (1823) and *Oberon* (1826). The first was his most extreme application of harmony to strengthen expression. In the second, he again made the forest a central feature. All three of the cited works show Weber's fully developed operatic style, which in time would prove essential to Schumann, Liszt, Wagner, Brahms, Bruckner, Mahler and others.

Weber helped to pioneer the calculated exploitation of an orchestra as a *tonal palette*, creating personal nuances of colour as in a painting. The instruments were blended in manifold ways, creating new sound values and responding to the dramatic action, the characters' emotions and, not least, the eternal presence of nature. Orchestration was gradually refined along Weber's lines, but the impact of his operas hardly faced competition until the appearance, forty years later, of Wagner's *Tristan und Isolde.*

Berlioz and the Fantastic Symphony

Parallel with German developments, the French continued to experiment with the orchestra. In Paris, at the age of only 27, Hector Berlioz made a sensation with his *Symphonie Fantastique* in 1830. Few single works in the history of the symphony orchestra have had such overwhelming importance as this. Berlioz' treatment of the orchestra went farther than either Beethoven's or Weber's, yet it also achieved a synthesis of the two.

According to Berlioz, these composers were in fact his chief sources of inspiration – in addition to an Italian, Gasparo Spontini, who had long written operas in Paris. Gluck's music was another of Berlioz' early experiences. He studied that of Beethoven intensively, and the Pastoral Symphony became his favourite work. It can reasonably be said that the latter was the starting point of his creativity.

Winds and choirs

But there was a further key factor, the specifically French music from the decades around 1800. While in his twenties, Berlioz had begun to study composition with Jean-François Lesueur. This was not a great composer, but an open and inspiring teacher who encouraged students to think originally (in contrast to Cherubini, the more traditional director of the Paris Conservatory). Lesueur brought Berlioz into contact with a good deal of music that would be of value to him.

Orchestral technique had been expanded by François Gossec with, among other things, conspicuous roles for wind instruments. Already when Mozart was five years old, Gossec had used the clarinet in a symphony, and it was he who

Hector Berlioz (1803-69) made a sensation with his rich musical effects and magnificent orchestration.

added the instrument to the Paris Opera's orchestra. Also important were the experiments of Étienne Méhul with orchestral timbre in symphonies and operas, for example in his popular *Joseph* (1807). He even wrote an opera without any violins in the orchestra! Moreover, he employed a *leitmotif* technique which directly anticipated Berlioz' *idée fixe* in the *Symphonie Fantastique*.

Another basis of Berlioz' rich orchestral effects was the general liking for wind instruments. After the Revolution, this emerged in reams of music dedicated to the glory of the Republic: marches, fanfares, hymns and cantatas. The Napoleonic era hardly diminished the need for such festive music. Frequently it relied on massive impact,

The Italian opera composer Gasparo Spontini (1774-1841) did much to inspire Berlioz.

with an enormous orchestra and a chorus of several thousand voices. Such features were to occur regularly in Berlioz.

Challenging the conventions

All these impressions would, of course, have been less fruitful if Berlioz himself had lacked an exceptional instinct for sound. Already in an early work such as the symphony called – in Hoffmann's spirit – fantastic, he demonstrated new ways of producing effects, combining instruments to reveal previously unknown sensations. From Beethoven he borrowed a sharp, fiery feeling and made it more glaring, exploiting the small E-flat clarinet and the piccolo. Trombones and tubas were used to depict the ravages of demons. Not even church-bells are missing in Berlioz' clash with conventions. Especially the last two movements of the symphony have an almost magical power, which even today captivates audiences. That this music was composed only a couple of years after Beethoven and Schubert is truly astonishing.

But Berlioz could also hearken to Weber's spirit and portray intimate, pastoral scenes, where instruments like the oboe and English horn – not to mention the strings – are used exquisitely. He often took advantage of the harp, which had once appeared chiefly in operas. And he was glad to let the woodwinds play in unison, a technique that would often be applied by Mahler.

Rehearsing for weeks

Berlioz' instrumentation aimed not primarily at gathering a splendour of sound, but at differentiating and generating variety in tonal, melodic and particularly rhythmical respects. Much has been written about his instrumentation, but his rhythmical imagination is worth the same attention. It may be the main reason why his music was often misunderstood by contemporary critics and audiences. Complex and unusual rhythms, combined with his transparent handling of orchestral sounds, imposed terrific demands on the players of that period. Berlioz asked for the ulti-

mate, and seldom received it.

The dilemma is that Berlioz' music has to be very precisely executed if his intentions are to be realized. Even today, an insufficiently rehearsed orchestra can make his rhythms sound clumsy and the tonal balance diffuse. Despite considerable growth in orchestras' technical ability by that time, and the introduction of better instruments, virtuoso orchestras in the modern sense were an unknown notion. Berlioz composed as though they already existed. A clear example is the virtuoso scherzo (Queen Mab) in *Romeo and Juliet*. Such pieces required weeks of practice. But orchestras cost a lot of money, which the composer frequently had to pay out of his own pocket.

A symbol of the future

For many young musicians in Europe, Berlioz became a beacon of inspiration and an emblem for the modern view of musical art. When the *Symphonie Fantastique* was first performed, Franz Liszt sat in the auditorium. Richard Wagner heard the "dramatic symphony" Romeo and Juliet, an experience that fueled him in *Tristan und Isolde*. Whoever failed to appreciate Berlioz could nonetheless hardly avoid taking notice of his epoch-making way of handling the orchestra.

His orchestration technique has been studied by the majority of later composers. Close links to it were forged by Wagner, Rimsky-Korsakov and Debussy.

From Wagner onward, a line of development ran through Mahler, Schoenberg and Webern, while a somewhat different one led to Strauss, Bartók and Lutoslawski. Another line ran from Rimsky-Korsakov to Stravinsky, Respighi and others. Berlioz created conditions for the symphony orchestra's evolution far into the twentieth century.

Berlioz collected his knowledge of orchestral instruments in a treatise on instrumentation (1844), the first textbook ever published on this subject. Both in original form and as revised by Richard Strauss (1905), it has remained fundamental for generations of musicians. Strauss' contribution was mainly to add examples from more recent music, especially that of Wagner.

Shakespeare's play "Romeo and Juliet" has inspired many artists. Berlioz wrote a dramatic symphony based on it, which in turn moved Wagner to compose his "Tristan und Isolde".

Symphonic grandeur

Ever since the great days of the *Concerts Spirituels* in the late eighteenth century, concerts had flourished in Paris. A modern French orchestra tradition was founded around 1830, but not by Berlioz, who was all too controversial to be given an opportunity to present regular concerts. Only a small circle realized that he was one of the real geniuses of music, and the French capital has never entirely accepted him.

A leader of quality

Instead, it was François Antoine Habeneck who established new standards. Of German origin, born and educated in France, he worked for many years as a violinist at the Paris Opera. During his last twenty-five years until 1849, he performed chiefly as a conductor. Among the important operas first conducted by him were Rossini's *William Tell*, Meyerbeer's *Les Huguenots* and Berlioz' *Benvenuto Cellini*. He also presided over the première of Berlioz' *Symphonie Fantastique*.

Habeneck led the *Concerts Spirituels* in the 1810s, but his most durable achievement was to launch a concert orchestra of his own, the *Société des Concerts du Conservatoire*. It played in the conservatory's sizable hall (with a thousand seats), which explains its name. The orchestra was as ample as many in our time: sixty string players, quadruple woodwinds, and a total of 85 members. As a comparison, the Leipzig Gewandhaus Orchestra, in that period, had only half this number of strings. Under Habeneck, the Conservatoire orchestra attained high class and was regarded as one of the best in Europe. It had a long life, its name surviving until 1967 when it was partly absorbed into the new *Orchestre de Paris*.

Three years of rehearsals

One of Habeneck's missions in life was to carry out maximally elaborate performances of the symphonies of Beethoven. When the orchestra made its debut in 1828, the *Eroica* was on the program, to be followed by the other symphonies in turn. From the outset, he worked bar by bar through the demanding ninth symphony (which still calls for exhaustive rehearsal). He instructed, corrected, and polished every detail until, in 1831, it was ready for the first French performance. By then, rumours of the orchestra's quality had spread, and visitors streamed in from near and far. One of them was the young Felix Mendelssohn, who learned valuable lessons there for his Gewandhaus

François Habeneck (1781-1849) was a great conductor who strongly influenced the orchestra's qualitative development. He led the premières of many famous works, such as Rossini's "William Tell". Here is a sketch of scenery for the latter's performance.

Orchestra at home in Leipzig.

The world of Wagner

Habeneck soon managed to cover all of the main works by Beethoven; but that was not all. When Richard Wagner visited Paris in 1839-40, fresh preparations were being made to play the ninth symphony. He heard Habeneck rehearse the first three movements, which overwhel-

med him. Never before had he experienced such a consummate and detailed orchestral event. His travel diary noted: "He who wishes to know Beethoven's ninth symphony completely must hear it performed by the conservatory orchestra in Paris... The presentation of German instrumental compositions at these concerts has made a deep impression upon me, and has initiated me anew into the wonderful secrets of genuine art."

As a result, Wagner's activity took a novel turn: he resolved to see that similar concerts took place at home in Germany. In 1846, with the court orchestra in Dresden, he gave a performance of the ninth symphony. The opera directors had tried to prevent this experiment, as the work had previously fallen through and was "obviously written by an insane composer". They thought that such a benefit concert on

*The Wagner tuba, named after the
composer who ordered its design, is a
development of the military bugle.
Resembling the French horn in its mouthpiece and number of keys, it is normally
used by the orchestra's horn players.*

Palm Sunday would draw too few people. But with clever advance information, Wagner instead attracted the largest audience on record!

Despite the opposition, he even
managed to get the podium rebuilt. The
orchestra was concentrated in the centre, surrounded as in an amphitheatre
by the choir at higher levels. "This," he
summed up, "was a huge advantage to
the powerful effect of the choral parts.
In the purely symphonic movements, it
lent the well-disposed orchestra enormous precision and energy." The concert was a colossal success and sent
echoes throughout Central Europe.

Long preparations

An important by-product of Wagner's
contribution was that he could show his
countrymen how far it was possible to
push an orchestra by means of careful
preparations. He put an end to the age
when a symphony was prepared at a
single rehearsal, something that had still
been common in Beethoven's time.
Other composers were now motivated
to create pioneering works that would
have been meaningless in the past.

No small requirements are posed by
Wagner's own music from the 1850s onward. *Tristan und Isolde* had more than a
hundred rehearsals at the Vienna Opera,
only to be cancelled before its planned
première. When the first performance
occurred at Munich in 1865, many
rehearsals were needed to prepare the
intricate counterpoint, as well as dynamic and tonal adjustments. Even when

Tannhäuser was presented by the Paris
Opera in 1861, more than 160 rehearsals
are said to have taken place.

Refined structure

During the 1840s, with *Tannhäuser*
and *Lohengrin*, Wagner had progressed
to an entirely personal style in terms of
melody and harmony. The orchestra's
significance deepened, and he exploited
it ever more masterfully. His basis was
Beethoven's organization with double
woodwinds. For the innovative wind
treatment in *Lohengrin*, these were increased to three. Leading roles were
granted to the English horn and bass
clarinet. Among the striking features is
also a division of the string instruments:
each group split into several independent sections, so as to create chords of
many notes. A superb example is the
prelude's shimmering violin sound,
from no fewer than four solo and four
tutti parts.

The orchestra plays a key role in Wagner's operas. Sometimes he relates the instruments to particular motifs, as when the contrabass tuba portrays a dragon. This setting was made in 1899 for a performance of "Siegfried".

Gods, giants and humans

At the time *Lohengrin* was finished, Wagner decided to write a musical drama based upon the Nibelungen legend. Here he mixed features of the Icelandic *Edda* and old Germanic mythology with ancient impulses from Aeschylus' *Oresteia.* The action of the dramatic *Ring* cycle, in which good and evil forces fight for world dominion, takes place on many psychological planes with strong symbolism. Its extremely complex story, traversing numerous generations, contains a rich cast of role types: deities, giants, mortals, beasts, creatures under the earth and on the bottom of a river.

In order to deal with this phenomenal epic, Wagner systematically widened the orchestra's range of expression. All sections were given more players, and unusual or new instruments were added. With quadruple woodwinds, each group could produce full and uniform chords, making it easier to achieve a tonal stratification. The horn quartet was doubled to eight, and the trumpets and trombones became four. Some passages use extra wind players behind the stage.

Melody in the bass

Until then, solo melodies had normally been presented by flutes, oboes and the like. Wagner entrusted comprehensive solos to the extremely low instruments as well: bass clarinet, double bassoon, bass trumpet and tuba. This alone gives the *Ring* new dimensions of sound, and

the Wagner tubas – built to his specifications – contribute to the diversity. An important factor was that, by this time, many brass instruments had become chromatically unlimited through the use of valves.

Such a determined emphasis on the wind orchestra naturally called for corresponding growth in the string section. However, this was not a matter of adding strange or novel instruments, but of flexible exploitation of the normal instruments in greater quantity. The

technique of division in *Lohengrin* was now developed further.

The more, the softer

In this context we should recall some general facts about the string group. Its expansion during the nineteenth century was concerned, in part, with balancing the winds and getting the sound to fill big opera houses and concert halls. But there were qualitative aspects as well. On the one hand, a large group of

The English horn's sonorous tone was well suited to Wagner's soft instrumentation.

string players is able, even in powerful passages, to focus on a beautiful supporting tone. If too small, the group must play more loudly and may sound stressed or even harsh. On the other hand, the former is also more suited to playing softly.

The paradox is only apparent. For a large group of violinists of average quality in unison produces a more even and appealing, as well as softer, *pianissimo* than do a few players, no matter how skilful. All musicians differ slightly in intonation, timbre and vibrato. In a large group, these divergences cancel out and one hears not the individual instruments, but their sum effect. Thus, a large enough quantity of players in each group is especially valuable when the strings are required to play *divisi*.

Leitmotifs

The text of the *Ring*, written by Wagner himself, consists of continuous speech, not formal poetry. Passages are not repeated as in traditional opera. The musical result is an "endless melody" without customary elements of form. To create coherence in spite of this, Wagner composed a great number of short, easily recognized "recurrent themes" (or "motives of recollection"). Each of these he connected with a particular character, event, action or the like.

The concept of leitmotifs was old, but nobody had yet systematically constructed entire operas from such elements. Usually they have a melodic profile; some are a rhythmical figuration, an instrumental tone, or a typical harmonic sequence. Occasionally they are allied to certain instruments. Not surprisingly, bird-song is executed on a flute and dragons are evoked on a double-bass tuba; other combinations are more sophisticated.

With the aid of leitmotifs, Wagner wove a fabric of associations backward and forward in the drama. Leitmotifs occur now and then in the song parts — but it is the orchestra, interestingly enough, that bears the main responsibility for them. While the characters talk, narrate and argue, the orchestra comments on their doings, revealing interrelationships that are not obvious from the text, or are unknown to the characters themselves.

Euphony

A feature of orchestral treatment that distinguishes Wagner, as much from his predecessors Beethoven and Berlioz as from his successor Mahler, is that he always emphasizes *consonance*. The instruments are certainly used for conspicuous solo passages, and are contrasted with each other individually or collectively. But they vary and enrich the total sound at a given time, rather than breaking away from it. In Beethoven, the trumpets sometimes depart from the unitary sound. Berlioz may employ the piccolo, E-flat clarinet, or tuba for very sharp passages. With Mahler, glaring and unattractive sounds would become a suitable way to depict the sombre secrets of existence.

Although Wagner often accumulates great power, he excludes raw, hard noises. Even at the most dramatic moments, his orchestra retains its euphony. He gradually "liberated" his early opera *The Flying Dutchman* from excessively sharp brass passages. In the *Ring*, *Tristan* and *Parsifal*, acute dissonances are commonly damped by soft instrumentation. We must go back to Mozart for a correspondingly rounded orchestral sound with no roughness or rebellion against euphony. In Wagner, the psychology of the text and music operates on its own; he had no need for superficially strengthening effects. This is all the more impressive in view of his youthful passion for the showy excesses of *grand opéra*.

Wagner's successors

Wagner exerted vast influence on his contemporaries, and on the immediately following generations. So pervasive were his achievements that almost no one could avoid being somehow affec-

The heckelphone was developed by Wilhelm Heckel and used, for example, by Strauss.

ted. Many attempted to copy him, but lacked his creative ability and his incredible sense of sound. Imitators appeared in many countries, and their works were generally short-lived.

Among those who made the best use of orchestration in Wagner's spirit was Anton Bruckner. However, he had quite a different artistic bent, and his symphonic structure was very personal. Another, who had been Wagner's assistant in Bayreuth, was Engelbert Humperdinck. With his idyllic, delicate folktale operas, such as *Hänsel und Gretel* (1893) and *Königskinder* (1910), he laid claim to a niche of his own. Also building largely on Wagner's musical drama and instrumentation was Hans Pfitzner, although he mainly followed the early Romanticism of Hoffmann and Schumann. He, too, was very individualistic, and his masterly "historical legend" *Palestrina* (1916) stands by itself.

Mahler enriches the orchestra

The above-mentioned quality is still more audible in Gustav Mahler, despite his explicit adherence to Wagner and his regular conducting of the latter's works. He blended ingredients from Bach, Haydn, Beethoven, Weber, Berlioz, Liszt, Wagner and others. Nonetheless, his music strikes us as unmistakably Mahleresque!

In his symphonic works, Mahler relied on the large orchestra of late Romanticism, whose components and use he varied constantly between works. He increased the late Wagner's quadruple woodwinds to five and, in some groups, even six. Already in his first three symphonies, the brass group is nearly up to Wagner's maximum size; it culminates in the eighth symphony's eight horns, eight trumpets, seven trombones and a tuba. Mahler's most limited orchestra is to be found in his fourth symphony with triple woodwinds (but four flutes), four horns and three trumpets, although no trombones or tuba.

Gustav Mahler (1860-1911)

Anton Bruckner (1824-96)

Typically, however, Mahler exploited his resources very restrictively in long parts. The middle movements often use far fewer players than do the rest (as was already the case with Haydn). Passages as transparent as chamber music occur constantly.

During the nineteenth century, few composers used any other percussion instruments than the kettledrums, bass drum, cymbals, triangle, and occasionally in operas a snare drum. Not even in Wagner do they play a strong role. Mahler was among the first to realize their potential: nearly twenty different kinds appear in his symphonies. And in each, a new combination is employed to produce the desired timbre and expressiveness. They are most conspicuous in the sixth symphony.

Strauss carries on

The Wagner tradition was taken further by Richard Strauss. It is especially clear in his early operas, but Wagner's advanced instrumental polyphony also underlies his later work. All of the instruments finally used by Wagner occur in Strauss, supplemented by new ones like the heckelphone (a baritone oboe) and, more surprisingly, old ones such as the *oboe d'amore* and basset horn.

There are admittedly significant differences between the tonal ideals of Wagner and Strauss. It was Mozart whom Strauss admired most. This is probably why he cultivated a clear orchestral sound with emphasis on the treble. His early symphonic fantasy *Aus Italien* has a light, transparent timbre, in contrast to Wagner's density and dark colour scale. The opera *Salome*, with its large orchestra, can – if adequately played – seem much like chamber music, as the composer explicitly intended.

Strauss depended on virtuosity to an extent that had seldom occurred in orchestral parts, except for solo passages. The same line had been taken by Berlioz, but orchestras of his time were not ready for it. By the end of the nineteenth century, the technical standards were considerably higher, not least as a result of greater familiarity with Wagner's music. Less adept orchestras certainly existed, but those available to Strauss were among the elite. They included those of the Munich, Berlin and Dresden opera houses, as well as the philharmonic orchestras of Berlin and Vienna. He could take for granted that his works would be performed by the finest players alive. It is no wonder that he did everything to make them shine.

For all that, his parts were regarded as very difficult. To execute them perfectly, an orchestra would need to contain nothing but virtuosi – and of course not even the best do so. On the other hand, Strauss did not expect every detail to emerge (as it unfortunately does on some modern CD recordings). What he wanted were the musical gesture, expression and colour. Contemporary witnesses say that, as a conductor, he emphasized the character and total effect of a work, rather than fanatical precision. The same is evident from his own gramophone recordings.

Richard Strauss (1864-1949) wrote music which was regarded as extremely hard to play. According to anecdote, he sometimes found it beyond his own abilities.

A relevant relic

When Strauss led a rehearsal, he took the musicians' problems with humour. According to an often-told anecdote, a horn player complained of the inhuman demands set by his part: "Herr Doktor Strauss, I am convinced that you can play this passage easily on the piano, but on a horn it is utterly unplayable." The disarming reply came fast: "No, you are quite wrong – I can't play it on the piano either!"

Strauss' orchestration technique was primarily a mixture of elements from Mozart, Berlioz and Wagner, but also drew influence from Debussy. Through his dominant position in European musical life for more half a century (he died as late as 1949), Strauss affected composers all over the world. Yet the first half of the twentieth century brought strong reactions against the Romantic ideals he represented. Many avant-garde composers have viewed him as a relic from an age that disappeared in World War I. Still, he has remained highly relevant for concert and opera audiences. All orchestras play his symphonic works, including those which were once heavily criticized, such as *Symphonia Domestica* and *An Alpine Symphony*.

The music of national identity

Our focus until now has been on Central Europe, where Romantic music was largely created. Works of great merit were written in many other areas, but often in the same basic style. Few composers managed to assert real independence, some of which will be surveyed here in two principal cases.

Russian innovators

During the late nineteenth century, a number of composers emerged to express the national spirit of Russia in various ways. Mikhail Glinka had made a sensation in 1836 with his opera *A Life for the Tsar*. Despite its native theme and occasional borrowings from folk music, it rested chiefly on German and Italian foundations. Six years later came his *Ruslan and Lyudmila*, where Russian features are more dominant. Although less popular, it became a strong source of inspiration to many musicians.

Little progress occurred for the next two decades. Then a young composer, Mily Balakirev, gathered some like-minded friends in St. Petersburg: the doctor Aleksandr Borodin, the civil servant Modest Mussorgsky, the naval officer Nikolai Rimsky-Korsakov, and the military engineer César Cui. Besides having different professions, several of these lacked a musical education. Balakirev helped them greatly, providing ideas and advice.

This gathering came to be known as "The Five", or "The Mighty Handful", and sometimes "The Regenerators" or "The New Russians". What primarily united them was the quest for national identity. At first, they fostered a belief that training in compositional technique was unnecessary, even restrictive for spontaneous inspiration.

Balakirev was fairly proficient as a self-taught professional musician, yet Borodin and Mussorgsky remained technically immature throughout their lives. Their music grew slowly and was continually reworked, limiting their production. Cui composed operas in a more Western style, but was a prominent journalist and defender of the group's ideas.

Scenery for Stravinsky's comic opera "Mavra" (1922).

Rimsky-Korsakov

One of the above-mentioned composers soon changed his attitude towards knowledge and trained himself thoroughly. Rimsky-Korsakov made musical history with his skill in orchestration. Among his models was Berlioz, whose clear, distinct, and often treble-coloured instrumentation he carried further. But he had less interest in Berlioz' penchant for glaring effects. He was more inclined to adopt some of Wagner's euphony, yet without the latter's density and emphasis of the lower register.

Influence by the chromatic harmony of Liszt and Wagner did not diminish the very personal nature of Rimsky-Korsakov's works, which often sound unmistakably Russian. He was fascinated with the country's history and folktales – ranging from European territory to the Asiatic peoples – and many of his operas were based on legendary themes. So were several of his orchestral works, the best-known being the symphonic suite

Nikolai Rimsky-Korsakov (1844-1908)

Scheherazade (1888) after tales from *The Thousand and One Nights*. There, as in his dance rhapsody *Capriccio Espagnol,* we meet a colourful orchestration rich in expressive solo passages.

Rimsky-Korsakov's passion for foreign lands, perhaps due to his long naval voyages, applied not only to legend and myth but also to music. Folk-melodic loans or tendencies appear in a majority of his works. Even Oriental ways of singing played a certain role in his treatment of the orchestra, using *melisms* or rapid sequences of notes. Such ornamentation is especially common in his woodwind parts and frequent violin solos.

From practice to theory

A "handbook of orchestration" has been seen in *Capriccio Espagnol.* Rimsky-Korsakov actually wrote a book of this kind: *Principles of Orchestration* (published posthumously in 1913). It is as important as Berlioz' basic treatise from 1843, which it supplements with no repetition. Berlioz had been content to describe the individual possibilities of instruments, but Rimsky-Korsakov discussed how they can be combined to produce a wealth of sounds and effects.

From 1871 until his death in 1908, Rimsky-Korsakov held a professorship at the music conservatory in St. Petersburg, later to be named after him. His mastery of orchestration was transmitted to a long list of students. Some of the most renowned were Aleksandr Glazunov, Sergei Prokofiev, Igor Stravinsky and Ottorino Respighi.

Contrasts in character

The most peculiar talent among "The Five" was that of Mussorgsky. He, too, left many incomplete works, largely because of insufficient training in compositional technique. Not a few of them were finished and reinstrumentated by Rimsky-Korsakov, with laudable respect for their musical value. It has been objected that the latter applied his own tonal ideals to his friend's creations, but it must also be remembered that his con-

tributions made possible the early international success of the operas *Boris Godunov* and *Khovanshtchina.*

Mussorgsky's orchestration may be considered clumsy, yet it shows a thoroughly distinctive sense of timbres. Dark, mysterious colours predominate, in close agreement with the historical subjects which he used. Certainly the lighter sound and glittering decorations

Modest Mussorgsky (1839-81)

of Rimsky-Korsakov contain more effects, but they clash with Mussorgsky's personality. A more faithful orchestration of the above-mentioned operas was later made by Dmitri Shostakovich.

In Rimsky-Korsakov and Mussorgsky, we confront two different approaches to the orchestra. Both are individual, and relatively distant from Central European principles. They well illustrate the national ideals of music that evolved in peripheral parts of the continent. However, this cannot be said of the composer who was perhaps Russia's greatest – Piotr Tchaikovsky. His well-known genius at instrumentation was essentially based on German and Austrian traditions from Mozart onward.

French orchestra music

All the new trends represented by

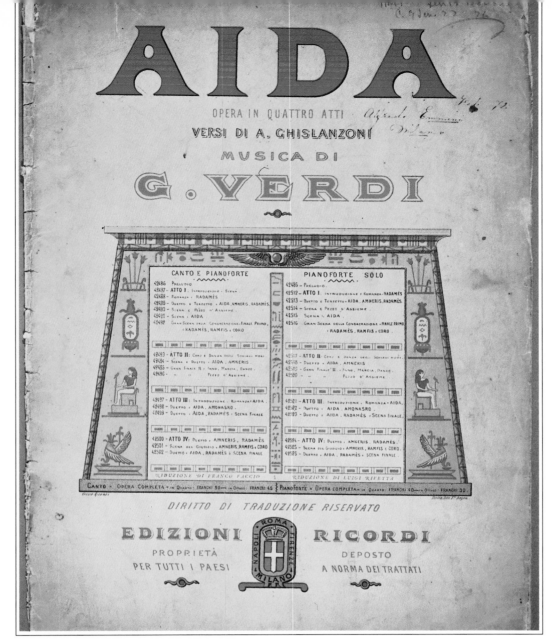

Verdi's "Aida" is a fine instance of fascination with the exotic. Motifs from Africa and the Orient became common in his day. Here is a programme of the opera's first performance in Cairo in 1871 (note the hieroglyphs).

Wagner were at first fascinating to musicians in France. A turning point came with the Franco-Prussian War of 1870-71. After France's defeat, many people regarded everything German with suspicion or even distaste. The composers who already had a nationalistic character were encouraged, and others joined them. But this was no uniform process: quite a few maintained a "love-hate" relationship to the master in Bayreuth. Camille Saint-Saëns, Emmanuel Chabrier, Ernest Chausson, Vincent d'Indy, and Belgian-born César Franck accepted influence from Germany, while at the same time striving to write in a "French" manner.

Once the war ended, an association was formed in Paris that acquired great significance: the *Société Nationale du Musique.* Among its founders were Saint-Saëns, Franck and Gabriel Fauré. Their aim was to promote native music and develop local styles. As a counterweight to the prevailing preference for opera and ballet, they focussed especially on orchestral and chamber music, and on songs. The orchestra was to be used primarily for creating atmosphere. Instead of spreading thick layers of colour as in heavy oil, the painting had to be done with light pastels. One of the

first who brought this ideal to perfection was Georges Bizet.

Exotic strains

Typical of the new French Romanticism was an interest in foreign cultures. Impulses were welcomed from North Africa, the Near East and India. The pioneer was Félicien David, a composer who had lived in Egypt, Turkey and Palestine when young. David wrote a symphonic ode named *Le Désert* (1844) and the opera *Lalla-Roukh* (1862), both using melodies and instrumentation affected by Oriental folk music. His orchestral colours intrigued contemporaries and were even praised by Berlioz.

David's music is unknown to most of us today, but we often find his influence in the Orientalizing features of Bizet, Jules Massenet, Charles Gounod, Léo Delibes, Edouard Lalo and others. Saint-Saëns' opera *Samson and Delilah* is a good example, and similar borrowings lie behind his titles for works such as *Africa, Egyptian Concerto* (both for piano and orchestra) and *Suite Algérienne.*

The colourful Carmen

Bizet became particularly important for the art of orchestration. In his twenties, he had taken David's *Le Désert* as a model and written a symphonic ode entitled *Vasco da Gama.* There and in his first mature opera, *The Pearl Fishers* (1863), an exotically coloured instrumentation is already conspicuous. Still, he had a classical outlook – with Mozart as paragon – and avoided excessively thick or luxuriant sounds.

Bizet's masterpiece is of course *Carmen,* in which he allowed the orchestra to sketch atmospheric backgrounds and to participate in the psychological interplay between characters. The score is rich in finely calculated colouristic effects, usually created with sparse but precise means. To bring them off, he did not need a lot of instruments: only a piccolo in addition to the winds that Schumann had used in symphonies, and Beethoven in the third *Leonora* overture.

For coming generations, and even musicians far beyond the borders of France, *Carmen* became an inexhaustible source of knowledge. Richard Strauss considered the opera to be a "textbook of instrumentation" on the level of Berlioz' and Wagner's works.

Saving on sounds

French music distanced itself increasingly from dense, homogeneous orchestral sound, in favour of a thin, transparent texture emphasizing the lighter instruments. Bizet had led the way and, towards the end of the century, it was most clearly followed by Claude Debussy. Yet not even he escaped the influence of Wagner. Like many other French composers, he made a pilgrimage to Bayreuth to learn on the spot, although he was soon frightened away.

Already in his early works, Debussy had developed a personal approach to orchestral expression. His cantata *La Damoiselle Élue* is an instance of the

Georges Bizet (1838-75)

Emma Calvé as Carmen, a role in which this great French soprano was famous.

Claude Debussy (1862-1918) found his own way of exploiting the orchestra's resources. He created new pictures with sound, partly by abolishing the dominance of string instruments.

transparent instrumentation which, during the next decade, would be further thinned out in his epoch-making *Prelude to the Afternoon of a Faun* and *Three Nocturnes.*

Debussy used the orchestra's full complement frugally. He preferred combinations of selected instruments. From then onward, the string group was no longer an obvious centerpiece – and this, after centuries of string supremacy, was a fundamental innovation. Together with an untraditional harmonic language of indistinct tonal relationships, whole-tone scales and polytonality, it created entirely new sound values.

Debussy went farthest during the years 1905-12 with *La Mer, Images* and the ballet *Jeux.* Here the aspects of timbre acquired an intrinsic value equal to that of harmony. Especially the ballet, in terms of subtle treatment of timbres and harmonies, belongs to the most remarkable music written before World War I. Half a century after its appearance, it became a cult object for many avant-garde composers led by Pierre Boulez.

Intense rhythms

Several of Debussy's contemporary or slightly younger compatriots devoted great attention to the symphony orchestra, but none of them contributed as much to its revitalization. Maurice

Ravel developed a fabulous virtuosity in his handling of its resources. A rather early work such as the song cycle *Scheherazade* (1903) is still related to Debussy's *Nocturnes.* In the ballet *Daphnis and Chloë* (1912), the expression was heightened with the aid of a large orchestra and energetic dance rhythms. The score is as colourful as it could be, and represents the zenith of the specifically French development of sonority to create atmosphere.

Impressions from folk music

We have seen how some Russian and French composers cultivated national and personal styles. Similar tendencies occurred elsewhere, yet seldom departed so consciously from the Central European ideals. The commonest approach was to embody melodic and rhythmic elements from local folk music. Traditional instruments occasionally inspired an attempt to imitate their sounds or playing techniques. Such were the guitar and castanets in Spain, and bagpipes in Britain and Eastern Europe.

How the folk musicians used popular variants of orchestral instruments was of no less interest to composers, a widespread example being the clarinet. The special ways of singing in Slavic countries left similar traces on symphonic music. So did certain sounds and accents in language, a focus that culminated with the works of Leos Janácek in Czechoslovakia.

Developments in music have naturally been paralleled in other forms of art. Debussy was often compared with the Impressionists, who also sought new modes of expression and rejected old conventions. Schoenberg, Stravinsky, Bartók and others experimented with rhythm and harmony in ways that recalled Cubist painting. This viola is by Picasso (Pushkin Museum, Moscow).

The growth of orchestras

Let us now survey the situation of some orchestras at the end of the nineteenth century. Symphonic music was being broadly cultivated, and new or reorganized orchestras sprouted frequently. The main centres of European orchestral music were London, Paris, Vienna and Leipzig.

Promenade concerts

London enjoyed a number of old concert associations. Most vital was the Philharmonic Society, founded in 1813 (and still active today, with the prefix "Royal"). The city did not, however, acquire a durable symphony orchestra until 1895. This was the Queen's Hall Orchestra, which subsequently gave the famous "promenade concerts" led by Henry Wood. It dissolved in the 1930s, when the London Symphony Orchestra (originally an offshoot of it) had long been established, and another orchestra had been started by the BBC.

Competitors on the Seine

The Paris Conservatory Orchestra was in full swing, but its repertoire had become more traditional than during the pioneer period of Habeneck. In 1861, the conductor Jules Pasdeloup began a series of alternative concerts, primarily with popular programs at low ticket prices. The emphasis was on German and some Russian music. A further series arose in 1873 under Édouard Colonne: reflecting the new ideas of the age (just after the Franco-Prussian War and the birth of the Société Nationale), it concentrated on contemporary French music. Through Colonne's persistent effort, the country's young composers soon reached out to a large public. The quality of playing was said to be considerably higher than Pasdeloup's. Yet a fourth Parisian series emerged in 1881, commanded by Charles Lamoureux, who also devoted himself to current French music but also to Wagner's.

All of these concert activities have continued until the present, apart from some interruptions. Normally, though, the orchestras have only worked part-time, enabling several musicians to play in more than one of them.

Vienna holds its own

In the Austrian capital, under the leadership of Otto Nicolai, players at the Court Opera formed the Vienna Philharmonic Orchestra in 1842 – the same year which gave rise to the New York Philharmonic, the oldest orchestra that still exists in America. The Viennese gave only sporadic concerts every year until 1860, when their activity became more regular. But even today, they are chiefly engaged in playing opera, leaving limited time for concerts. At the turn of the century, they were joined by the *Konzertvereins-Orchester* and the *Tonkünstler-Orchester*, which merged in 1919 to become the *Wiener Symphoniker*, now very familiar.

A small city with a prominent orchestra

While dwarfed by the world's metropoli (in the late 1800s it was only 3% as populous as London), Leipzig has always been culturally important. Its *Gewandhaus Orchestra*, active without a break since the 1780s, has set an enduring stamp on the city. Still longer has it been the publishing headquarters of Central Europe.

A brilliant period began in 1835 when Felix Mendelssohn was appointed conductor of the Gewandhaus concerts. He proved to be a leader with ma-

ny interests. Already in 1829 he had awakened Bach's *St. Matthew Passion* from a hundred-year slumber, and thereby initiated a Bach renaissance on a large scale. Moreover, he campaigned vigorously for works by contemporary avant-garde composers, such as Berlioz and Wagner. From the 1830s onward, Leipzig also had an alternative concert series, known as *Euterpe*, pronouncing a modern type of repertoire.

At the court of Meiningen

One town which, although it received no new orchestra, should be mentioned here is Meiningen. From the late seventeenth century until 1918, it was the capital of the central German duchy of Saxony-Meiningen. These dukes were lovers of theatre and music, employing many good musicians who included several from the Bach family. In 1831, Duke Georg II built a theatre which became renowned for its modern performances. He hired high-class conductors to lead its orchestra, and granted them unlimited time for rehearsals.

Especially after Hans von Bülow, conductor of the Munich Opera, arrived to take command in 1880, the Meiningen group undertook comprehensive tours and won fame as a principal orchestra of its time. Priority was given to impeccable performances of Brahms' music. His fourth symphony was originally presented in Meiningen, and many other works were played, occasionally under his own baton. It was in fact the orchestra's superb clarinettist, Richard Mühlfeld, who inspired Brahms to write his four works of chamber music for that instrument.

However, the orchestra was by no means as large as might be imagined. Usually it seems to have comprised only about forty players – enough, at any rate, for Beethoven's symphonies, which were its second specialty.

Progress in Berlin

Berlin, like Dresden, was an important opera city, but its concert orchestras tended to be short-lived. One that operated for many years was Benjamin Bilse's excellent entertainment band. He paid the musicians such low salaries, though, that they decided to start their own group.

In 1882 they attended a guest performance by von Bülow's orchestra from Meiningen, and were deeply impressed by its high quality. That same year, the Berliners began to give philharmonic concerts, which were the starting-point of the famous Berlin Philharmonic Orchestra. For some years around 1890, von Bülow was its chief conductor. More than a quarter century followed under Arthur Nikisch's leadership, securing the orchestra's worldwide reputation.

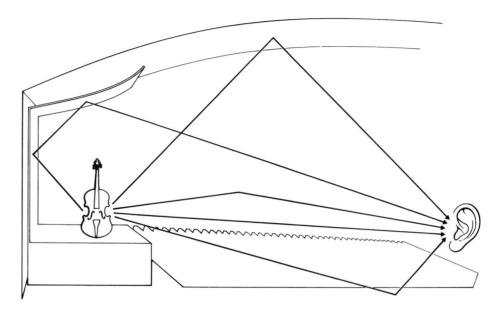

A listener in a room is reached by both direct sound and reflected sound. The reflections begin as indicated here, and they may multiply rapidly, producing a diffuse echo. Their speed and distribution greatly influence our appreciation of the music.

Great concert halls

The nineteenth century witnessed many of the building projects that have provided famous homes for orchestras. Since then, of course, the science of acoustics has been considerably refined – but it remains true that the best sounds can often be heard in halls dating from more than a hundred years ago. With the aid of practical experience, spaces for music were designed which have yet to be excelled even by modern methods of calculation. Some of them were planned from the very beginning for symphony concerts. Others were taken over, or reconstructed, after having served purposes with different – if any – acoustic requirements.

To the last category belonged the Russian nobility's palace in St. Petersburg, erected during the 1830s. When the Petrograd (later Leningrad) Philharmonic Orchestra was formed in 1921, the building opened its white, marble-like concert hall, which is still ranked among the world's best.

In the 1850s, a couple of halls opened which have become well-known as

THE ROYAL ALBERT HALL WAS BUILT IN 1867-71, PARTLY DUE TO PROFITS FROM THE
INDUSTRIAL GREAT EXHIBITION OF 1851. LONG AFTERWARD, ITS RESONANCE LED SIR THOMAS
BEECHAM TO REMARK THAT IT OFFERED MODERN COMPOSERS A UNIQUE CHANCE TO HEAR
THEIR WORK REPEATED.

acoustically ideal for concerts, although originally intended as opera houses: the Teatro Real in Madrid, and the Academy of Music in Philadelphia. These successful transformations from opera to concert usage are remarkable in view of the rather different acoustic needs of the two arts.

Vienna acquired a home for the *Gesellschaft der Musikfreunde* in 1870, a building known as the *Musikverein*. Its gilded concert hall, too, is among the finest in existence.

A sonic colossus

In 1871 a more special arena for music was dedicated to concerts in London. The gigantic Royal Albert Hall, seating 10,000, is one of the biggest that functions acoustically for normal symphony orchestras (and, indeed, even for little ensembles). As a rule, perfect sound is thought impossible to achieve in spaces with more than 3,000 seats; all of the preceding halls are smaller than that. The Albert Hall lies far beyond this

Carnegie Hall in New York City, built in 1891.

limit and, while it cannot compare with rooms of more modest proportions, its sound is amazing with respect to the vast volume. It is best suited to splendid music with a large orchestra and chorus, such as Tchaikovsky's *1812 Overture* (including cannons and a separate military band) or Mahler's eighth symphony. The British conductor Sir Thomas Beecham, who never missed a chance for a good joke, is said to have commented upon the Albert Hall's echo that it was "a contemporary composer's sole opportunity to hear his work twice"!

Three prominent halls arose during the 1880s. First, when the Berlin Philharmonic Orchestra was born in 1882, it moved into a roller-skating hall! This acoustically inadequate space was remodelled some years later to create the superbly sounding *Philharmonie*. There the city's concert life centred, until a ruinous bomb attack in 1944.

In Leipzig, the *Neues Gewandhaus* was opened in 1884. Then a hundred years old, the original hall had become too small for the growing orchestra and public. The new hall became the scene of the Gewandhaus orchestra's second heyday, in the early decades of our century – with chief conductors such as Nikisch, Wilhelm Furtwängler and Bruno Walter. In 1944 the building was

destroyed by bombs, its successor being an entirely fresh edifice from 1981.

Yet another phenomenal orchestra house emerged in 1888. Many generations of music-lovers have enjoyed the Concertgebouw in Amsterdam. Oddly enough, it was the place that inspired an orchestra to be founded. This group earned world renown under almost fifty years of leadership by Willem Mengelberg.

More recent monuments

New York got its Carnegie Hall in 1891, among the most prestigious of all concert arenas. Innumerable stars have appeared there ever since Piotr Tchaikovsky conducted his *1812 Overture* at the building's dedication. During the 1960s, it stood in danger of being demolished, but was saved through the efforts of the violinist Isaac Stern, and it has continued to please a steady stream of musicians and listeners.

Back in London, the Queen's Hall opened in 1893. It became especially well-known for the Proms, started a few years later by Henry Wood and led by him for half a century. The hall was wrecked by bombs in 1941, since when the "promenade concerts" have taken place in the Albert Hall.

The expanding orchestra

With the First World War, 150 years of consistent development in the symphony orchestra came to an end. Many forms of organization were used during the Baroque period, but the number of instruments had depended mostly on practical factors and was not changed in any definitive way. The special eight-part form that was standard-ized in the mid-eighteenth century, however, supplied a starting point for steady growth among the instruments.

Although works for very large orches-tras had existed earlier, they were isolated occurrences. The most famous example from the seventeenth century is a festival mass for Salzburg – thought to have been composed by Orazio Benevoli of Italy, yet possibly by Heinrich Biber of Bohemia. A huge work for six orchestral groups, several organs, four choruses and fifteen solo singers, it has a score of no fewer than 53 parts.

To illustrate the eighteenth century's gigantic concerts, we may recall the Handel festivals arranged in London since 1784. His *Messiah* was then per-

ces. For the requiem, Berlioz specified "at least" 108 strings, twenty woodwinds and twelve horns. Among other requirements are four separate brass groups, with about ten players in each. The percussion section includes sixteen kettledrums and ten cymbals! In total, over 200 instrumentalists and even more singers contributed to the première in 1837 at *Les Invalides* in Paris.

Massive effects appealed to Berlioz, but they were only one motive. What he considered primary was to differentiate the sound apparatus as much as possible, so that truly subtle mixtures of colour could be created. He pointed out that a collective use of the whole orchestra must be saved for a few grand climaxes. And the *Grand Messe des Morts* shows that he meant it seriously.

Ultimate power

Orchestral size and diversity reached their extreme during the decades just before World War I. This trend was emphasized for opera by Strauss' *Elektra*, presented in 1909 – and for symphonic music by two immense works in 1910 and 1912, Mahler's eighth symphony and Arnold Schoenberg's *Gurre-Lieder*. Both of the latter employ, in addition to the orchestra, three separate choirs and, respectively, eight and six vocal soloists.

Symphony of a Thousand

Mahler's eighth symphony was given the name of *Sinfonie der Tausend*, although not by him but in the interests of publicity. At the first performance, which the composer conducted in Munich, an or-

chestra of about 150 musicians accompanied 500 singers in two mixed choirs and a boys' choir of 350. The score calls for five or six of each woodwind instrument (with various side-instruments), eight horns and trumpets, seven trombones and a tuba, percussions for at least four players, a mandolin, two harps, and four keyboard instruments: celesta, piano, harmonium and large organ. The symphony's climaxes are among the most overpowering that have ever been written. On the other hand, the second movement, nearly an hour long, primarily consists of restrained, atmospheric music for smaller groups.

Even stronger gusts blow in *Gurre-Lieder*, with 25 woodwinds and as many brass instruments. Of the ten horn players, four also use Wagner tubas. Half a dozen percussionists are needed, as well as four harps.

Metaphysics

Mahler and Schoenberg were certainly aware that they balanced on the outer edge of feasibility. Their willingness to wield such formidable resources is perhaps less understandable today than it was at the beginning of the century. While already criticized at that time, they were building on 150 years of continuous tradition. Most importantly, they lived in a period of mysticism and spiritual fervour. It is no coincidence that Aleksandr Scriabin in Moscow simultaneously, from 1903 until 1910, composed his metaphysical orchestra works *The Divine Poem, The Poem of Ecstasy* and *The Poem of Fire (Prometheus)*.

formed in Westminster Abbey with over 500 participants, half of them in the orchestra. Shortly afterward, there were twice as many! But in this case it was a matter of inflating music that had not been intended for such multitudes. The original calls for a quite small orchestra.

Music in stereo

The large choirs have been mentioned which, supported mainly by military bands, came into fashion for celebrating *la gloire* after the French Revolution. Inspired by them, Hector Berlioz designed his *Grande Messe des Morts (Requiem)* and *Te Deum* in a colossal format, with "stereophonically" positioned instrumental and choral for-

A new world

Stravinsky used the orchestra in many different ways. His ballet "The Firebird" still displayed the influence of Rimsky-Korsakov. This scenery was by the French painter Jacques Blanche.

Igor Stravinsky
(1882-1971)

The Great War had a sweeping influence on culture, and nothing seemed the same in its wake. With the old world gone forever, modernists took the lead in music: Stravinsky, Prokofiev, Hindemith, Bartók and Schoenberg. They had chiefly traditional roots:

Stravinsky in the school of Rimsky-Korsakov, Schoenberg as a follower of Brahms, Bartók as an admirer of Strauss' orchestral language. Yet soon they bade farewell to the aesthetics and exaggerations of Romanticism. They advanced a more realistic attitude towards creativity itself, avoiding the cult of genius.

Many processes were accelerated with the War, but probably music would, sooner or later, have taken more or less the same course anyhow. A number of works advertising the new era had already emerged: *Five Pieces for Orchestra* by Schoenberg (1909), *Bluebeard's Castle* by Bartók (1911), the two first piano concertos by Prokofiev (1912-13), and Stravinsky's *The Rite of Spring* (1913).

Chamber orchestras

Several of the composers who brought the giant orchestra to its culmination were now the ones that took an opposite approach. Schoenberg had initiated it with his Chamber Symphony for 15 solo instruments (1906), a work which inspired composers in many countries for decades. Stravinsky, after his display of elementary power in *The Rite of Spring*, wrote orchestrally inclined chamber music – including a melodrama, *The Soldier's Tale* (1918), with only seven players.

Even Strauss, following his lavish operas *Salome*, *Elektra* and *Der Rosenkavalier*, composed a chamber play, *Ariadne auf Naxos* (1912). The orchestra was reduced to thirty-six members, barely half of them string players. The instruments were used frequently for solo passages, and individually in varied combinations. It is remarkable how Strauss, with such small forces, managed to extract a variety of sound that – apart from its power – is hardly second to *Elektra* with an orchestra of 110 players.

Igor Stravinsky

The ballets *The Firebird, Petrouchka,* and *The Rite of Spring* (1909-13) represent three different ways of using a large orchestra. In the first, Stravinsky exhibited his teacher Rimsky-Korsakov's shimmering tonal palette, which undeniably suits a legendary theme that the latter might equally well have treated. In *Petrouchka*, the tale's noisy market-place setting is depicted by orchestral sounds rich in stark contrasts. Soloists free

In "The Rite of Spring", first performed in Paris in 1913, Stravinsky's suggestive and sometimes "ugly" sounds have had great significance for twentieth-century composers, inspiring many imaginative works. Here we see the final scene in the Stockholm Opera version of 1987.

themselves from the orchestra to draw portraits of the characters. Especially conspicuous are the trumpet fanfares and the virtuoso piano passages – a reminder of the music's origin as a "concert piece" for piano and orchestra.

In *The Rite of Spring*, what dominate are the wind and percussion instruments. The string orchestra is of secondary importance almost throughout the work, except in the irregular stamping rhythm just after the introduction. Wind players are as numerous here as in Mahler's sixth symphony, and more so than in Strauss' *A Hero's Life*: quintuple woodwinds, eight horns, five trumpets, three trombones and two tubas, as well as two Wagner tubas and a bass trumpet.

Even the percussion section is comprehensive. This story of sacrifices in pagan Russia paints a picture of prehistory with complicated, irregular rhythms and sharp, unlovely sounds – all contributing to exceptionally suggestive expression. No single composition in the twentieth century has influenced the music world so greatly. Scarcely any creator of music has been able to avoid its impact.

Back to the sources

For Stravinsky it was now important to reduce the orchestra and depart from the standard complement which had reigned for 150 years. He turned against the development of instrumentation into an

Arnold Schoenberg (1874-1951)

independent art. The many-voiced, colourful Romantic orchestra, he thought, does not convey the musical course but drowns it in a sea of harmony.

A Soldier's Tale, mentioned above, is admittedly chamber music but meant an important transition to Stravinsky's future orchestral works. In 1919, with the ballet *Pulcinella*, he adopted an eager devotion to music for chamber orchestras, often influenced by the Baroque and by Classicism. *Pulcinella* builds on melodies by Pergolesi and is designed for two each of flutes, oboes, bassoons and horns, a trumpet and a trombone, besides strings (but no clarinets, since Pergolesi did not use them).

The virtue of clarity

Music from the past was evidently still relevant, and for several reasons. Most significantly, priority had been given to clarity. A Bach or a Mozart dedicated the orchestra to the service of musical structure. The tonal peculiarities of instruments made a contribution to diversity and enjoyment, but were granted no special status on the level of other resources. The same can be said for many of Stravinsky's works from the late 1910s onward, when he tested one instrumental combination after the other. Surprisingly enough, not even in the colourful *Firebird* suite (1919 version) did he need more than a piccolo and tuba in addition to the wind group used by Beethoven's third *Leonora* overture!

A year later came the original *Symphonies of Wind Instruments*, dedicated to the memory of Debussy. High Romanticism's normal wind group, without any string or percussion instruments, serves here in an ascetic spirit that is the very opposite of Romanticism. Similar features are found in an *Octet* for the unusual combination of a flute, a clarinet, two bassoons, two trumpets and two trombones.

Percussive pianos

In 1923, Stravinsky composed a ballet that is one of his strangest works in terms of orchestral constitution: *The Wedding (Les Noces)*. He used neither strings nor wind instruments, relying on four pianos and an arsenal of percussion equipment that require half a dozen players. Even the piano parts

S	A	T	O	R
A	R	E	P	O
T	E	N	E	T
O	P	E	R	A
R	O	T	A	S

The magic of combinations. Schoenberg's twelve-tone method of composition, invented in 1921, is based on the same principle as an arrangement of letters which can be read in opposite sequences to form a complex pattern.

have a distinctly percussive quality and function as an integral section of the percussion ensemble. The latter is also joined, in a sense, by the ballet's song parts with their staccato, repetitive sequences. Breaking completely away from the traditional orchestral approach, this work marked the beginning of a tonal disintegration which has characterized much music in the later twentieth century. Interestingly, Bartók's percussion-like first piano concerto was written only three years afterward.

In his later works for orchestra, Stravinsky continued to vary the combinations. His *Symphony of Psalms* (1930) employs quintuple woodwinds (although no clarinets), while the string group is reduced to cellos and double basses. The *Dumbarton Oaks Concerto* comes close to Bach's *Brandenburg Concertos* – with a flute, clarinet and bassoon, two horns and ten string instruments. The jazz-inspired *Ebony Concerto* (1945) uses a saxophone section and a trumpet section, with five players in each, as well as a horn and three trombones, percussion, a piano,

harp, guitar and strings. In the *Mass* (1948) he reduced the orchestra to a "double wind quintet", while making it unconventional by means of a combination of three oboes, two bassoons, two trumpets and three trombones.

Stravinsky had enormous importance for the development of twentieth-century music in virtually every field. The orchestra was only one of these; and here alone, he introduced a host of new ideas, as the preceding illustrations show. Many others have taken part in this process of regeneration, but nobody in such a versatile and inspiring manner.

Arnold Schoenberg

From the 1920s onward, Schoenberg was to be most famous for his twelve-tone technique. This did not primarily have to do with the orchestra, but another of his ideas did: so-called *timbre melody*. According to him, just as an ordinary melody is formed by alternating pitches, a kind of melody can be produced by instead changing the timbre combinations and relative degrees of

strength among the instruments. The best-known instance occurs in the third of his *Five Pieces for Orchestra*, a movement which he called "Colours". His proposal was not widely adopted, but in the mid- twentieth century it was revived by the latest frontiersmen, Luigi Nono and Pierre Boulez.

Pointillistic music

Of deeper significance for contemporary methods of orchestration was Anton Webern. He worked in the chamber-orchestra format, chiefly with individual wind parts. The revolutionary feature was his frequent alternation between the instruments. This completed the dissolution which had gradually occurred during the orchestra's past history. At first, every instrument had stuck to its part throughout a composition. In Haydn's day, for the sake of contrast, the instruments were changed from one appearance of a theme to the next. With Berlioz and Wagner, they could relieve each other even during a given melody. Webern took the last step and shifted the instruments from note to note, often jumping between registers at the same time.

There is seldom any *tutti* in Webern's extremely economical music. On occasion, just one or two parts are active at a time. Melody, harmony, rhythm, and timbre are as fluid as colours in a kaleidoscope. The sounding notes are mixed with pauses, a quality that gave rise to the term "pointillistic music". His only piece designated as a symphony (1928) lasts for a mere ten minutes; it is pure chamber music for clarinet, bass clarinet, two horns, a harp and a quartet of string parts (no double bass). After World War II, Webern's method influenced many composers such as Boulez, Nono, John Cage, Karlheinz Stockhausen, and their successors.

An age of fragmentation

The orchestra's evolution during the twentieth century cannot be summarized briefly. Despite the special traits of past composers, there is a certain degree of unity in such concepts as Baroque, Classicism and Romanticism. But we lack a corresponding term for the last seventy-five years. Stylistic trends have become ever more numerous, and composers have approached the orchestra in strongly individual ways. We must leave the task to future musicologists of finding common denominators with the help of a wider time perspective.

As seen above, the seventeenth century was dominated by the string orchestra, while the eighteenth became an age of woodwind instruments and the nineteenth one of brasses. Our own century has been consecrated to percussion instruments. Among the first (after Mahler) to systematically develop this outlook was Edgar Varèse, a French-American, in works such as *Ameriques*, *Offrandes* and *Arcana*, all from the 1920s.

However, the progress of percussion has been accompanied by other hallmarks of the times. Entirely new instruments have been built – for example in the 1920s, the electrical *Ondes Martenot* which was used particularly by French composers, such as Olivier Messiaen. The traditional instruments' areas of application have also been widened further, as when the *prepared piano* came into use by John Cage during the early 1940s.

Fresh sensations

Composers interested in unexploited sounds have discovered, from the majority of instruments, effects that never occurred to their original constructors. String instruments are being scraped, knocked on, bowed between the bridge and tailpiece (to make them squeak) and much else. On wind instruments, too, players have rapped and honked, shouted or sung into loose or adapted mouthpieces, and overblown so hard that the sound has become an uncontrolled noise. Such techniques tend to be used in a drastic manner, and are experienced by many listeners as ugly, perhaps unmusical. Yet there is no doubt that they can also be employed more delicately.

Electro-acoustic music, often called "electronic", is occasionally integrated with the orchestra. More relevant to our subject, though, has been its influence on György Ligeti, Krzysztof Penderecki and many younger composers – to orchestrate in new ways. Sometimes a large number of individual parts occur, forming tonal *clusters* without distinguishable pitches. Here the exploitation of *microtones* (intervals less than a half tone) can make the tonality even more diffuse.

Since World War II, most composers have thus strayed very far from the conception of sound that appealed to Mahler, Debussy, Webern and Stravinsky at the beginning of the century. Paradoxically, this same "quartet" has been the decisive inspiration for many creators of modern music. Tradition, then, is by no means defunct!

The present chapter began by asking which criteria should be obeyed if a collection of instruments is called an orchestra. The limits proved difficult to draw, when traditional music was involved. And they are still less clear in the case of music today. As was noted previously, Stravinsky already reduced the orchestra in some of his works to small, carefully chosen groups. The ten wind players in his *Mass* are, formally speaking, a chamber-music group, but in this context they nonetheless give a rather orchestral impression to the listener.

Percussion and organs

Once a work for a symphony orchestra was ordered from a young composer. What he finally delivered was a piece designed for 48 percussion instruments and four Hammond organs. Had he cheated the customer? At least not consciously, as it turned out. In his opinion, he had written a truly symphonic opus "in the spirit of our age", and had used the tonal resources he considered necessary. For him, the concept of a symphony orchestra possessed no fixed boundaries. That the music would be laborious and expensive for an orchestra to perform was something he had not thought of.

Such a composer may seem nonchalant, but his self-defence is an interesting sign of how relative the idea of a symphony orchestra can be. Does the reader recognize that his vision, in fact, resembles that of Stravinsky, many years earlier in *The Wedding*, with a throng of percussion instruments and four grand pianos?

For all that, as we approach the end of our century, it is obvious that the orchestra has remained surprisingly intact on the whole. The mainstream of symphonic music is still based upon the arsenal which was available a hundred years ago. Percussion instruments have multiplied, but the string and wind instruments have seen nothing really new during this century. Perhaps future students will be more struck by our composers' ability to extract fresh sounds from old instruments, than by the new devices which have appeared. The traditional symphony orchestra's possibilities are certainly not yet exhausted.

Musicians at our discretion

One method of composition in recent decades has been to allow passages of varying length in a work to be guided by chance, or else freely improvised by the players. An intriguing example of a contemporary composer who applies this principle even to the choice of instruments is Arvo Pärt, an Estonian. Some of his music is written for an "arbitrary ensemble". At times he adds tips in the score about how to combine the instruments. In *Fratres* (1977), he himself has created alternative versions for violin and piano, for twelve cellos, for a mixed string orchestra with a couple of percussion instruments, and for solo violin with old or new instruments. The instruction "old or new" is, in fact, a recurrent one in Pärt's works. With him, the orchestra's 400-year development has, so to speak, come full circle: our age extends a hand to the sixteenth century!

The future of the symphony orchestra

Seventy-five years ago there were many who wanted to declare the symphony dead. This attitude was soon put to shame. Instead, the composers filled the old form with vital contents, stressing Mahler's view that "the symphony is like life itself – it must contain everything from the highest to the lowest". New symphonies have continued to appear in a ceaseless stream. Even composers who began with a different orientation have often created fundamental works of art for what they had thought to be an anachronism.

During the 1960s, amid joy over the endless opportunities of electro-acoustic music, it was prophesied that symphony orchestras would become superfluous, at any rate for contemporary music. Here, too, developments have been opposite. The interest in orchestral music has gone on growing, and the 1990s fully justify a bright faith in the symphony orchestra's future.

The quest for novel sounds and exciting effects has taken many forms. Pebbles inside a "prepared" piano move when the keys are struck and the strings vibrate, creating unexpected tones.

2
The Conductor

*H*ow can we understand the
mysterious signals a conductor
gives to the orchestra?
Does he wave his wand as he
pleases, or are there rules
for him to follow?
A modern conductor is the
orchestra's unchallenged leader,
with a charismatic personality
that marks the music — but it
has not always been so.

An art is born

EW PROFESSIONS HAVE GIVEN RISE TO AS many cults and myths as the conductor's. This, however, is a relatively recent phenomenon. It was not until the later nineteenth century that conducting began to become an independent activity. Even a hundred years ago, the leaders of orchestras were primarily active as composers – and such a personal bond survives to some extent today. For example, Stravinsky, Tippett and Lutoslawski have been eager to conduct their own compositions; Hindemith, Britten and Penderecki have now and then conducted that of others as well. In certain cases, the balance has been more even between the two interests, as is illustrated by the careers of Bernstein and Boulez.

The vast majority of conductors in our century have devoted themselves exclusively to conducting. Yet many have studied composition, as an important aid to understanding the creative process behind musical works. Although quite a few have proceeded to write works of their own, these have seldom been of more than mediocre quality. Great conductors such as Wilhelm Furtwängler and Otto Klemperer spent much time in composing symphonies and other music, but the results have not become part of the standard repertoire.

Despite the late emergence of pure conductors, a need for leaders of large musical groups has always existed. In ancient Greek theatre, the chorus – chiefly of dancers – was coordinated by stamping on the ground. Choir leaders in medieval churches must have acted more quietly, and the monophony of

Gregorian chant required only rough hand-signals for the melodic line. But the gradual development of polyphony heightened the demands. In the Renaissance's artfully modelled masses and other choral works, musical interpretation of a text was emphasized. Besides his coordinating role, the choir leader served increasingly as an artistic director.

The conductor's staff

Stehgeiger and staff-striking

During the orchestra's first two hundred years, music that called for many participants was led by a musician whose directions could be seen by all. Sometimes this was the leader, who played while standing up. The others could then also take cues from his play-

Gregorian chanting follows a single melody and does not need precise conducting.

Whether to conduct with a baton is largely a matter of taste. These are the hands of Herbert von Karajan.

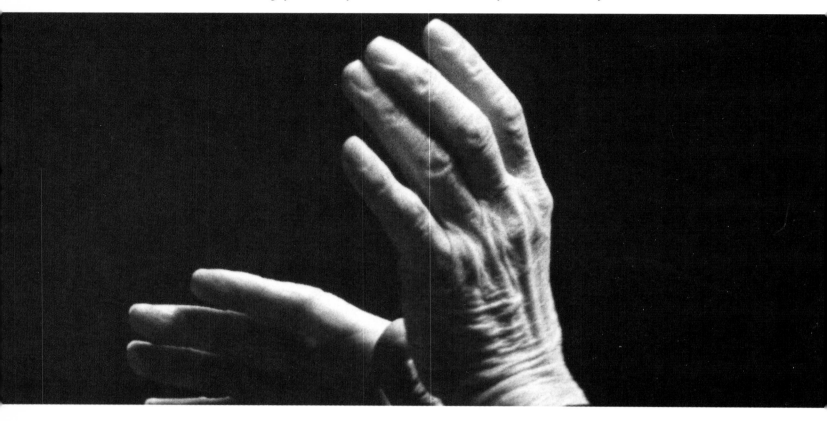

Haydn often conducted while playing the harpsichord, together with a concert master. His 76th birthday in 1808 was celebrated in Vienna as illustrated here.

ing, as in phrasing and bowing. Here we have the prototype of the *Stehgeiger* (standing violinist) who led nineteenth-century dance and salon orchestras in Vienna and elsewhere.

One could also conduct by using only the hands, or by slapping rolled-up music sheets against one's palm. Another method was to strike the floor with a heavy staff, occasionally several metres long. This peculiar, and disturbing, custom was rather common in the

seventeenth century. Surprisingly, even the ambitious innovator Jean-Baptiste Lully relied on so inartistic a procedure. His fate shows that it was not entirely safe, either: he hit himself on the foot and died of the injury! We might think that the staff soon fell out of use, but it could still be heard in some places as late as the mid-nineteenth century. In Paris, it was a barbarism that infuriated Berlioz.

Conducting in pairs

The normal practice during the 1600s and 1700s, however, was to have no separate conductor at all. Orchestra music, opera and minor choral works were led, instead, by a participating musician. The Baroque orchestra was generally small, often with only three or four independent parts, and simple in structure. On the whole, a constant tempo was maintained throughout a composition or movement. The director's task was limited to indicating the tempo and starting the ensemble off, as well as signalling at some critical points. At the opera, of course, cues were needed for the singers.

At the orchestra's centre stood the thorough-bass group, with a chord-playing instrument and a bass-supporting cello or bassoon. Whoever sat at the harpsichord or organ could usually do

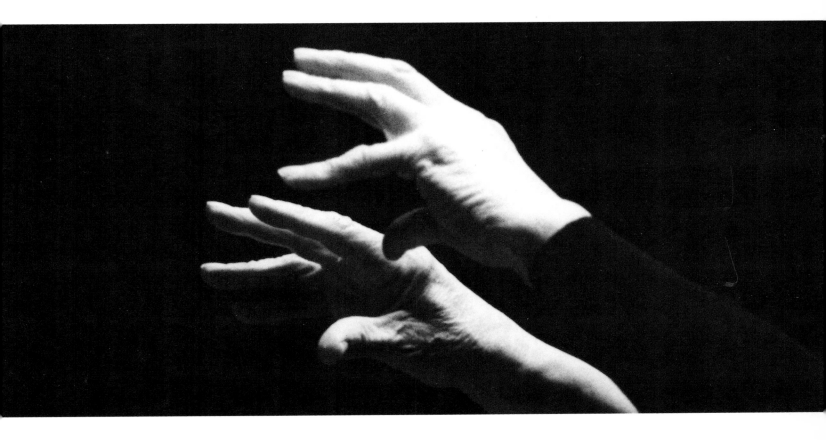

the conducting while he played. In passages that required his full attention to the keyboard, the concert master (leader) substituted for him. Frequently one of these men was the composer.

This dual leadership was sufficient for a great deal of orchestral music, until the end of the classicistic era. When Haydn gave his celebrated concerts in London during the 1790s, he conducted his symphonies from the harpsichord, aided by the leader Johann Peter Salomon. The same approach has been revived today by some orchestras specializing in old music.

Independent conductors

By the early nineteenth century, music had become so complex – with its frequent changes in tempo, delicate balancing of timbres and so on – that the process of conducting had to be freed from the playing in an orchestra. François Habeneck still tended to conduct from the leader's place, but Beethoven and Weber stood before the orchestra in the modern fashion.

It was now ever more common to use a thin baton, and to be content with waving it in the air, rather than knocking something with it. A notable propagandist for this technique was the German composer and conductor Ludwig Spohr. Towards the mid-nineteenth century, almost everyone else had followed suit.

Nonetheless, in accordance with tradition, orchestras were still directed mainly by composers. Some, for example Beethoven, chiefly presented their own works – yet others concentrated on a wide repertoire of contemporary and past music. Among the most versatile, in the early half of that century, were Weber, Spohr, Mendelssohn and Liszt.

Important contributions were now and then also made by Berlioz and Wagner.

Ludwig Spohr (1784-1859) was the first conductor to use the baton.

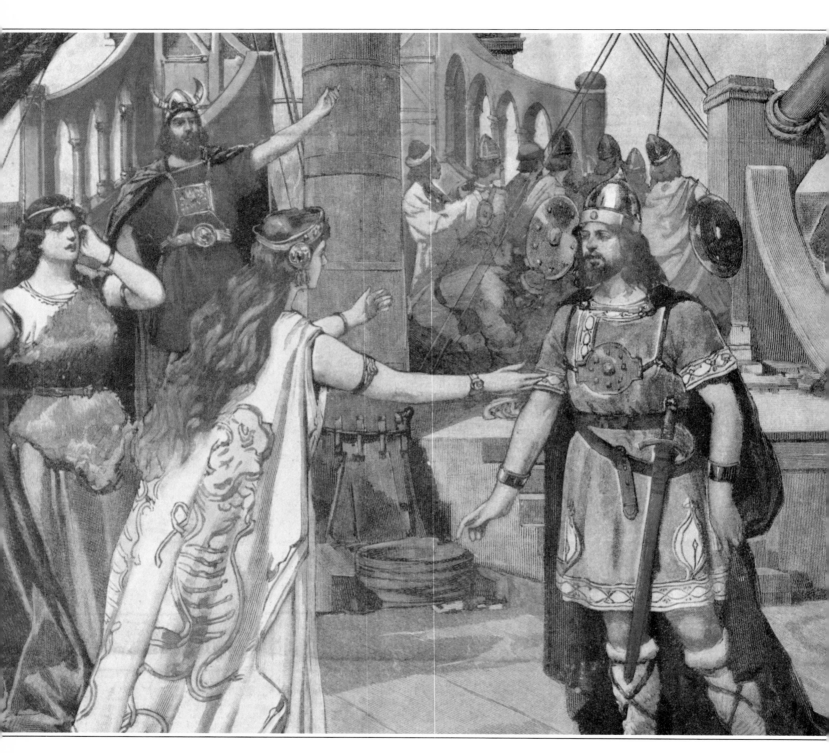

Scenery by Max Bruckner for Wagner's ''Tristan und Isolde'' in 1886,
first conducted by Hans von Bülow.

Professional conductors

We begin to see conducting as a special profession in the 1850s, when a young German named Hans von Bülow – inspired by Wagner – launched his brilliant career. He, too, played a dual role, but not as a composer: after studying with Liszt, he became one of the foremost piano virtuosos of his day. It was he who played the solo part at the first performance of Tchaikovsky's now-famous first piano concerto.

Bülow made history, though, primarily as a conductor. During his time at the Munich Opera, he conducted the first performance of Wagner's *Tristan und Isolde* as well as *Die Meistersinger von Nürnberg*. The little court orchestra in Meiningen was developed by him into one of the finest in Europe. At the recently formed Berlin Philharmonic Orchestra, he became one of the first permanent conductors. In addition, he was a busy guest conductor in many musical cities.

Bülow's style was both passionate and analytical. His quality-conscious renewal of the art of playing was his most important single achievement. It laid the foundations for performing virtuoso orchestra music, such as Richard Strauss' symphonic poems. And Bülow's success spurred

The Vienna Court Opera was directed by Gustav Mahler in 1897-1907.

many others to make careers of orchestra conducting. He became the prototype of the modern concert conductor, and the first star in the profession.

How we would regard Bülow's performances today is hard to say. Ideals and tastes change quickly. In the spirit of his age, he often retouched and modified the musical score – although with the conviction of serving the composer's intentions. Naturally we might sneer (as did his contemporaries) at

some of his theatrical exaggerations. For instance, he is said to have conducted Beethoven's *Eroica* wearing white gloves, and replaced them with black ones for the second movement, the funeral march!

Mahler and Nikisch

During the decades around 1900, two giants dominated the world of conducting: Gustav Mahler and Arthur Nikisch. The former worked primarily at the opera houses in Budapest, Hamburg, Vienna and New York. With his uncompromising demands, he contributed strongly to higher standards of quality – especially in Vienna, whose court opera he conducted from 1897 until 1907. For his contemporaries, Mahler was above all the celebrated conductor, whereas his own music was controversial. Not before the 1960s, half a century after his death, did it win the universal acclaim that we take for granted today.

Nikisch began as a violinist, and was deeply influenced by playing under Wagner's leadership. Through his work as a conductor of the theatre in Leipzig, the symphony orchestra in Boston, and the opera in Budapest, he was promoted during the 1890s to the head of both the Leipzig *Gewandhaus* orchestra and the Berlin Philharmonic. These posts he held until his death in 1922.

Opposite natures

The Berlin musicians' shift from Bülow to Nikisch may seem peculiar, since the

Arthur Nikisch (1855-1922)

Arturo Toscanini (1867-1957).

La Scala in Milan has lived through many a heyday, not least under the leadership of Toscanini.

one stood in absolute contrast to the other, and both were distinctive archetypes in their character. Bülow was a purposeful, methodical stickler for details, who stubbornly trained the public as well as the orchestra. Nikisch was unreflective, anti-intellectual, lacking in pedagogical ambition or ability – but he had a charismatic radiance. The former was pedantic and demanding, and never seemed to be satisfied; the latter was generous with praise, and forever courteous in company with the musicians.

Bülow had rehearsed even well-known music down to the last note, often with the enervating manner of a schoolteacher. Yet Nikisch was content to rehearse briefly, without any thorough instructions. When he looked out over the orchestra, all the players had the feeling that his glance was meant for each of them personally. Nikisch relied on their own knowledge, and on his almost hypnotic power of firing them up to great achievements. The broad contours, the beauty of sound, and the poetry of expression were his focus. Structure, form and "content" interested him little.

The Berlin Philharmonic must, therefore, have undergone a huge adjustment. But the players seem to have vastly appreciated both conductors. They realized that Bülow was responsible for their lofty stature among contemporary orchestras. After the constructive years with him, a great inspirer was just what they needed.

The cult of Toscanini

Most conductors in later times have stood somewhere between the above extremes. However, the tendency has been an increasing emphasis on the details of the music. Oddly enough, it seems to have originated mainly with a single person: Arturo Toscanini. This Italian conductor enjoyed an exceptionally long career (68 active years until 1954), and made a reputation as a profound innovator. The opera house of La Scala in Milan, and the Metropolitan in New York, experienced brilliant periods under his leadership. The same was true, during his last twenty-five years, of the New York Philharmonic and a group specially established for him in that city, the NBC Symphony Orchestra.

Toscanini became the object of veritable worship, which was actually foreign to his nature. He never stepped intentionally into the limelight, but considered himself a humble servant of creative geniuses. All his energy was devoted to their benefit and to art in its purest form. His goal was to produce performances that were scrupulously prepared. The music had to sound pre-

Jean Sibelius (1865-1957) wanted "A Saga" to sound as soft as a forest, and disliked Toscanini's sharp articulation of notes in the score.

cisely as it appeared to him in the score. Spontaneous interpretations and impulses at the performance were out of the question; nothing was to be left unprepared at rehearsals. By tireless effort, he reached a degree of exactitude and rhythmical strictness that was unknown until then.

Fidelity to the score

Both a strength and a weakness lay in following the score so closely. Written notes can never be more than an approximate indication of how a composition should be executed. The dead symbols come alive only when filtered through the recreating artist's temperament. Despite the enormous admiration for Toscanini, it is therefore not surprising that some composers opposed his approach.

Jean Sibelius is said to have become terrified when he heard a performance of his tone poem *En Saga*. The string section's introductory arpeggios had been rehearsed so that each semiquaver sounded like a polished diamond. "No, no," he protested, "it should be a diffuse sound, like the forest whispering..."

Toscanini himself evidently had a blind faith that his way was the only right one. Here is a characteristic utterance: "People talk about Furtwängler's Beethoven, Mengelberg's Beethoven, Bruno Walter's Beethoven. I am only interested in Beethoven's Beethoven!"

Differing opinions

We cannot know what Beethoven or Mozart would have thought of Toscanini's strict, sometimes hardhanded way of presenting their music. Judgements about his view of the classical masters have diverged widely. On the other hand, performances that have seldom produced disagreement are those of music by composers whom Toscanini knew personally – such as Verdi, Puccini, Respighi, Debussy and

The gramophone transformed conductors into international stars.

Strauss. In these cases, he was able to supplement the score with living testimony about the creators' own intentions.

Posterity remembers Toscanini perhaps best as a concert conductor. Yet it may be that his contributions were greatest in the art of opera. At that time, most music theatres had a large current repertoire. Even when a work had been abandoned for months, it was not uncommonly performed without any new rehearsals. As a result, in many theatre pits considerably lower standards were accepted than for symphony concerts. Toscanini's opera performances showed what high quality was attainable. His example came to influence the majority of contemporary conductors, including those who did not share his general principles.

Controversial artists

Between the World Wars, the Philadelphia Orchestra grew to an elite level in the hands of Leopold Stokowski, of Polish-Irish parentage. His orientation was not that of Toscanini. He had no exaggerated respect for the score and did not hesitate to "improve" it when he thought necessary. He worked intensively with the sonorous features of the music (which interested Toscanini less). Half a century after he left Philadelphia, the orchestra – with entirely new players – still retained much of the special sound which he created.

Stokowski's artistic ideas, too, were hotly debated. It was said that he made the music wallow in an exuberant tonal costume, which did not always suit its nature. Moreover, he was an exhibitionist and sometimes let the visual aspect of his appearance dominate over the musical content. But we should not forget that, besides his work with the Philadelphia Orchestra (and several others), he championed a great deal of new and seldom-played music. He contributed actively to giving the American public a wider perspective and a better musical appetite.

The modern ideal of an international virtuoso orchestra is largely based on what Toscanini and Stokowski achieved during the first half of this century. With the huge improvement in sound quality of gramophone recordings in the late 1920s, listeners all over the world could appreciate their achievements. Both were among the first great conductors to be extensively recorded.

Momentary magic

It was, of course, inevitable that such strong personalities as Stokowski and Toscanini would arouse conflicting reactions. So, at times, did a third charismatic conductor in the same period: Wilhelm Furtwängler of Germany. Widely regarded as the opposite of Toscanini, he laid much significance on the impulse of the moment and the atmosphere of the concert hall. Performances of a given work could therefore be quite different from one night to the next. The audience changed and the conditions were never quite identical.

How closely should a conductor stick to the score? Do we want, as Toscanini put it, "Furtwängler's Beethoven" or "Beethoven's Beethoven"?

The Chicago Symphony Orchestra has been conducted by Fritz Reiner among others.
He was one of those who dealt strictly with the musicians, causing opposition from their union.

But Furtwängler was by no means an unreflective impulse-musician like Nikisch. Deeply rooted in Central European cultural traditions, he took his calling most seriously. He speculated constantly about every aspect of music and performance, as well as of life itself. In his own symphonies, profound thought is conspicuous. Furtwängler rehearsed conscientiously – yet instead of a Toscanini's demand for transparency and precision, he cherished a more poetic style with dense, suggestive orchestral sounds. Rather than polishing details, he emphasized the unitary effect, often monumentally designed and, at fortunate times, with much inner tension.

Despotism and democracy

Toscanini and Stokowski were decided dictators. In their day, many orchestras, especially American ones, depended entirely on the conductor's whims. If he was not satisfied with players, he had the power to dismiss them instantly. Among those who displayed this tyrannical attitude longest were two Hungarians, Fritz Reiner and George Szell. They had held leading positions at prominent German opera houses, and became even more famous when, after World War II, they brought the symphony orchestras in Chicago and Cleveland, respectively, to the superb level which we know from many extraordinarily fine recordings.

Today hardly any orchestra would accept the kind of treatment that had to be tolerated under these despots. Toscanini often showered insults and wild denunciations over his musicians. In contrast to some others, however, he did not do so out of cruelty. He had a dream, an artistic vision, which meant everything. When the orchestra failed to realize it, his southern temperament took over and he vented disappointment with a child's unreasonability. Actually the hand-picked NBC Symphony Orchestra was one of the most adept in its time.

The conductor's authority endured longer in America than in Europe. Later generations have, to some extent, had to pay for the roughness of such despots. The hard rules established by the professional unions of orchestra musicians are a product of their experiences during that period.

Social legislation, too, has expanded and the employment conditions of our age are less uncertain than before. Yet an orchestra's activity is still mostly governed by its "music director", although within narrower limits.

Leonard Bernstein (1918-90)

Herbert von Karajan (1908-89)

Two superstars

Finally let us consider two great conductors who have been as important in our time as Toscanini and Furtwängler were for earlier generations. Leonard Bernstein in America, and Herbert von Karajan of Austria, were regarded from the 1960s until the 1980s as the most brilliant of all conductors. They won their "superstar" status primarily through enormous exposure in media, such as recordings and television. Their worldwide careers sped up during the first decades of television, and both knew how – in very different ways – to exploit that innovation.

Perfection

Karajan received much influence from Toscanini and Furtwängler. He himself declared that their contributions, which once were thought incompatible, had been decisive for the shaping of his personal approach to conducting. The for-

mer inspired him to ask for the utmost in precision and homogeneity, the latter to seek the core of the music. One might add that, especially in his later years, he cultivated a tonal beauty that could best be compared with Stokowski's.

Karajan soon became known as a serious, extremely demanding trainer and tamer of orchestras. His concerts and

opera performances were studies in perfection, with every unevenness peeled away and every difficulty overcome. But perfection does not always mean having great character. He did not escape criticism for being too static or predictable, and allowing the opulent sound to outweigh the vivid expression.

Among Karajan's foremost qualities

Many of von Karajan's performances have been visually recorded.

was a full mastery of the music's form, something that benefitted his opera work in particular. A ninety-minute act in a Wagner opera was performed with the same firmness as a ten-minute symphonic movement. One could have a presentiment of the end already as one heard the beginning.

World dominion

Around his personality and diverse activities, Karajan built up a literal empire with global ramifications. His company arranged orchestra tours, ran festivals, made video recordings and so forth. At the centre stood his own Berlin Philharmonic.

He held everything in an iron grip. To control all the stages of an opera production, he took an active part in the whole artistic process – including the scenery, lighting and direction. For video, he was even his own picture producer.

In the 1980s, Karajan put a lot of energy into video laser-disc recordings

Bernstein's comradely attitude towards the musicians created a perfect atmosphere for fine performances.

of his main repertoire. No other conductor has yet devoted as much attention to this medium, and these recordings are of great documentary value for those who wish to study an outstanding conductor at work. But there is also a drawback. Karajan is exhibited for so much of the time that the result is occasionally visual monotony. His own explanation is said to have been that "orchestra players are so ugly to look at"! The belief in his personal radiance never abandoned him.

Full of feeling

Karajan was superficially like Bernstein in some ways. Both had unparalleled success, and were TV stars admired throughout the world. Here, though, the similarities end – for as artists and human beings, they were unusually different.

Compared with Karajan's often haughty image as a self-conscious diva, Bernstein seemed open and relaxed, with humour and infectious enthusiasm. In orchestra work, he was the players' friend.

While even Bernstein was certainly aware of his greatness, he evidently had less need to parade it. What he did reflect was the common treatment of idols as public property. They are forced to surround themselves with a protective wall that keeps out a storm of admirers who want to share their shining presence.

Bernstein was a distinct example of an individual who fulfilled the American Dream of success. That he became the artistic director of the New York Philharmonic had much symbolic significance, since the country's principal orchestras were almost always led by Europeans until then.

An impulsive spirit

For Bernstein, conducting did not involve pushing technical brilliance to the brink of absurdity. He preserved the music's freshness and avoided freezing every detail of interpretation in advance. It did, to be sure, happen that purists criticized imperfect playing and excessive emotion. Bernstein was impulsive and threw himself into the music's drama, passion, joy and triumph. And that was just why the public adored him. The well-controlled perfection of a Karajan would have been a strait-jacket for Bernstein.

His music-making rested on a deep love for music. This was what he wanted to give other people, by every possible means. One can easily remember the famous TV series "Omnibus" and "Young People's Concerts" in which, with irresistible enthusiasm and pedagogical insight, he clarified the music's elements and its complexity for his youthful audience.

When it came to popularizing "serious" music, Bernstein had the great advantage of being equally at home with popular music. His successful Broadway musicals contributed to blurring the borders between genres. All were amazed that *West Side Story* could be composed by a philharmonic *maestro*. His importance cannot be overestimated as regards the spread of classical music among listeners who had previously ignored it.

How does a conductor work?

We have now surveyed a number of interesting personalities in command of orchestras. Our choice has been guided not simply by their stature, but chiefly by the fact that they embody distinct types of artists. Many other excellent interpreters could be named, but this is not the purpose of the present chapter. It has been thought more generally useful to supply a basic grasp of the development of conducting than to pause before a long series of portraits. The next step will be to see what a conductor does as he stands on the podium.

Here we shall concentrate on the performance of music as it is traditionally written. Quite a lot of works composed during the last half-century demand additional, or quite different, methods of conducting. These frequently differ even between individual works, and a universal practice is difficult to recognize. Sometimes the composer gives instructions in the score, but a conductor is often required to shape effective ways of communicating instructions to the players.

Gestures and signals

For the concert-goer, a conductor's pantomime of movements can seem confusing and even incomprehensible. It is not made any clearer by the tendency of every conductor to act in his own special way. Yet common features do exist, which are internationally accepted and understandable to orchestras around the world. Among them are the patterns for marking *metre*, or rhythmical time.

Normally it is the right hand that keeps time (although a few conductors are left-handed). The basic patterns are illustrated here. In reality, however, the beats are seldom executed so distinctly. The gestures usually become softly rounded, particularly in music that is not sharply rhythmical.

The right hand

Metre (time signature), tempo, dynamics and, to some extent, character are all indicated by the right hand. It has

Right-hand patterns for two, three and four beats.

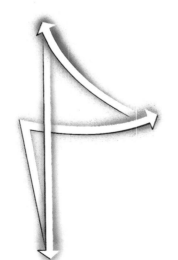
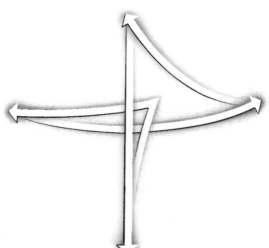

Movements of the right hand are often proportional to the strength of the music.

the primary responsibility of governing the music's flow and helping the players to locate themselves, even in passages with complex rhythm. Sometimes, several time signatures occur simultaneously in different voices of the score. The conductor may then temporarily leave the "mainstream" and turn towards a certain group or individual to signal another rhythmical division. On occasion, he may even show a separate metre with each hand, which demands extreme control of his arm muscles.

The right hand can indicate various dynamical nuances – weak ones with small movements, and strong ones with larger gestures – as well as successive transitions between them. Accents are shown by more emphatic movements. A skilful conductor is thus able, with one hand, to convey many instructions at once.

However, there is no guarantee that he will make, for example, four beats in a 4/4 measure. This depends mainly on which tempo is involved, but also on how much is "happening" in the music, or how complex it is. In a slower tempo, one bar of the music takes more time, so the beats may come too far apart for complete control of everything that is going on. Consequently, two beats are often made for each beat of a measure – a total of eight beats in a 4/4 measure. Division into even more beats may be needed to clarify the process.

In a fast tempo, the opposite is done: one beat for every two beats of the measure, or only one beat per measure. Depending on the nature of the music, we may even see one beat for

every two measures, or for still more measures in exceptional cases. The important thing is how much help the players require at the point in question. This also means that a conductor may behave differently with a virtuoso orchestra than with a less adept group.

If the players are not to become confused by the changing rhythmical division during a concert, it should be indicated during the rehearsal. Often the conductor makes it clear, for instance, by using his left hand to signal "two" just before his right hand changes from four to two beats per measure. It is also important that his "first beats", the downbeats, are always made distinctly, so that they cannot be misunderstood.

The left hand

Further roles of significance fall to the left hand. It is used to "cue" (or signal) important entries, and it can moderate the dynamics, articulation, intensity of expression, vibrato, touch, and so on – of the whole orchestra, of a group, or of a single instrument. Thus it has an artistically formative function, rather than the more strictly unifying one of the right hand. Making the hands and arms work independently can be difficult for a person who is not born with this ability. Even experienced conductors occasionally (and unnecessarily) use both hands to mark time, as if they were following each other in a mirror.

A less common approach was represented by Richard Strauss. "The left hand," he declared, "has almost noth-

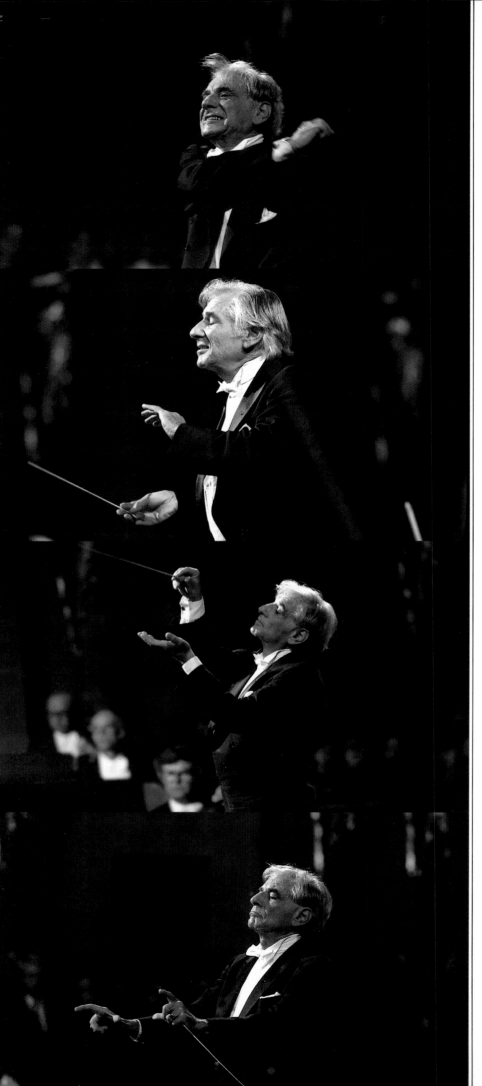

ing to do with conducting. It should preferably be kept in the pocket, and only once in a while give a little softening wave, or some passing sign. For such purposes, a scarcely noticeable glance is otherwise sufficient." We know from films that he worked in this very way, at least during his later years (he gestured more vigorously in his youth).

The face

Whatever one may think of the left hand's duties, Strauss was referring to an essential matter: the part of the conducting which *is not* done by the hands and arms. An orchestra is influenced by the conductor's entire body language, ranging from his general posture to the faintest bend in his back or legs. Most important of all is his face: with the greatest conductors, it is often more determining than the hands. A glance of the eyes can indicate an exact entry, or encourage the player before a demanding solo. It may also show that something is going wrong. In addition, during the playing, certain conductors smile briefly to thank individuals or groups for their performance. Facial variations indicate the character of the playing, and help the musicians collectively to find the right expression.

But this must not go too far. Too much grimacing – like excessively powerful movements of the body – can be a distraction from the playing. Nor is it useful for anyone to watch the sufferings of the world reflected in a conductor's face when Tchaikovsky's *Pathétique* Symphony is on the program. The conductor is not supposed to reproduce the music visually: he should inspire the orchestra to do so acoustically.

The conductor's face exhibits a good deal of giving and taking, which the audience seldom notices or is meant to notice. Not even when we see him frontally, on television, do we recognize or understand more than a part of the silent communication between him and the players. A gesture or a glance can be a reminder of something that was done during rehearsals – or on the contrary, it may be a forewarning of something unexpected.

An ability to give such warnings is typical of the greatest conductors. It provides players with some preparation for even the most spontaneous of whims. Leonard Bernstein possessed this talent in abundance. Once the present author had an opportunity to observe it, in a work with rapid changes of tempo and expression: Mahler's fourth symphony. When discussing the performance with him afterward, Bernstein remarked: "Well, it's the audience who should be surprised. If the orchestra is, then I have an awful job to get it together again!"

The style of movement

Conductors have very different ways of moving. Some are edgy or jerky, while others constantly seem to wave the baton in circles. Still others resemble skiers, pushing themselves forward with poles. Some are as tense as steel springs, others relaxed and good-natured. One may wave eagerly throughout the concert, whereas another saves his gestures for the occasional climax.

To the last of these categories belonged Fritz Reiner, whom we have already mentioned, and the French conductor Pierre Monteux. It was sometimes impossible for the audience behind their backs to tell whether they were doing anything at all. The tip of Reiner's baton was said to circulate in a space the size of a postage stamp!

Certain conductors work intensively with every muscle. An example is Georg Solti who, in a television program of music by Richard Strauss, emphasized that one always perspires if one really is "into the music". Strauss himself thought, on the contrary, that a conductor must never perspire: "It is only the public who should get warm."

Ballet on the podium

There is no definitive answer as to which movements are most functional for a conductor. But it can be said in general that extremely violent movements seldom promote convincing results of musical execution and expression. Conductors who give a veritable ballet performance in front of the orchestra distract both the players and the audience.

Curiously, many conductors seem to confuse dramatic behaviour with musical intensity. In fact, these two features are often opposed. A conductor who employs sweeping gestures to announce an intensification, a climax or surprise, is taking away the musical impact that the composer intended. The psychological effect will have passed when the sound from the orchestra reaches us. Experience shows that the expression becomes more lively if the conductor gestures moderately.

Surplus energy

An interesting example of this occurred some years ago in Paris, when a famous conductor presented one of the great Mahler symphonies. During the first movements, he continually bounced around with excess energy. Living out every detail of the music, he appeared to be going through the same inferno as Mahler did when composing it. Yet the orchestra's scale of expression came nowhere near his state of exaltation. It

A conductor's face conveys much communication with his musicians, which is seldom noticed by the audience. One glance can suggest the music's character or prepare a player for a solo.

played quite mundanely, with beauty but not much commitment, indeed somewhat reserved.

Towards the middle of the symphony, the conductor seemed to have tired all his muscles. He clearly resolved to change his tactics. Throughout the rest of the work, he mostly stood still, making calm movements and giving only essential signs. Now the orchestra displayed an entirely new attitude. Its sound sprang forth in full bloom, roaring or singing in turn; the soft nuances shimmered mysteriously, and the outbursts exploded with demonic power. So charged was the atmosphere that the work itself seemed reborn. This was an instructive experience, which one wishes that all the world's hyperactive conductors had been there to witness.

Race horses

Some conductors behave like champion steeds about to plunge around a course. They can barely bridle their zeal to cast themselves into the music's whirls. When the moment to set off arrives, it often does so loudly, commencing the composition with a noise or a grunt instead of music. Most performances of a work like Strauss' *Don Juan* are started with a distinct thud of the conductor's foot on the floor. Such a signal must be needless, since there are others who obtain superb coordination with only a discrete, precise gesture. The orchestra's dramatic beginning then has a much stronger effect.

Wrong keys

To a large extent, these manifestations of temperament are unconscious. The same

Conductors vary widely in their physical involvement with the music. Here we see Berlioz, caricatured by Geiger.

is true for some conductors who grunt, groan, or inarticulately sing while the music is being played. Fortunately, their vocal punctuations seldom carry farther than the first row of seats. But the orchestra may find them bothersome, especially as they tend to be uttered in a

quite different key than the music.

Such sounds are also easily picked up by microphones. Radio audiences may be disturbed to hear music that is mixed with ecstatic cries. Many conductors have been shocked when recordings reveal the noise they have produced.

Becoming a conductor

Let us review the qualifications that make a top-rate conductor:

The artistic gift of musicality

Strong inner conviction

Charismatic personality

Natural capacity for leadership

Pedagogical inclination

Psychological insight

Good body coordination

A feeling for stringent rhythm

Ability to maintain a given tempo

Knowledge of counterpoint, harmony, form, music history and other "theoretical" topics

Familiarity with the characteristics and techniques of all instruments in the orchestra

Instrumental proficiency, preferably on both string and wind instruments

Knowledge of musical styles, both general and personal, through several centuries

Awareness of performance practices in different periods

A capacity for "dramatic" program composition

Talent and training

Certain aspects of a conductor's "equipment", notably those that concern knowledge, are accessible to many people. The most prominent conductors usually also have a general humanistic education and wide cultural interests. Knowledge is all very well, but an ability to use it creatively is not as common, and requires more abstract qualities such as imagination, taste and empathy. Some of them can be refined and deepened by practice, study and experience, yet nothing can replace inborn talent.

Conducting "by heart" is sometimes taken to be a proof of great artistry. However, what it demands is not musicality but prodigious memory. Several of the best conductors have never given a concert without a score! Similarly, while a mastery of theoretical topics is important, it does not ensure that the conductor's performance will be worth listening to. An ability to keep time in complex patterns, though also quite helpful, shows nothing about musicality either.

Thus, in order to progress farther than perfect time-keeping, a conductor must possess attributes that are more or less intangible. It is probably just this "mystical" element that has given rise to the romantic myth of the conductor as a genius. There is a familiar saying that the conductor's profession involves fifty percent talent and equally much hard work.

Rehearsal techniques

An excellent way to begin conducting is to spend some years playing in an orchestra. This provides invaluable understanding of how the whole group functions and responds. By experiencing good and bad conductors from behind an instrument, one can avoid many mistakes later on.

Among the main things to be acquired is a capacity for rehearsing. Orchestras are expensive to run, and must be utilized effectively. Time is frequently too short for a conductor to work on as many details as he wants. He then has to recognize quickly what is most important and how to do it. Moreover, he should develop a "selective" ear that can detect individual parts and instruments within the orchestra's sound.

It usually takes years to learn all this, and it is possible only with practice. The best approach is to train in a minor orchestra, where mistakes are acceptable and kept out of the limelight.

Formerly, an ideal schooling could be obtained as an assistant at one of the many small opera houses in Central Europe. Whoever showed talent, and had a little luck, might suddenly find himself taking over an entire performance when the regular conductor fell ill. A number of great conductors started their careers by such means. Another lesson was the value of attending rehearsals by experienced conductors. Some beginners studied privately with older masters, although they were seldom given any practice.

Formal education

The conductor's "instrument" is the orchestra, and orchestras are rarely available for practice. Often a conductor has made his *début* after just a few hours of work under professional conditions. It has even happened that a musician takes over a concert or opera performance without having once stood in front of an orchestra.

Education in conducting, at conservatories and universities, has become common only in recent decades. Gradually its basis has widened and the general level of knowledge has risen substantially. Today many students can flawlessly beat through a complicated work such as Stravinsky's *Rite of Spring*, which was previously reserved for the most talented individuals. These institutions have produced a large quantity of knowledgeable, competent conductors for orchestras.

Nonetheless, if we look at those who work for the world's leading orchestras, those who appear regularly are hardly more than a couple of dozen! Can a

shortage of first-class conductors still exist, or is this an illusion?

There are several answers, one being that top orchestras frequently promote a person who has good relations with a record company before one who is "only" a superb musician. Obviously, this reduces the selection a good deal.

However that may be, it is clear that orchestras themselves have become far better – or rather, that many more orchestras have become really good. And the consequence is that their demands on conductors have increased sharply.

Uniformity versus integrity

The age of conductors with distinctive personalities may, in any case, be gone forever. The interpretations of the orchestra's central repertoire have been smoothed out, and much music is now steeped in a melting-pot of international

standards. Could this be the cause of the limited supply of fine conductors?

Many great conductors in the past were by no means virtuosi. They succeeded on the strength of superior musicality, artistic integrity, and a power to inspire the orchestra and audience with their very presence. Their primary resource was a depth of spirit.

A famous example was Wilhelm Furtwängler, whose indistinct motions were confusing for players that did not know him well. According to legend, a member of his Berlin Philharmonic was asked how the orchestra could be so perfectly coordinated in spite of his vague gestures. The revealing answer was: "Ah, when we see him enter through the podium door, we all begin to count. When we reach forty-two, we start playing!"

The test of time

It is amazing how rapidly an orchestra can estimate a conductor's ability. Already after a minute or so of work, the players have a fair notion of the newcomer's potential. Some claim that he bears the signs before the rehearsal begins. Indeed, unexpected qualities may emerge in time, dispelling their first impression. Yet strikingly often, the latter turns out to be right.

Then must a conductor exhibit every bit of his knowledge and acquired experience within the first sixty seconds? Of course not. There is no point in pretending: seasoned musicians invariably see what is not genuine. Nor are many of them interested in attempts to display profound learning.

A young conductor is naturally afraid to make a fool of himself in public, and nervous of being exposed by scores of weather-hardened orchestra veterans. But, when stepping onto the podium, a conductor does not necessarily meet a sea of strict critics, ready to attack every trifle. Most players tend to be generous, eagerly searching for indications of musicality and leadership, rather than for flaws. Even nervousness – within reasonable limits – and faults in routine are regarded as unavoidable. Musicians realize these restrictions and seldom allow them to decide a judgement.

The orchestra's assessment of a conductor is largely intuitive, not based on conscious weighing of his "pros and cons". For a good orchestra, his manner of conducting is not crucial. The important thing is that it feels natural to make music with him, that he knows the score, shows conviction and a definite view of the music, is able to communicate without talking too much, and conveys real confidence – in both artistic and human terms.

3
The Instruments

*E*very instrument in a symphony
orchestra has a history of its own,
which may be even longer than
that of the orchestral form.
Here we meet many familiar
tools of sound, and some
of the most fanciful.

WHEN WE SIT IN A CONCERT HALL AND listen to a symphony orchestra, we can naturally hear that the various instruments produce different sounds. A trumpet is not like a French horn, nor a viola quite like a violin. Our ability to distinguish between them by ear depends on several factors. Most of these have to do with the individual instruments' construction, and others with the musicians' ways of playing them.

What we can see is that the instruments nearest in front of us are made of wood and have strings, which are rubbed with a bow or plucked with the fingers. They are collectively known as *bowed instruments*. Farther back sit musicians with many instruments – both wooden and metallic – which are played by blowing air into them. These *wind instruments* are divided into two groups, the *woodwinds* and the *brasses*. At the rear, or at either side of the podium, we find the musicians who strike, shake, or scrape on their *percussion instruments*. Occasionally there is a harp, with an often artfully shaped frame, in which is stretched a large number of strings that are plucked by finger. Like bowed instruments, this is a *stringed instrument*. The latter term also comprises some of the instruments which are played on a keyboard, primarily the piano and harpsichord.

More crafts than craftsmen

During a concert each of the string players ordinarily wields a single instrument. Only in very unusual works of music do they change instruments. But some of the wind players do so commonly, replacing their usual instruments with smaller ones (as when a flutist uses a piccolo) or bigger ones (a clarinettist may play a bass clarinet).

The largest orchestras frequently have special musicians for these *side-instruments*. Yet even there, for example, French-horn players can switch to a so-called Wagner tuba. Such exchanges are standard procedure among percussionists, who may need to handle ten or twenty instruments with different techniques for the same piece of music. Thus a symphony orchestra of 100 musicians might well employ 125 instruments in the course of one concert!

The Gothenburg Symphony Orchestra

This chapter will concern the contemporary symphony orchestra's normal range of instruments. A few unusual devices are included, but our survey is not meant to be exhaustive. Certain string and wind instruments have variants which rarely occur in a symphony orchestra. Exceptions are more the rule in the percussion section, where equipment as odd as stones and iron chains, or instruments from non-Western music cultures, may be heard. Composers today are ingenious at adding new tools of sound to the orchestra. It would be neither possible nor meaningful to describe everything, at any rate for the purposes of the present book.

We shall discuss the instruments according to their main groups. In this connection, several old terms have become misleading with time. One might, for instance, think that all woodwind instruments are made of wood, but such is not the case – any more than brass instruments are always of brass. As general designations, though, they are so ingrained and internationally accepted that they will doubtless endure.

Here, instruments and their groups are examined in the order of their appearance in a normal score. This is basically shown in the adjacent illustration, which covers all the principal instruments and the most common side-instruments, as well as some eccentric ones.

Wind instruments

A wind instrument's sound is created by producing regular vibrations of the air within it. These resonances of the *air column* can be created in different ways. On a flute instrument, the musician blows against a sharp edge of the device's own body, so that the air stream divides and the air inside the instrument vibrates. Players of the *reed instruments* (oboes, clarinets, bassoons and their relatives) blow against the edge of one or two thin membranes, called reeds, set in the mouthpiece. On brass instruments (the French horn, trumpet, trombone, tuba and so forth) it is the musician's lips which perform this function, vibrating in order to make the air column resonate.

A wind instrument is essentially a pipe in which sound generated by blowing at one end is influenced and, so to speak, refined until it emerges at the other end. The initial sound has no definite pitch and is usually not enjoyable. It may resemble a quacking duck, or a wheeze on blades of grass – and yet the final result can be the sweetest tone of an oboe!

Many sounds to a note

A given note may sound in diverse ways, even when it comes from the same type of instrument. What we actually hear is a blend of numerous ingredients. To begin with, there are the reed's quality and elaboration; on a flute, the size, shape and angle of the mouth-hole (*embouchure*), and so forth; on brass instruments, the inner form of the mouthpiece. Then we have the pipe's dimensions and design

(cylindrical, conical, or a combination of shapes), its materials (sometimes several) and density, its interior surface (smooth, rough or porous), as well as the geometry of its end (more or less flared in a curve like a funnel or bell).

But more about all this later. Other parts of the instrument may also affect its sound by their material and shape. We can thus easily understand that the manufacture of musical instruments is a highly specialized handicraft, with no use for industrial mass production. Indeed, until now we have considered only the instrument itself. Equally important, of course, is the player whose years of education and training enable him or her to control an often unruly instrument with unfailing precision.

Harmonics

On a piano we are familiar with the fact that each note has its own key, a black or white one. The pianist cannot alter the pitch of the notes – their frequency of vibration. This is the task of a piano tuner, who adjusts the strings. But wind instruments work differently, as we shall see. In their original form, they could produce only certain tones, some very impure. They are built on the basis of the harmonic series, comprising *fundamental tones* and the *overtones* that these generate. (A note which is completely free of overtones – called a sinusoidal tone, due to the shape of its sound wave – has musical significance only for electro-acoustic instruments and associated compositions.)

The harmonic series is always the same in relation to the chosen fundamental tone (or "first harmonic"). Its first overtone (or "second harmonic") is twice as high in frequency (number of cycles per second) as the fundamental; its second overtone is three times as high, and so on. This is because the air column in the instrument – like a string on, say, a violin – can only vibrate along

The harmonic series starting from a low C.

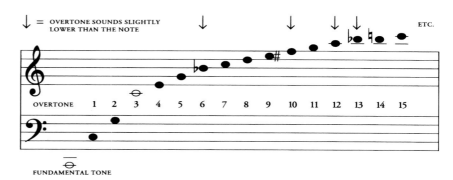

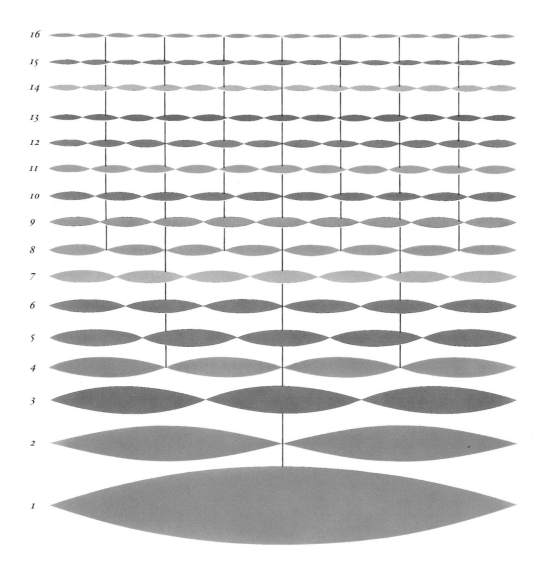

The harmonic series for any fundamental tone. Each tone is a vibration at a certain frequency with a corresponding wavelength. Only waves that reach a peak or node at the ends of the air column or string are possible, so the allowed tones increase in frequency as simple fractions of the fundamental tone.

its entire length (thus producing the fundamental tone) and along simple fractions of its length (such as 1/2 and 1/3 for the first and second overtones). These kinds of vibration, and an example of the resultant notes, are shown in the accompanying illustrations.

Equal temperament

Overtones are physically "pure", but some of them – starting with the sixth – differ from the tones of the system of *equal temperament* to which we have become accustomed in recent centuries. This system divides an octave (frequen-cy doubling) into twelve *semitones* (separated by equal "half steps"). It is a compromise among other possibilities, enabling us to shift easily between dif-ferent tonal keys, as on a piano. Overtones that disagree with the system of equal temperament are marked with an arrow, indicating that they sound flat

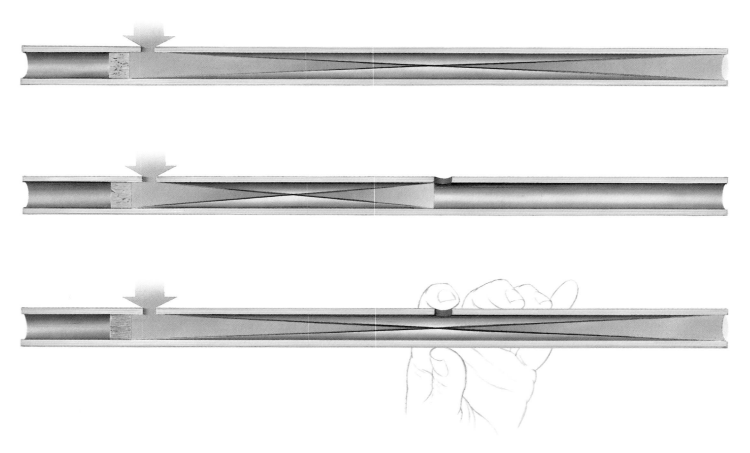

Different tones can be created on a wind instrument by using the fingers to open or close its holes.
These change the length of the freely vibrating air column, and thus the frequency of the sound.

(too low) compared to the scale of that system. They would seem false to our ears, and must be corrected when played on a wind instrument.

One might expect impure overtones to make noise out of music. Yet they are weaker than the fundamental keynote, and we do not hear them independently. Their strengths depend greatly on the instrument which produces them. Moreover, their intensity in relation to each other, and to the keynote, are what create the quality of sound that we call *timbre*, or *tone colour*. Differences in the acoustic spectrum of overtones, for instance between an oboe and a violin, give our ears the means to tell such

instruments apart from each other.

Techniques of blowing

In order to produce the fundamental tone on a flute, the player must blow carefully and not too powerfully – or nothing comes of it. The same happens when we blow on the top of a bottle: excessive force yields no tone. If the musician blows harder or suddenly, the result is instead an overtone; and the more power or "surprise" to the air column, the higher this overtone is. Such *overblowing* is, however, not a mistake but a necessity for the function of many wind instruments. Overblowing can be done

in numerous ways for different instruments, and will be discussed later.

The simplest blown device, for example a whistle or a wooden pipe, gives only a single tone – its fundamental. One method of getting more tones is obviously to join several pipes of varying lengths, each with its own tone; such a construction is called a *panpipe*. Another is the very technique of overblowing, which allows player to generate certain overtones. For this purpose, special instruments known as *natural trumpets* and *natural horns* were once built, lacking holes or keys for the fingers.

When overblowing, an air column of constant length is used. If the musi-

*One way of controlling the air column is with keyed holes, as on the clarinet.
Another, for example on the slide trombone, is to telescope a section of tube:
a shorter air column raises the tone.*

cian shortens the air column, he gets a new fundamental tone, which is ever higher as the column becomes shorter. This fact has, of course, also been employed in wind instruments. It avoids at least some of the difficulties with overblowing. Best of all, it gives access to tones which are not in the harmonic series of the fundamental tone of the key in which the instrument is tuned.

Usually the shortening is achieved through a number of holes that are bored in the sides of the instrument's body. By opening or closing them with his fingers in different combinations, the player can command a reservoir of notes; an elementary instance of this construction is the *recorder*. To go further and extract more tones, one must elaborate the fingering and combine it with overblowing.

Mechanical aids

Diverse inventions have been contrived to exploit more tone-holes than the fingers can cover. In particular, keys are added to open or close the holes. Such a key is a small metal plate, its inner side padded with leather to seal the hole. Some keys have springs that return them to normally open or closed positions when they are released by lifting the finger. To move a nearby key, the musician pushes directly on its pressure plate. If a hole is farther away, he pushes a plate that is linked to the key by a lever or axle running along the instrument. Several keys may be linked together and manoeuvred with one finger. Combined arrangements of this sort have become increasingly clever.

In sum, the keys fulfill a range of functions: they seal effectively, serve as elongated fingers for holes that are inconveniently or distantly located, can control several holes at once – even

more than the player has fingers – and they can cover holes which are too big to be sealed by fingers.

Tone-holes are rarely used on contemporary brass instruments; there are other ways of changing a vibrating air column's length. One is to couple in, or out, extra tube sections of relatively short size. This is how a modern trumpet, tuba or French horn works. Alternatively, a tube section can be telescoped into another to shorten the air column, raising a tone proportionally. Such is the principle of the symphony orchestra's most common form of trombone, the so-called slide trombone.

Articulation

Playing on a wind instrument offers several choices of articulation. One blow can be made to produce a sequence of *legato* notes that merge together, or a separate blast may create each note. The latter is done at a slow tempo by means of *single tonguing*: the musician articulates a consonant, usually "t" or "d" (for a hard or soft note respectively). When the pace is faster, *double tonguing* becomes more practical, shifting between tongue-tip and tongue-base consonants like "t-k" or "d-g". A technique of *triple tonguing* is also used: "t-t-k" or "d-d-g".

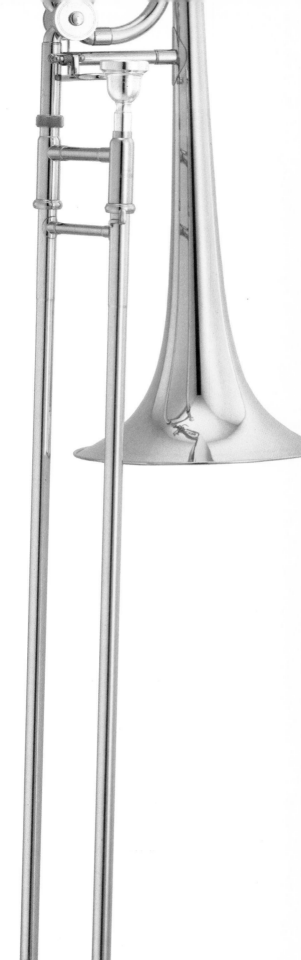

Musicians at the wedding of Joseph II and Isabella of Parma in 1760. The boy at right is Mozart.

The woodwind instruments

This orchestral group consists chiefly of flutes, oboes, clarinets, bassoons, and the English horn (which is related to the oboe). Here, too, belongs the saxophone. It is a motley assemblage: flutes obey a different principle of sound generation than do other woodwinds, and saxophones as well as most present-day flutes are made of metal. Novel materials have often been experimented with. Formerly some instruments were constructed of glass, porcelain or ivory, whereas lately hard rubber and synthetic substances such as plastic have been tried. Since density is important, flutes are occasionally built of gold and platinum. Equally influential is the nature of the interior surface; if too porous, it dampens rather than amplifies the sound, while rough and smooth surfaces yield distinctive sounds.

The flute is an *edge-tone instrument*, meaning that one blows against a sharp edge on it to produce air vibrations in the pipe. As also noted earlier, oboes, clarinets, bassoons and saxophones are *reed instruments*. In them, the membrane whose edge the player blows against is a thin tongue of soft cane-wood that vibrates as a result.

Key systems

All the woodwinds in an orchestra have systems of keys to open and close holes in their sides. The types used nowadays are some 150 years old, but the idea goes back much farther. Keyed instruments were illustrated in the early fifteenth century, and well-developed key

The piccolo

systems existed already before 1600, for instance on the Renaissance *sordone* (a relative of the bassoon).

Originally there was no unified method of holding the instruments. One musician would place his right hand, and another his left, closest to the mouthpiece. The tone-holes or keys were thus positioned so that they could be reached from any side. Certain keys acquired double pressure plates which stuck out in particular directions. As the number of keys and mechanical aids grew, however, it became harder to provide such ambidextrous accessibility. Towards the end of the eighteenth century, a consensus arose that the left hand should always be nearest to the mouthpiece.

Few tonal keys

Still in the time of Haydn and Mozart, every work was composed within a limited framework of tonal keys. This was essential if the contemporary wind instruments were to be sufficient. As we have seen, they operated on the basis of

the harmonic series. By then, some of them had indeed been augmented with key systems which made it possible to play *chromatically*, using all the twelve semitones. But no instrument could produce these purely except in its own fundamental key and the most closely related keys. When a composer ranged into more remote keys, the musicians had to take up instruments that were tuned differently. A consequence can be noticed in Baroque pieces with the trumpet. Since trumpets were normally tuned in the key of D, much of this music was written in D major!

The most thorough development of key systems occurred during the first half of the nineteenth century. Its main motive was the new aesthetic ideal of music in early Romanticism. Composers wanted to exploit all tonal keys and shift between these effortlessly. They also wished the sound to be as similar as possible over the whole register of tones. Changing instruments while playing was no longer feasible. Woodwind instruments had to be modernized so that every note was pure, and every semitone step equally long. Such a tuning of equal temperament had long been used on many keyboard instruments.

In the first decades of that century, instrument-makers experimented with new key systems to satisfy these needs. One of the most successful was Theobald Boehm, himself a prominent flutist. He worked primarily with his own instrument, but his constructions became influential. We shall return to Boehm in connection with the transverse flute.

Flute instruments

Two types of edge-blown flutes:

End-blown

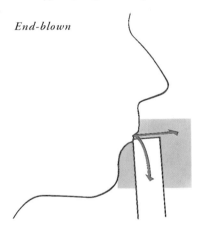

Side-blown

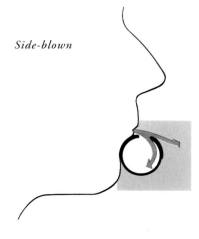

The flute is one of the very oldest musical devices. In simple forms, it arose as soon as human beings began to produce sounds by blowing on hollow objects, such as shells or tubes made of reed, bark, animal horn or bone. By puffing air against the object's edge or into the tube's end, sound could be generated in the same manner as when one blows into a hollow door-key.

Flute instruments are known to have existed as early as 20,000 years ago. One kind was probably Chinese, and came to Europe through Byzantium two thousand years ago. But so primeval a tool of sound must have been created independently in many places. Flutes found in northern Europe have been dated to nearly 10,000 years old.

The simplest pipes gave only one note, but several of them could be combined as a panpipe. Before Christian times, it had been discovered how to increase the choice of notes with tone-holes as well as by overblowing. This opened a path to playing real melodies.

What primarily distinguishes the flutes from other wind instruments is the sharp edge dividing the air stream blown against it. The air changes direction repeatedly between both sides of the edge, causing the vibrations that are transmitted through the tube.

There are two ways of leading the air to the edge, and thus two rather different methods of producing the tone. One way is to blow directly against the farther edge of the mouth-hole. Its advantage is that the player can influence the note's quality by changing the tension and position of his lips and the angle of the air stream. Instruments for such "direct blowing" are called *embouchure flutes*. The best-known example is the ordinary *side-blown* transverse, or "cross", flute.

In this case the mouth-hole is placed on the tube's side near one end. But other, *end-blown* embouchure flutes are blown into the end itself. While contemporary orchestras normally have only side-blown flutes, the end-blown type is occasionally played in special works, such as the panpipe in Mozart's opera *The Magic Flute*.

The other means of conveying the air is through a channel in the mouthpiece at the instrument's end. After its passage, the air meets the dividing edge

Flutes have been enjoyed in traditional cultures since the Stone Age. This representation of a player was made around 2,000 years ago in the region of Ecuador.

in a manner which is always the same, so the sound cannot be influenced much. This channel or duct has given such instruments the name *duct flutes*, the most common instance being the recorder.

From marches to romances

In Western countries, both side-blown and end-blown flutes have been in general use for at least a thousand years. While their principles of sound production remain unaltered, their design has varied. So, too, have the sounds which are expected of them, often due to purely practical considerations. A medieval fife's sharp and piercing tone was desirable for playing outdoors. It often served as a military march instrument in combination with drums. The soft sound ideal that we are familiar with, as in a symphony orchestra, is of later date. This began to appear in the late seventeenth century, becoming widely accepted since the Romantic period in the early nineteenth.

The recorder

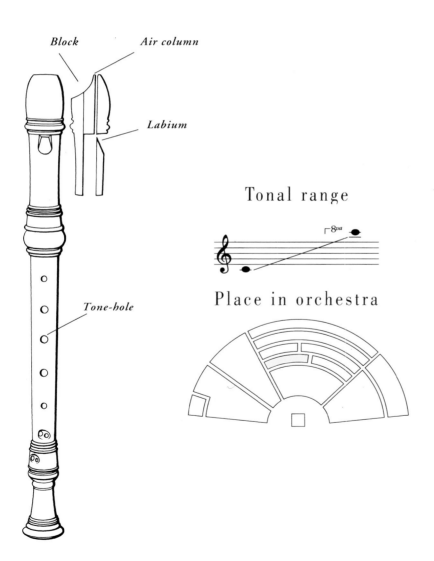

Block

Air column

Labium

Tone-hole

Tonal range

Place in orchestra

For a long time the transverse flute and the recorder were played side by side. Thus one of Bach's famous *Brandenburg Concertos* calls for recorders, whereas a couple of others prescribe the transverse flute. From the Renaissance onward, recorders were made in various sizes to be played in groups – rather like subsequent string quartets. Their heyday began in the seventeenth century and lasted until the mid-eighteenth, when they were overshadowed by the transverse flute.

The recorder, called a "block flute" in some languages, has a wooden block mounted at the tube's upper end. Between the block and tube is a thin slit, through which the air passes to the dividing edge. The mouthpiece is tapered so that the lips can hold it easily, and this has led to the name *beak flute*.

The tone-holes of a recorder, usually numbering seven, are covered partly or wholly with the fingertips in different combinations. A soft, intimate sound is produced in the lower register. In the upper register, the fingering must be coordinated with overblowing, so the player has to blow harder and the sound is more penetrating.

The transverse flute

Ancient Etruscan paintings are our earliest evidence of side-blown flutes. In sculptures and pictures of Hellenistic times, from the centuries just before Christ, we can see that they were already provided with tone-holes, usually six. The next thousand years are pretty quiet about them, but apparently they began to spread across Europe in the twelfth century. In the late Middle Ages, they came mainly from Germany and Switzerland, under the common name of *German flutes*. These were usually made of boxwood, yet sometimes of other materials, even glass.

Towards the end of the seventeenth century a new ideal arose: the transverse flute's sound became milder. A centre of inspiration was France, where members of the Hotteterre family developed many woodwind instruments. The transverse flute acquired a wider, more conical tube and its tone-holes were positioned for easier playing. One key was built onto it, and became standard for more than a hundred years.

Until then, small flutes had been made in a single piece. Now they were assembled from three parts: the "head-joint" (with mouthpiece), the "body", and the "footjoint" (with tone-holes and optional key). This designation continues today. In the early eighteenth century, the body was sometimes made interchangeable so that the instrument could be adapted to different tunings.

At this time, composers increasingly wrote solo music, especially for oboes and flutes in the treble range. Oboes won immediate popularity, yet the flute had to wait until the middle of the century – and it turned into the high fashion of the Enlightenment period. Suddenly everyone wanted to play a flute, whether amateur or professional. Even Frederick the Great of Prussia devoted much time to both playing and composing for the flute, and musicians around him created a wealth of flute works. Notable was Johann Joachim Quantz, the king's flute teacher, whose pedagogical importance also resulted in a flute textbook, published in 1752 and still very readable.

The word "flute" had not extended beyond the recorder, and side-blown instruments were explicitly termed transverse flutes. However, as the latter gained favour over the former, people began to say "flute" for the transverse flute alone.

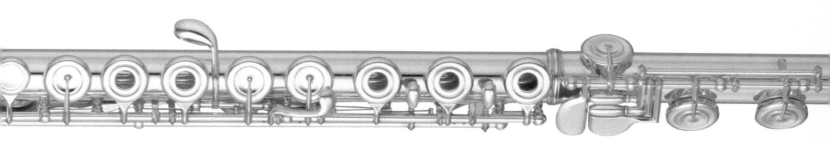

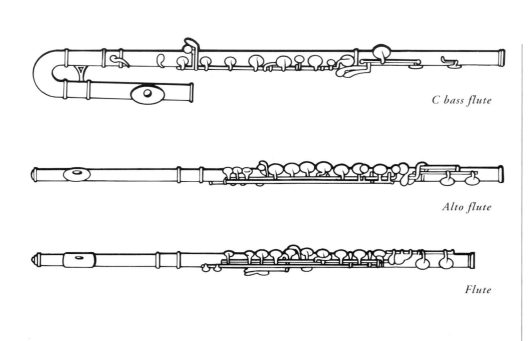

C bass flute

Alto flute

Flute

Piccolo

In the second half of the eighteenth century, many experiments were made with different designs of the mouth-hole, tube and tone-holes. Instruments with a fuller sound and better opportunities for changing the tonal key were desired. New materials were tested, the tone-holes multiplied, and the number of tone-keys grew to eight. The fingering became simpler and every effort was made to satisfy the composers' need for chromatic instruments.

The Boehm flute

But the most drastic development occurred only some ways into the nineteenth century. In the court orchestra of Munich was a solo flutist named Theobald Boehm, also a trained gold-

Tonal range

Place in orchestra

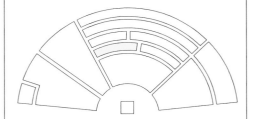

Repertoire examples

Piccolo

<u>Orchestral works:</u>
Beethoven symphonies 5 and 6 (4th movements), Rossini overture to "The Thieving Magpie", Tchaikovsky symphony 4 (movement 3), Rimsky-Korsakov's "Scheherazade", Ravel piano concerto in G major, Shostakovich symphony 9, Britten's "The Young Person's Guide to the Orchestra"
<u>Solo works:</u>
Vivaldi concertos (actually for flageolet)

Flute

<u>Orchestral works:</u>
Gluck's "Orpheus and Eurydice" (Dance of the Blessed), Mendelssohn's music for "A Midsummer Night's Dream" (scherzo), Brahms symphony 4 and Dvořák symphony 8 (4th movements), Debussy's "Prelude to the Afternoon of a Faun", Shostakovich symphony 15 (movement 1)
<u>Solo works:</u>
Bach orchestral suite 2, Telemann suite in A minor; concerts by Vivaldi, F. Benda, Quantz, Mozart, Reinecke, Nielsen, Ibert, Jolivet

Alto flute

<u>Orchestral works:</u>
Ravel's "Daphnis and Chloë" (suite 2), Stravinsky's "Rite of Spring", Lloyd Webber's "Requiem"
<u>Solo works:</u>
Holmboe's flute concert (movement 2), Fukushima's "Mei"

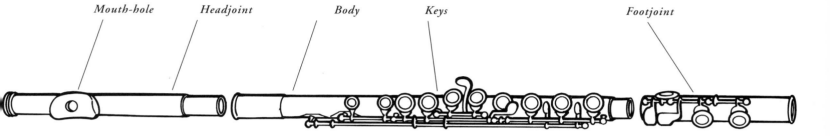

Mouth-hole   Headjoint   Body   Keys   Footjoint

smith and familiar with fine handicraft. For many years he worked on flute constructions to obtain all the chromatic tones as purely as possible, with an even timbre across the entire register and a fuller sound. He made the tube's inner form mostly cylindrical (as it had been in the Middle Ages), and enlarged both the mouth-hole and tone-holes.

In particular, Boehm placed all the holes where they operated best acoustically, regardless of how easy it was to finger them. Yet this required a huge refinement of the key mechanism. Among other things, he used *ring keys* that enable a finger to cover one hole and, at the same time with a rod or axle from the ring, influence a hole farther away.

The first "Boehm flute" appeared in 1832, and fifteen years later came his final design. Its highest honour is that, throughout the following century and a half, no significant changes in it have been needed!

Many musicians were initially wary of Boehm's flutes, finding them to have a less individual sound than the old wooden ones. But thanks to their improved intonation and greater evenness, they gradually achieved wide acceptance. Berlioz, as always, was quick to exploit these advances, though Wagner was at first doubtful because of a certain change in timbre. Richard Strauss, and the French in the early twentieth century, made full use of the Boehm flute. In addition, Boehm applied his experience to other woodwind instruments, and some of his structural details were valuable there as well, even though no such breakthrough occurred for "Boehm oboes" and so on.

With Boehm, it became a rule to manufacture transverse flutes of metal, as is still done. Those in symphony orchestras are usually of silver, their timbre being rich in overtones; gold and platinum are also employed. Each material has its own qualities, which can even be combined by using diverse alloys. Wooden flutes, too, play a role in some orchestras.

The transverse flute is the orchestra's most agile wind instrument, and composers often turn to it for rapid runs and leaps. The playing can be articulated in many ways, including trills and tremolos. The timbre is also variable. In the middle register, it has a basically clear and soft character, suited to melodious music. In the depths, it sounds hollow and rather desolate, yet at the heights it becomes light and glittering. Its range is extensive, enabling a good player to command more than three and a half octaves. On the other hand, its dynamics are more limited than on some other wind instruments.

Despite the metal construction of most transverse flutes, they are thus grouped among the woodwind instruments. Historically, this is quite understandable. The important point is that flutes, in a musical sense, form a natural unit with their wooden cousins — the oboes, clarinets and bassoons.

There is a long list of transverse flutes apart from the "large" orchestral

The piccolo's sharp tone is easily distinguishable in a large orchestra.

flute, with imaginative names such as the *flute d'amour* and the "Swiss fife". We shall focus, however, on those that are common in today's orchestras: the piccolo and the alto flute (called a bass flute in some countries). While the former is universally used, the latter occurs now and then in special works.

The piccolo

This may be called a miniature version of the ordinary flute. It sounds an octave higher and has about as wide a range, almost three and a half octaves. It first came into use towards the end of the eighteenth century, evolving from the military fife. But the designation *flauto piccolo*, meaning simply "little flute", existed even earlier. During the Baroque and as late as Mozart's time, that term meant a soprano recorder, or else the small flageolet which was also endblown.

Like many other novel instruments, the side-blown piccolo was initially employed in opera orchestras, for instance by Gluck. We find some of the earliest symphonic examples in Beethoven's fifth and sixth symphonies. In the former, it contributes to the triumphant mood of the finale by delivering piercing fanfares up in the treble – while in the latter its shrill tone makes the storm imagery more effective.

In the nineteenth century, the piccolo was improved along with the large flute, notably by Theobald Boehm. Its modern construction is similar, apart from its usual lack of a separate footjoint. In contrast to the large flute, piccolos are still often made of wood for the sake of a softer timbre. Yet pure and alloyed silver do occur, and occasionally a wooden piccolo is played with a silver mouthpiece.

Composers use the piccolo for conspicuous solo passages and effects, as well as for accentuation or colouring of other instruments – in particular, of the large flute or the violins. Brass instruments, too, sound more brilliant when a piccolo is added.

The alto flute

Bigger than the ordinary flute, this version is normally pitched a perfect fourth lower. Its design and material are otherwise the same. Invented by Boehm on the basis of, among others, the older bass transverse flute of wood, it came into use during the later nineteenth century. It is said to have been Boehm's favourite instrument, but has never enjoyed much popularity. The tone is relatively weak (requiring a lot of air) and has difficulty in penetrating. However, its hollow and fateful character is distinctive and can heighten the tension when played solo against a restrained background. Ravel employed the alto flute in *Daphnis and Chloë*, Stravinsky in *The Rite of Spring*.

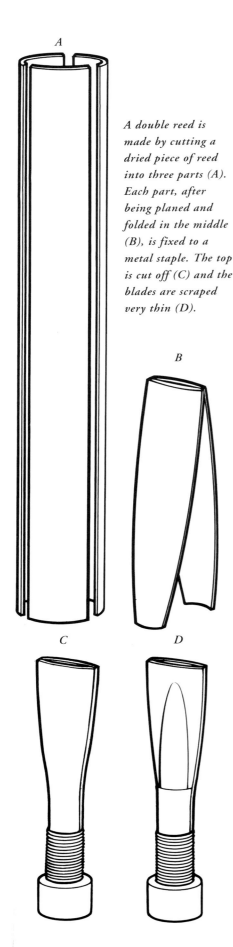

A double reed is made by cutting a dried piece of reed into three parts (A). Each part, after being planed and folded in the middle (B), is fixed to a metal staple. The top is cut off (C) and the blades are scraped very thin (D).

Reed instruments

On all woodwinds except the flutes, sound is produced by blowing against the edge of a thin membrane, known as a reed. A *single reed* consists of a wooden tongue, stretched over an opening in the side of the mouthpiece, and vibrating when blown on. A *double reed* means that two parallel tongues are attached to the instrument, and vibrate against each other when their ends are blown on. Oboes (including English horns) and bassoons have the latter type.

Here the principle of sound generation is the same as when one blows across a stretched blade of grass. The shrill noise that results is refined in the instrument's sound tube. To vibrate easily, the reed must be made from soft, elastic wood of the cane variety. Most commonly used today is a cane species, *Arundo donax*, which grows in southern France and Spain.

The birth of a reed

In manufacturing a double reed, firstly a well-dried piece of cane is cut into three parts. Each part is planed in a special tool to the required thickness (for an oboe, only slightly more than half a millimetre). It is then soaked, folded across, and cut along the sides with another device. The fold is cut up to give two blades which are scraped thin until they can vibrate easily. They are tied together round the narrow end of a conical brass *staple*, which is attached in the sound tube's opening with a socket of cork. The staple's material and form have a great influence on the playing, and musicians sometimes need to switch between several different reeds.

A reed's personality

Every reed must be exactly suited to the instrument and to the person who will play it. Therefore, orchestral musicians do not buy finished reeds, but the raw materials – sections of worked cane or even parts of the original plant. It is essential to get pieces of just the right thickness, so that they will fit into the shell-shaped planing bed and so that the reed will have the correct tension.

For many hours afterward, the player sits in his room and planes, scrapes, measures, and tests the reed. Its quality is decisive for the musical outcome. During a concert, as well, the reed must be checked and kept sufficiently moist. Perhaps you have seen an oboist who

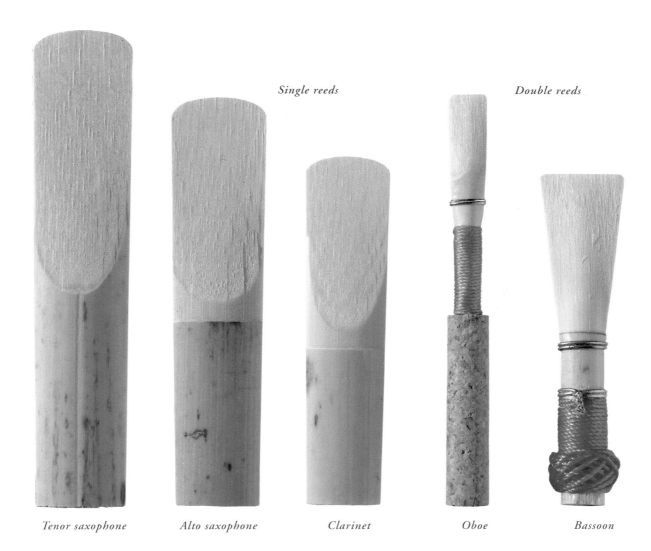

Single reeds   *Double reeds*

Tenor saxophone   *Alto saxophone*   *Clarinet*   *Oboe*   *Bassoon*

punctuates an imperfect performance by giving his reed an accusing glance as though it were a living creature!

From the shawm to the dulcian

Musical reeds have ancient roots. In the old Mediterranean cultures, double-reed instruments were familiar during the millennia before Christ. Egyptian paintings around 1500 BC show simple oboes with two almost parallel sound tubes. A similar Greek instrument, the *aulos*, was used in theatres and at festivals of the god Dionysos. It resembled the later shawm, and was related to the popular folk instruments that still occur in some countries.

The Renaissance introduced serious changes in these devices. Only then did true art music begin to emerge, free of religious or military rituals. Loud, shrill instruments were not enjoyed indoors, and milder types were developed. At the same time, soft- sounding recorders and viols appeared.

Towards the end of the Renaissance, features of the dulcian and other instruments were adopted by the first bassoons. In the mid-seventeenth century, the treble shawm entered the scene, laying a foundation for the oboe. A single-reed type of shawm may, indeed, have been the inspiration for the clarinet around 1700.

The oboe

During the early Baroque, violins were the most frequent solo instruments for indoor use. Nothing else sounded as expressive and gave the player so many technical opportunities. Thus, when oboes arrived, a revolution followed. They were invented in the mid-seventeenth century, probably by Jean Hotteterre with his musical colleagues at the French court. Having only two keys, yet built very precisely, they could be wielded with great virtuosity — which explains how they managed a breakthrough in just a few years.

The high quality of these original oboes was due to their construction in three separate parts. This made it possible to test their acoustic characteristics fully, with exact boring and positioning of the tone-holes. Boxwood was their usual material, and several sizes of oboe were made for playing in groups. The soprano and alto ranges soon became predominant for solo roles.

Oboists of the Sun King

There was an immediate need for the oboe at the court of Louis XIV. His

The oboe has a warm, but still penetrating, tone and is well suited to playing melodic passages or quick runs.

musicians had moved from the open air to entertain in the salon – and their leader, Jean-Baptiste Lully, thoroughly revised the selection of instruments. Particular renown awaited *Les douze grands hautbois du Roi* (the King's twelve excellent oboists), some of them playing the bassoon. In other words, the name "oboe" derives from *hautbois* (loud wood), indicating that its sound was still quite robust.

The oboes were often arranged chorally, like the string instruments in a modern orchestra. One famous example is Handel's *Fireworks Music,* whose original version called for no less than twenty-four oboes, in addition to twelve bassoons and many brass instruments.

A golden age of oboes

At first, oboes were often used to enrich the sound of string ensembles, but they quickly earned more individual assignments. During the late Baroque and almost the whole of Vienna classicism, the oboe remained the orchestra's

leading wind instrument.

By a few decades into the eighteenth century, its construction had been perfected and an increasing number of virtuosos took to them. Composers such as Albinoni, Vivaldi and Handel produced large quantities of solo concertos for the oboe. These were eventually to become scarce: between the works of Mozart in 1778 and Richard Strauss in 1946, hardly any concerto of international fame can be found!

The modern key system

While Boehm was working on his flutes, the oboe's sound tube was being elaborated in France by Guillaume and Frédéric Triébert, who designed a corresponding key system. Some of Boehm's ideas proved useful to them, but their modernization went less far than the flute's. In spite of that, only minor adjustments have been needed since the mid-nineteenth century.

The complicated key system, however, required a more stable wood than

Baritone oboe   *English horn*   *Oboe d'amore*   *Oboe*

The English horn with a bell

box, which could warp and crack. Hard species such as grenadillo, ebony and rosewood were introduced, the last being most common today.

The orchestra's tuning pitch

An oboe has a limited dynamic register, but its bright and clear tone has no trouble in getting through. It has always been especially appreciated for melodious music. Fast runs, as in Rossini's overture to *The Silken Ladder*, can also be executed on the oboe. Its capacity for distinct staccato is often exploited in the orchestral repertoire.

When an orchestra tunes up, the pitch is given by the first oboist. This eighteenth-century tradition has been maintained because the oboe's timbre is easy to hear throughout the orchestra.

Oboes for hunting and love

Around the year 1720, several oboes with a somewhat deeper sound were launched. One, the *oboe da caccia*, was crescent-shaped and had a large metal bellpiece; another received the name of *oboe d'amore*. Whether they had anything to do with hunting or love is uncertain, but they were widely used – as by Bach – to create variations in timbre. Only a few composers have subsequently specified the "love oboe", for instance Ravel and Strauss.

Tonal range

Place in orchestra

Repertoire examples

Oboe

<u>Orchestral works:</u>
*Beethoven symphony 6 (movement 3),
Schubert symphony 9 (movement 2),
Rossini's overture to "The Silken
Ladder", Brahms violin concerto
(movement 2), Ravel's "The Tomb of
Couperin", Stravinsky's "Pulcinella",
Shostakovich symphony 1*
<u>Solo works:</u>
*Concertos by Albinoni,
Vivaldi, Telemann, Handel, Haydn,
Mozart, Vaughan Williams,
R. Strauss, Martinu*

English horn

<u>Orchestral works:</u>
*Rossini's "William Tell" overture,
Berlioz' "Symphonie Fantastique"
(movement 3), Wagner's "Tristan
und Isolde", Franck's symphony
(movement 2), Dvorák symphony 9
(movement 2), Sibelius'
"Tuonela's Swan", Shostakovich
symphony 11 (movement 4),
Copland's "Quiet City"*
<u>Solo works:</u>
*Donizetti's "Concertino", Honegger's
"Concerto da camera" (with flute)*

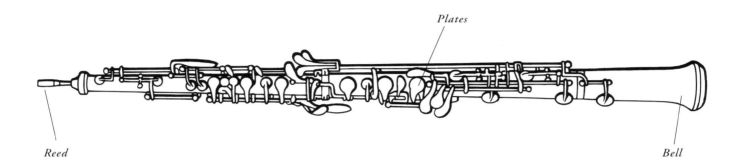

Plates

Reed

Bell

The English horn

Near the end of the eighteenth century, though, the "hunting oboe" turned into the English horn. This name is misleading, as the instrument is not at all English. It might be a mistranslation of the French *cor anglé* (angled horn) taken to mean *cor anglais*. For the instrument did originally often have an angular shape, although the straight form soon prevailed. The mouthpiece is extended with a slightly bent metal crook that carries the reed.

The Vienna classicists seldom used this instrument, but it gained general acceptance with Berlioz and Wagner. A modern English horn's sonorous timbre is clearly distinguishable from the lighter oboe's. It may be considered more elegiac, and has thus been frequently employed for solo parts, as in *The Swan of Tuonela* by Sibelius.

The bulb bell

All of these instruments in the alto range have, at their lower end, a thick section like an egg or pear. This bulbous *bell* (German: *Liebesfuss*) was popular during the mid-eighteenth century and built into many woodwinds to soften their tone. Exactly what gives such instruments their special timbre has been debated. It is not the bulge alone, but probably a combination of the bulge and the crook, as well as the fact that the slightly conical sound tube is made a bit narrower before the bell joint.

Baritone oboes

Still lower-sounding oboe instruments occur in some music. One, invented at the beginning of our century by Wilhelm Heckel in Germany, and is named the *heckelphone*. Its bell is shaped rather like a pepper-grinder. Among the first to use it was Strauss in several of his operas. Today's orchestras occasionally replace it with a *bass oboe*, which is also in the baritone range.

The hunting oboe's secret

We do not know whether there was much difference between the Baroque *oboe da caccia* and an English horn. Some Baroque purists insist on playing the former, while others think that the choice is a matter of appearance. A British writer tells of an oboist in the early part of our century who toured as a specialist on the *oboe da caccia*. But the beautifully upturned bell was only a dummy which he tied to his English horn. Everyone admired the supposed hunting oboe, until a conductor asked just where the difference lay. And the player's reply was forthright: "The difference is five pounds per concert!"

The heckelphone

The clarinet

Whereas flutes and bassoons were introduced in the sixteenth century, and the oboe in the middle of the seventeenth, the clarinet arose in about the year 1700. It was probably invented by Johann Denner in Nürnberg, on the basis of a recorder-like instrument, the *chalumeau*, whose mouthpiece had a single reed. The name "clarinet" came later, meaning "little clarion", because it was thought to sound like a trumpet in the high clarino register.

Every second overtone

Overblowing distinguishes a clarinet from flutes, oboes and bassoons. While they yield all overtones, the clarinet's cylindrical pipe and single reed produce only the even-numbered ones.

Thus the first playable overtone is not at the octave, but at the twelfth (an octave and a fifth), above the fundamental. Early clarinets had holes for the diatonic scale from the fundamental tone up to the ninth (an octave and a whole tone), leaving a gap of one fourth to the first overblown tone. To bridge the gap, instruments were provided with two keys, but this bridging has remained one of the clarinet's problems.

Chromatic playing of all the semitones was impossible, so different tunings were needed in order to command more tonal keys. Ever since the days of Vienna classicism, B-flat and A have been the usual tunings, suitable for flat and sharp keys respectively. The A clari-

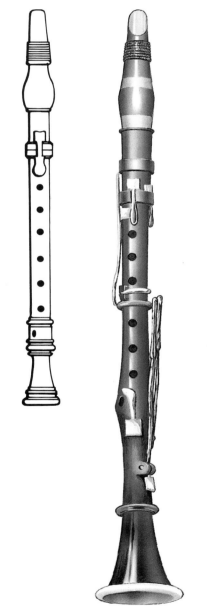

The chalumeau and (at right) an early clarinet from the eighteenth century.

net has a somewhat darker timbre (appreciated not least by Brahms).

Müller's clarinet

The original clarinet, very like a chalumeau, developed during the eighteenth century in terms of both its sound and playing technique. As the need for versatile instruments grew, its number of keys was increased to five or six, and the bell acquired its slightly outcurved form. A leap forward was taken, a decade into the nineteenth century, by the Russian-born virtuoso Iwan Müller. His clarinet was the result of extensive experiments with the boring of the pipe, the form and placement of the tone-holes, and the keys as well as how they were sealed against the holes.

This type of instrument, with thirteen keys, became widespread in several variants for a century. In Germany it was elaborated during the 1840s by Johann Adam Heckel, who is better known for his bassoons; also some decades later by the clarinettist Carl Bärmann, and subsequently the instrument-maker Oskar Oehler in Berlin. Thus it acquired more than twenty keys. In Belgium, Müller's system was refined during the 1840s by Eugene Albert and Charles Mahillon. Particularly Oehler's "German clarinet" has been used long into our time by many German, Austrian, and some East European orchestras. Elsewhere, it has declined sharply in recent years.

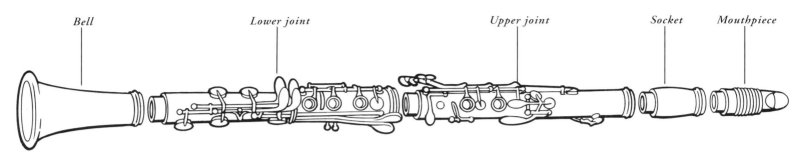

Bell   Lower joint   Upper joint   Socket   Mouthpiece

Repertoire examples

Clarinet
Orchestral works:
Mozart symphony 39 (movement 3),
Schubert symphony 8 and
Brahms symphony 4 (2nd movements),
Sibelius' "A Saga" and symphony 1
(movement 1), Bartók's "The Miraculous
Mandarin", Kodaly's "Dances of Galanta"
Solo works:
Concertos by C. Stamitz, Mozart,
Krommer, Weber, Spohr, Crusell, Nielsen,
Hindemith, Copland

E-flat clarinet
Orchestral works:
Berlioz' "Symphonie Fantastique"
(movement 5), R. Strauss' "Till
Eulenspiegel", Ravel's "Bolero" and
"Daphnis and Chloë" (suite 2),
Stravinsky's "Rite of Spring"

Bass clarinet
Orchestral works:
Smetana's "Hakon Jarl", Wagner's "Tristan
und Isolde" (act 2), Stravinsky's
"Rite of Spring" (beginning),
Khachaturian's piano concerto

Tonal range

Place in orchestra

Adolphe Sax (1814-94)

The French approach

Another path was taken in France,
where Adolphe Sax built his own clarinet in the 1840s. Most successful was a
type made by Auguste Buffet, in collaboration with the teacher Hyacinthe
Klosé. Buffet's "French clarinet" is also,
rather improperly, called a "Boehm clarinet". It was strongly influenced by
Boehm's key system, but he never participated in its design. During the twentieth
century, it has become ever more popular
and now predominates even in countries
which once preferred Oehler's system.

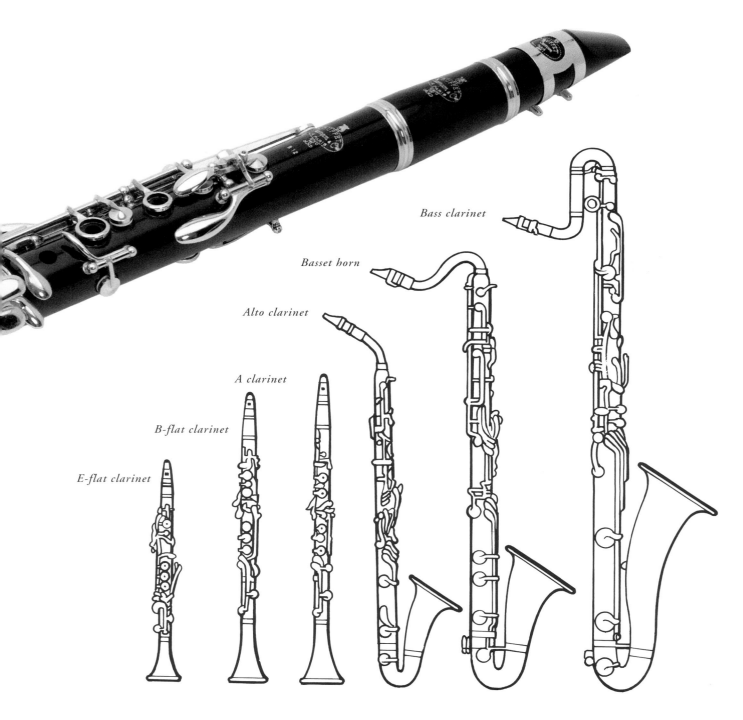

Bass clarinet

Basset horn

Alto clarinet

A clarinet

B-flat clarinet

E-flat clarinet

The great distance up to the over-blown register makes a large number of keys necessary. On standard instruments, there are usually 24 holes and 17 keys.

Inverting the mouthpiece

When clarinets were in their infancy, the reed was attached to the upper side of the mouthpiece. But players soon noticed that a beautiful tone could be produced more easily if the reed rested against the lower lip. This is how mouthpieces have been made ever since the mid-eighteenth century. The reed is fastened by a metal ligature with two tension screws. It was once tied on, as is still done for Oehler instruments.

Early clarinets already consisted of four or five parts: the mouthpiece, the barrel or socket (more outcurved at that time than today), the upper or left-hand joint and the lower or right-hand joint (with keys), and the bell. Essentially

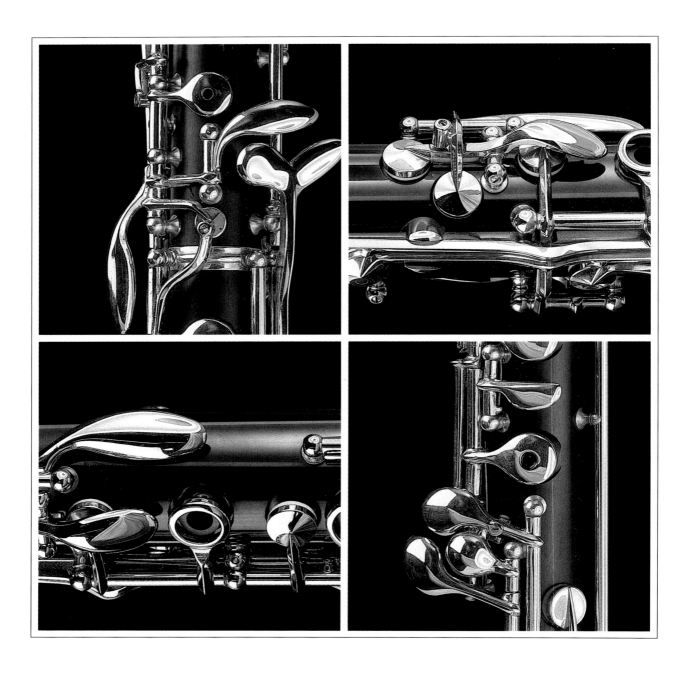

they are still built in this way. Their material, originally boxwood, was replaced by the harder ebony and grenadillo. The beak-shaped mouthpiece continued to be made of wood far into our century, but is now made of ebonite or sometimes glass.

Shifting tone

It is easier to reach high notes by overblowing in the twelfth. Hence the clarinet's range is greater than those of other woodwinds – nearly four octaves. Its tonal character also changes significantly. In the low *chalumeau* register (the latter instrument was played without overblowing) it becomes gloomy and mysterious, especially in soft nuances. Yet the overblown *clarinet* register sounds bright and clear, even sharp and penetrating at the highest notes.

This contrast in character has sometimes been intentionally exploited by composers. A good example is the trio part of the minuet in Mozart's symphony No.39, where two clarinets play in separate registers – the melody line is entirely of overblown notes, and the underlying accompaniment is of chalumeau notes. Normally, though, one of the clarinettist's tasks is to hide the break between registers as fully as possible. Learning to do so requires years of training.

The bass clarinet

Playing violin parts

The clarinet's single reed can be affected over a wide range, enabling it to produce anything from a barely audible *pianissimo* (such as the beginning of Weber's overture to *Der Freischütz*) up to a potent *fortissimo*. It is a very flexible instrument which can (when blown by a virtuoso) easily produce runs, leaps, trills and other ornamentation. One thus understands why the clarinets in brass bands play the masterly role of the violins.

Late acceptance

It may seem astonishing that the clarinet won approval only after some 75 years of use. During late Baroque times, few composers cared for it – among them Handel, Vivaldi and Rameau in occasional works. The reason is that, for a long while, this instrument was much less flexible or nice-sounding than oboes and flutes.

In the second half of the eighteenth century, clarinets were adopted by the excellent orchestra at the court of Mannheim, where Carl Stamitz composed a number of solo concertos. Presumably it was there that Mozart became acquainted with the instrument, and his many clarinet works soon established it in orchestras. Haydn used it in some of his last symphonies; Beethoven and Schubert had it from the start.

Romantics like Weber and Wagner took imaginative advantage of the clarinet in their operas – not least its ability to convey ethereal poetry and mysterious natural settings. Its opportunities for virtuoso performance have been cultivated since the end of the last century by Strauss, Debussy and many others.

Clarinets on high...

Several clarinets are tuned higher than the usual ones in B-flat and A. Most familiar in orchestras is the little E-flat clarinet, which has existed since the late eighteenth century. It lends an impression of scorn in Berlioz' *Symphonie Fantastique*, and its screeching tone is appropriate to just that sort of grotesque ridicule. The decades around 1900 saw its frequent use by Mahler, Strauss, Schönberg, Ravel, Stravinsky and others.

A somewhat lower, less sharp version in D was common during the childhood of clarinets, continuing long into our day with Central and Eastern European orchestras. A clarinet in C has also been employed, for instance by Strauss' operas.

There are also lower variants than the standard clarinets. Only the bass clarinet, tuned an octave lower in B-flat, is a permanent member of orchestras. When introduced in the 1770s, it sometimes had a zigzag shape for easier access to the tone-holes. Yet it was not generally used until modernized by Adolphe Sax in 1838.

Its rounded, pleasing tone served the Romantics well. Berlioz and Meyerbeer wrote characteristic solo parts for it, soon followed by Liszt and Wagner, then for example by Strauss, Schönberg and Ravel. The *contrabass* clarinet, a further octave deeper with a soft, full timbre, occurs in isolated cases in twentieth-century music, such as Webern's *Six Pieces for Orchestra*.

All of these low clarinet instruments have a straight sound tube, with a mouthpiece angled towards the player and an obliquely upturned bell of metal.

The basset horn

Around 1770 in Germany, yet another special design arose – the *basset (little bass) horn*. By adding more keys, the clarinet's range was extended downward a perfect fourth to F. This instrument took on various forms to make the tone-holes accessible: an angle, U-shape, zigzag or crescent. Normally the tube was also curved back and forth inside a box-like wooden piece, following the pattern of the Renaissance rackett (see the bassoon below). Today, the basset horn resembles a small version of the bass clarinet, with its bell obliquely upturned.

That the basset horn acquired some popularity was due to Mozart, who loved its deep sound – more neutral than the clarinet's. It scarcely appealed to nineteenth-century orchestral composers, but Strauss (an admirer of Mozart) benefitted from it in numerous operas and other works.

The alto clarinet

Tenor saxophone

Soprano saxophone

The saxophone

The Belgian instrument-builder Adolphe Sax was also an adept clarinet-tist, and could immediately test his own constructions. A truly versatile professional, Sax contributed to the development of many wind instruments. His main clients were brass bands, which he provided during the 1840s with a large family of brass instruments, generally

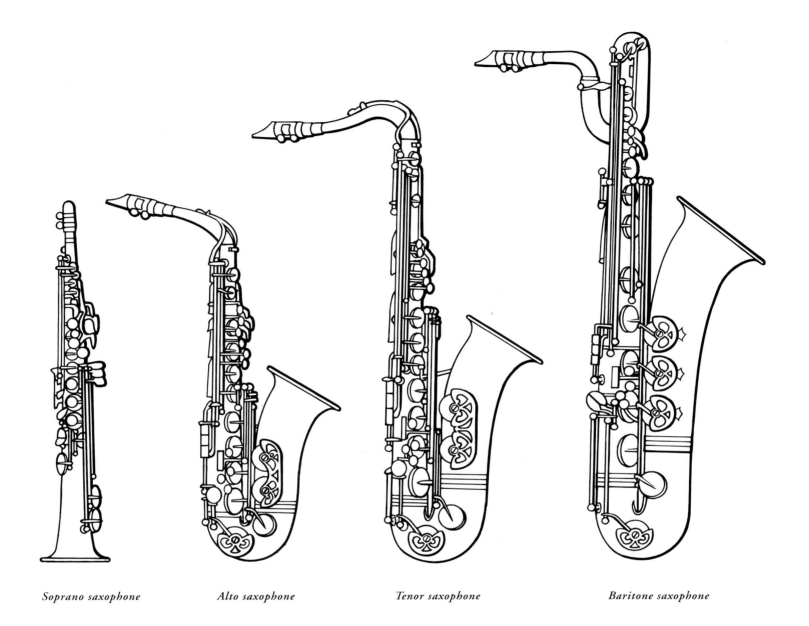

Soprano saxophone   *Alto saxophone*   *Tenor saxophone*   *Baritone saxophone*

called *saxhorns* after their inventor.

Alongside these, Sax created another new type: the *saxophones*. They had features from diverse sources: a single reed like the clarinet, a conical tube like the oboe, and a Boehm-type key system. Although made of metal, they are grouped in the clarinet family – and thus as woodwind instruments – because of the reed. Their external form,

with the upper part turned towards the player, a straight sound tube, U-shaped lower section, and obliquely upturned bell, was established already by Sax. However, the soprano versions are usually straight like clarinets.

Saxophones were originally manufactured in no less than fourteen sizes! Eight have been focussed upon later, most commonly those in the soprano,

alto, tenor and baritone ranges. Still chiefly used in brass bands, as well as in jazz and popular music, the instrument nonetheless occurs at times in symphony orchestras. Prominent solos – in particular for the alto saxophone – have come from Bizet, Ravel, Prokofiev and other composers.

The bassoon

Some of the low-sounding Renaissance reed instruments were built in a way that permitted deep tones without being too unwieldy. Just as the sound tubes of brass instruments had been curved, so were they now in wood instruments. Either the tube was made of metal, or a piece of wood was bored with a row of parallel holes whose ends were joined. The most elaborate example was the *rackett*, in which a tube coiled up and down for several metres in a can-like body. The bassoon's tube folded only once, but its Italian name *fagotto* really means a "bunch" of tubes.

Early bassoons came in many sizes for use by ensembles. From the outset, their low variants were most popular. Their construction was in principle the same as today, except that they were initially made in a single piece. The sound tube was slightly conical, widening

Playing the bassoon

downward to the U-shaped joint and then upward to the bell. There could be six to eight holes, and one or two keys existed at an early date.

Chromatic growth

We have mentioned the instrument-maker Jean Hotteterre of Paris (actually a family of important musicians). Together with colleagues at the court of Louis XIV, he also became interested in the bassoon. By building it in separate parts, they could bore the tube and place the tone-holes more precisely.

Late Baroque bassoons usually had three keys. Around the end of the eighteenth century with its greater need for chromatic playing, the keys increased in number to eight or so. During early Romantic times, work proceeded to make the instrument fully tempered

and its timbre more even.

The French and German schools

From then on, the manufacturers went their separate ways, and two approaches emerged with considerably different ideals. In France the basic eighteenth-century design was kept, with practical improvements. A certain unevenness in tone and playability remained, but these instruments continued to be used for a long while in other Latin countries as well, and in Russia.

In Germany, however, the bassoon underwent extensive changes. Several generations of instrument-makers from the Heckel family, in particular, imposed far-reaching technical modernization. New materials such as rosewood were adopted, and the sound tube's

boring was modified, as were the holes' shape and positioning, the keys and the entire mechanical apparatus.

Yet so radical a revision could not be achieved without altering the device's acoustic properties, even if it was a question of taste whether they became better or worse. The Heckel bassoons, and similar ones from other makers, have gained ever more ground during our century. Musicians all over the world – lately also the French – now prefer these finely equipped and more easily blown instruments with their softer tone.

Still, it cannot be overlooked that this conformity has dubious aspects. Much of the older music, and some of the more recent French, is intended for bassoons with a light "pre-Heckel" timbre. The difference is considerable in, for example, works by Debussy and Rimsky-Korsakov. Ultimately the issue must be one of stylistic fidelity, a concept which has a broad following in other respects today.

Crooks and joints

Hotteterre's design did not do badly: after more than three hundred years, a bassoon is assembled from the same four sections, in addition to the mouthpiece. First the air passes through the reed and the crook, which opens into the *tenor joint* (also called the wing). Then comes the *double joint* (or butt), in which the passage turns upward to the *bass joint.* Finally there is the bell, once given diverse forms, but nowadays hardly outcurved at all. Modern bassoons are often made from various sorts of maplewood.

Previously, problems arose in reaching the widely spaced holes on large instruments. Bassoons found a simple but ingenious solution. The sound tube was led through a thicker section of wood, in whose sides the tone-holes were "lengthened" by obliquely bored channels (giving the tenor joint its wing-like shape). The distance between holes was thus made shorter at the fingers than inside the sound tube. Seventeenth- and eighteenth-century bassoons also had holes and keys on the butt. Today there are keys on all four sections of the instrument.

Singing and lamenting

The bassoon's timbre varies a little between registers. At the bottom, it is dry

but full, a good foundation for the woodwind group. The same role is sometimes played for the string instruments when the composer wants a more distinct bass. Most flexible is the middle range, especially suited for melodious solos. One fine example can be heard in the second movement of Tchaikovsky's fourth symphony. At the top, the sound is more nasal and "lamenting", put to effective use by Stravinsky at the beginning of *The Rite of Spring.*

The contrabassoon

Deeper-sounding bassoons appeared already in the early seventeenth century. A hundred years later, Handel inspired a new design for his *Fireworks Music.*

Haydn exploited the contrabassoon (double bassoon) in his oratorio *The Creation,* and Beethoven in the fifth and ninth symphonies. Yet it was not used very often, long being thought too limited. Even Berlioz, otherwise enthusiastic about innovations, called for it only exceptionally. The same is true of Wagner, who included it in *Parsifal* but not in the entire *Ring.* Only during the past century has it seen regular use, mainly due to the substantial improvement in its construction by Heckel around 1880.

A modern contrabassoon's sound tube, almost six metres long, is folded in four parts. At the end is a metal bell, somewhat outcurved. In contrast to the ordinary bassoon's, it turns downward. The instrument is supported on the floor.

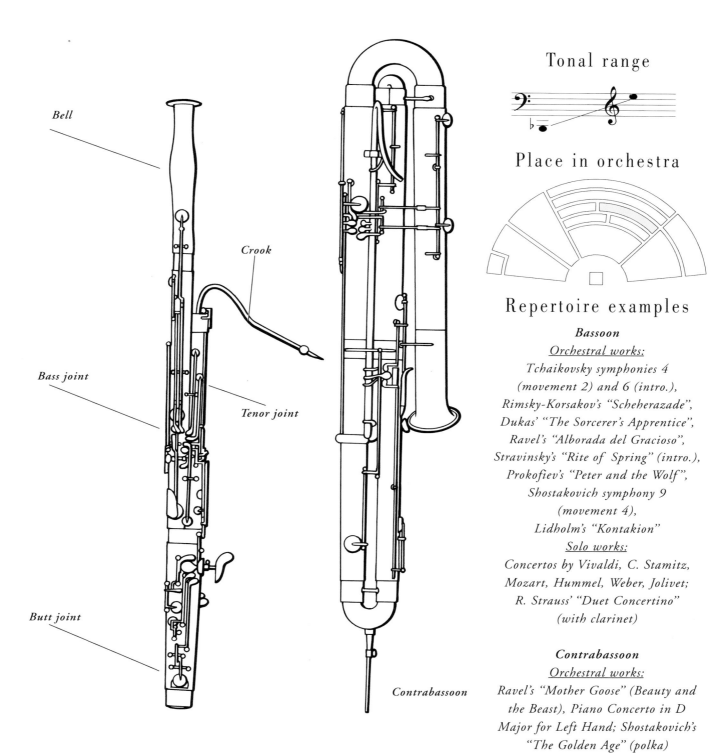

Bell

Crook

Bass joint

Tenor joint

Butt joint

Contrabassoon

Tonal range

Place in orchestra

Repertoire examples

Bassoon
Orchestral works:
Tchaikovsky symphonies 4
(movement 2) and 6 (intro.),
Rimsky-Korsakov's "Scheherazade",
Dukas' "The Sorcerer's Apprentice",
Ravel's "Alborada del Gracioso",
Stravinsky's "Rite of Spring" (intro.),
Prokofiev's "Peter and the Wolf",
Shostakovich symphony 9
(movement 4),
Lidholm's "Kontakion"
Solo works:
Concertos by Vivaldi, C. Stamitz,
Mozart, Hummel, Weber, Jolivet;
R. Strauss' "Duet Concertino"
(with clarinet)

Contrabassoon
Orchestral works:
Ravel's "Mother Goose" (Beauty and
the Beast), Piano Concerto in D
Major for Left Hand; Shostakovich's
"The Golden Age" (polka)

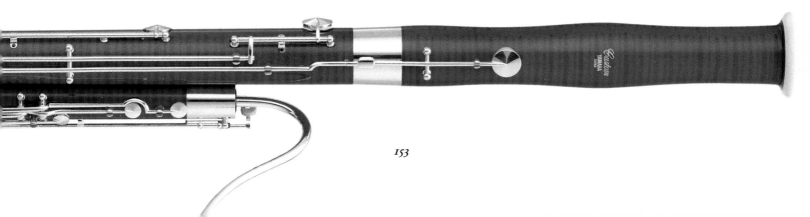

The brass instruments

Before continuing, let us acquaint ourselves with an important factor: the relation between inner length and diameter of a sound tube. A narrow, long tube differs from a comparatively wide and/or short one, in regard to which notes can be produced and to their character. Narrow instruments are rich in overtones, and thus sound light; wider instruments are softer or "rounder".

The tube's shape also influences the resultant timbre, a conical form making it soft and dark, a cylindrical one giving sharp and light tones. Most instruments employ combinations of different tube forms, so there are many intermediate kinds of timbre.

On this basis, brass instruments can be divided into three main groups: those with a long tube that broadens conically (as in the French horn) or has a constant cylindrical width (as in trumpets and trombones), and those with a short tube that often broadens conically (as in cornets and tubas).

That the tuba's sound passage is called "short" may surprise us, since it looks quite long with all its curls. But the principle involved does not concern the absolute length of the passage. Even

in a tuba, it is short in relation to its considerable width!

From prehistoric to medieval times

The brasses in an orchestra have much the same origin – signalling instruments of the Middle Ages. Their evolution began, however, thousands of years earlier with simple devices made of hollow bone, tusk and horn, or pipes of wood, bamboo and bark. The method of producing sound was essentially as in our day. When the player blew into the tube's opening, his lips vibrated and the movement was transmitted to, then amplified by, the air inside the object.

As for the craft of using metal to make instruments, it arose at an early date. Such inventions existed, for example, in ancient Egypt, and Bronze Age Scandinavians blew on imposing, S-shaped *lur* horns. The latter were built in oppositely turned pairs, and had a mouthpiece of the type that was to occur long afterward on trombones.

In Roman times, at ceremonial and especially military events, signals were sounded on long instruments, either

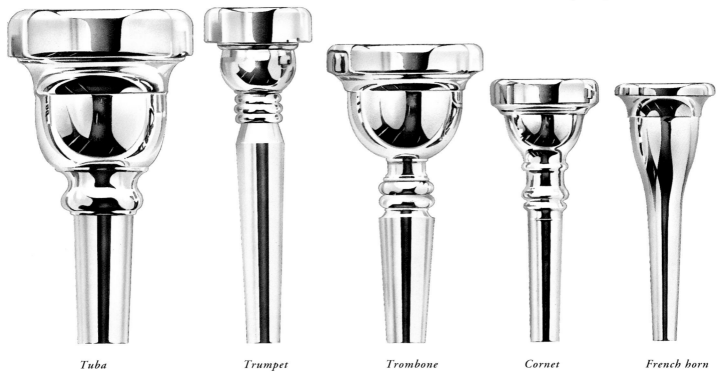

Tuba   *Trumpet*   *Trombone*   *Cornet*   *French horn*

straight or curved like a G. Their names – *tuba, cornu, buccina* – descended to some of our modern instruments: the tuba, horn and trombone (German: *Posaune*). A medieval buccina, the *buse*, meant a straight signal trumpet. It is, in fact, still of interest because Respighi, in his orchestral work *The Pines of Rome*, used buccine prominently.

Postal riders and clarion specialists

Brass instruments in the Middle Ages were of the natural type. Each could produce only notes belonging to the harmonic series for its own fundamental tone. As we have seen, a series begins with the intervals of an octave, fifth, octave, third, and fifth (expressed here in a simplified way). Thus the resultant tones form a "major triad": starting at

The post horn

C, for instance, they are C, E and G. This limitation in the lower register explains why military trumpet signals are simple triad melodies. The same is true of signals on hunting horns, and of the tunes on post horns which *postillons* once used to announce their arrival. These are simply the sole notes that can be obtained from such instruments.

In the upper part of the register, notes are closer together and can be

played in sequences with whole-tone or (a few) semitone steps, known as *diatonic* or *chromatic* melodies respectively. But this requires great skill. During the seventeenth and eighteenth centuries, royal trumpeters and, in particular, specialists in the high clarino register, were socially respected professionals. Those of Germany became members of a special guild, with monopoly rights in many cities. Not until the early nineteenth century was it permissible for anyone to be a trumpeter.

The first modern brass instrument

One means of overcoming the natural instruments' restriction to a few notes in a single key was developed at an early date. Already before the end of the fifteenth century, someone got the idea of equipping a bass trumpet with a loose U-shaped tube section: it could be slid gradually in relation to the rest of the tube. This changed the length of the air column, enabling the player to produce several alternative fundamentals, each with its own harmonic series. The *slide trombone* was thereby created, and after 500 years it still works in basically the same way!

Horn and trumpet hand in hand

In former times, no clear distinction existed between trumpets and horns. A trumpet might be made either partly conical, or in the round shape that we associate with a French horn. Likewise, some horns had tubes which were almost cylindrical, or curved in a noncircular manner. The important thing was that a trumpet's tube should be mainly cylindrical and a horn's mainly conical, while the two used different types of mouthpiece. Yet even in the days of Bach, horns permitted less agility than did trumpets, and therefore were considered less serviceable. They earned a permanent position in orchestras only well into the eighteenth century.

Keyed instruments

We have already described how instruments with tone-holes emerged and were eventually provided with keys. The latter began to be employed on woodwinds in the second half of the seventeenth century, but only later was this technique applied to brass instruments. Keys were added to trumpets during the 1760s, and to horns around 1810. A trumpet usually had five keys, whereas a horn could have up to ten.

Some solo music was composed for these instruments, but they never won acceptance in opera and symphony orchestras. Their chief role was played in

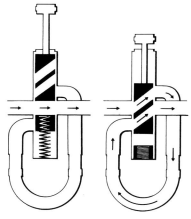

Pushing down a piston valve lengthens the air passage in the instrument.

military orchestras, until taken over by cornets and flugelhorns during the mid-nineteenth century. Unfortunately for them, valves were developed at about the same time and proved to be more practical, especially on trumpets.

Valve systems

In the Baroque and Vienna classicistic periods, each piece of music was normally confined to the instrument's tonic key and its closest relatives. Beyond that, some essential notes were missing from the scale, and others in their new context became too impure to be corrected. The musician then had to pick up an instrument with a different tuning, which was obviously inconvenient (other methods are mentioned below). But composers in the early nineteenth century wanted to change freely between keys, so the manufacturers strove to provide fully chromatic instruments with tempered tuning – that is, with all semitone intervals equally long.

The first valve construction was presented just before 1820, and improved during the following decades. In contrast to the slide trombone with stepless shifting of the fundamental tone, valves lower the fundamental in fixed steps.

The number of valves can vary, yet three valves are most common on the smaller orchestral instruments of our time (French horns, trumpets). When a valve is pushed in, the air stream takes a detour through an extra tube section. One valve lowers the fundamental by a single semitone, another by two semitones, and the third by three semitones.

A player operates the valves in different combinations. When all three are pushed in, the lowering is thus by six semitones, bridging the gap of a fifth between the first and second overtones. On instruments where the fundamental is usable – namely those of wide bore, such as the trombone and tuba – the entire octave between it and the first overtone must be covered. This is usually done with a longer section which gives a further lowering by five semitones, coupled in through a special fourth valve.

Piston and rotary valves

There are two types of valves. A piston valve has several air-holes bored cross-

Piston valves

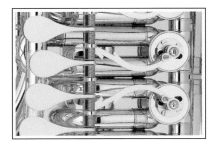

Rotary valves

wise through a piston that slides within a cylinder. A rotary valve contains a similar piston, which is instead rotated back and forth. While they work differently in mechanical terms, their purpose is the same. As a musician pushes on a piston valve, or on the lever of a rotary valve, the direct path of the air stream is closed and the longer passage through an extra tube section is opened. The valves are spring-loaded to return when the finger is lifted.

No completely consistent rule exists as to the type of valve used on each kind of instrument. Internationally speaking, the most common are rotary valves on French horns, and piston valves on trumpets (with exceptions in Vienna for example). Cornets are generally piston instruments, and tubas use rotary valves.

Continual corrections

A problem with valve systems is that the extra tube sections produce pure (tempered) tones only when they are used one by one. Suppose a single extra section extends the air column by 1/12 of its length. But if another extra section is coupled in at the same time, the air column is already longer, so the former section extends it by less than 1/12. The consequent tone becomes ever less pure as more extra sections are introduced. To compensate, the musician primarily corrects the tone with his lips – and on horns, also by changing the position of his hand inside the bell. On larger instruments, one or more additional sections have to be coupled in through extra valves.

Thus, despite the high technical standard of modern instruments, they have to be played with continual corrections. In addition, the use of a mute involves changes in pitch that require correction. For those who are used to a piano or other instrument with all pitches fixed in advance, such demands may seem almost insurmountable. It does, indeed, take many years of training to control a brass instrument perfectly.

The bugle

Brass instruments with wide bore and chiefly conical tubes are customarily designated as bugles. This name is not quite adequate, though, and the group has no unambiguous definition. It includes old natural instruments as well as modern forms with valve systems. Among its treble instruments we find the *cornet* and the *flugelhorn*. Both of these sound a bit softer than the ordinary trumpet. The middle register is played by the *alto, tenor and baritone horns* (the last is also called a euphonium), and the bass by, for example, the *ophicleid* (with keys) and the *tuba*.

Bugles vary greatly in appearance and one can easily forget that they are

Mutes are used to soften and change the sounds of brass instruments.

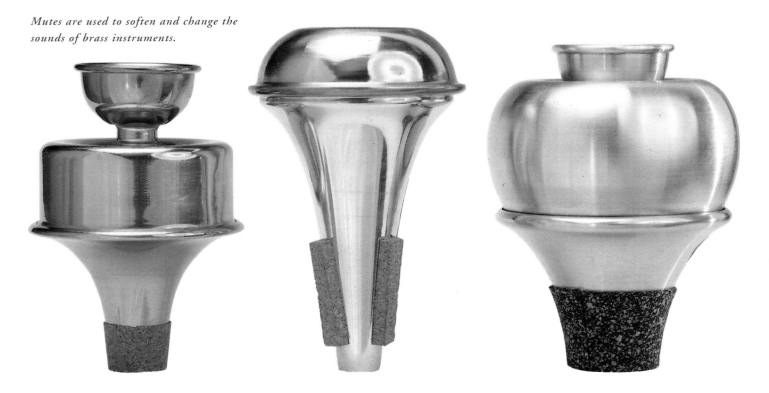

close relatives. There are elongated trumpets, circular tubes like the French horn's, oval tubes and so on. The bell may have different sizes and be directed straight or obliquely upward, forward, or obliquely backward.

Mouthpieces

The timbre of a brass instrument is influenced not only by the relation between its length and width: the mouthpiece is important too. A shallow, bowl-shaped mouthpiece presses the player's lips together more tightly than a deep one. This makes high notes easier to reach and yields a sound that is sharper – richer in overtones. A deeper mouthpiece has the opposite effect of facilitating low notes and softening the sound.

The main types are generally known as a *cup mouthpiece* and a *funnel mouthpiece*. Their forms are somewhat diverse, as are the resultant characteristics of sound and playing technique. As a rule, the cup mouthpiece is used on trumpets, cornets, trombones and tubas, while the funnel mouthpiece occurs on French horns and Wagner tubas.

Mutes

A brass player can dampen and change the instrument's timbre to a high degree by inserting an object into, or holding it in front of, the bell. Such a "mute" may have various designs and materials, usually being of metal or wood. For insertion, it tends to have a conical shape and produces numerous effects. Some mutes make the timbre sharp and penetrating (although dynamically weaker), whereas others create a softer character. With a mute, one can also make the instrument sound hushed as if from a distance. French horns may be moderated either in this way or by inserting a hand into the bell.

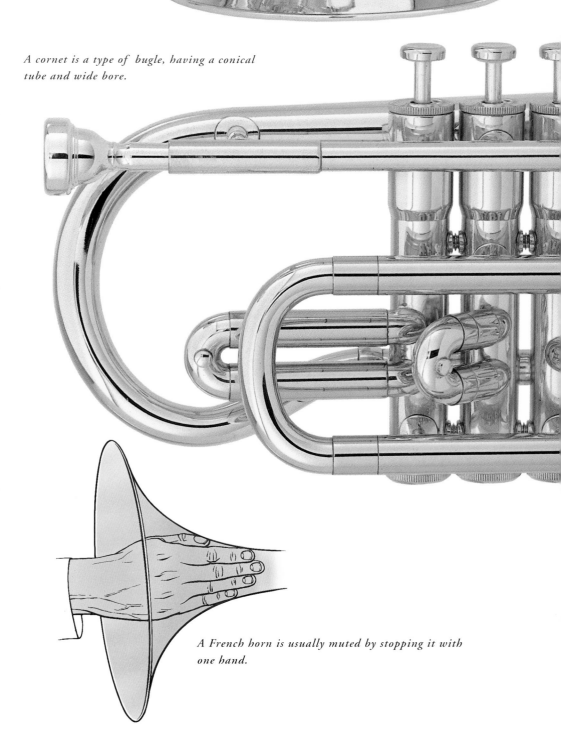

A cornet is a type of bugle, having a conical tube and wide bore.

A French horn is usually muted by stopping it with one hand.

The French horn

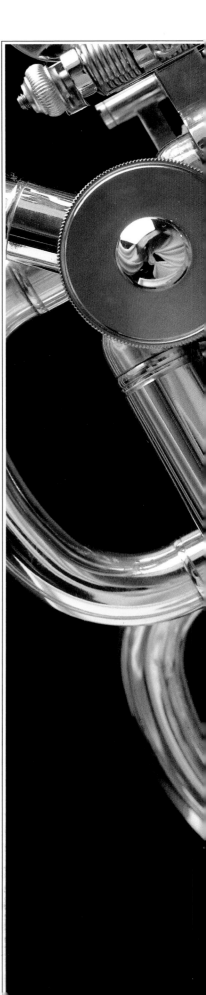

Most primitive cultures have used instruments fashioned from the head-gear of animals, such as the bull-horn and ram-horn. When horns began to be made with other materials, it was but natural to imitate the same old shapes. This is one reason why present-day instruments look as they do. In addition, their development has involved many practical considerations.

For instance, a metal tube several metres long was found clumsy to carry about, and was therefore rolled up in a suitable form. Circular shapes have been common since the fourteenth century, though other forms have also occurred. It is believed that the bell was often pointed obliquely downward or backward because this was most convenient for musicians on horseback; the rider held the reins with his right hand, and the horn with his left.

During the Middle Ages and the Renaissance, many kinds of horn instruments were developed – some for playing natural tones, and others with tone-holes such as the *cornett* (or *Zinke*)

and the *serpent*. But the form which we call the *French horn* was first established in the seventeenth century (its German name *Waldhorn*, from the word for a forest, arose only around 1700). While it was not yet as flexible as the trumpet, composers began instead to exploit its special qualities of timbre. Bach, not least, wrote frequently for both the

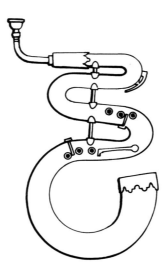

The serpent

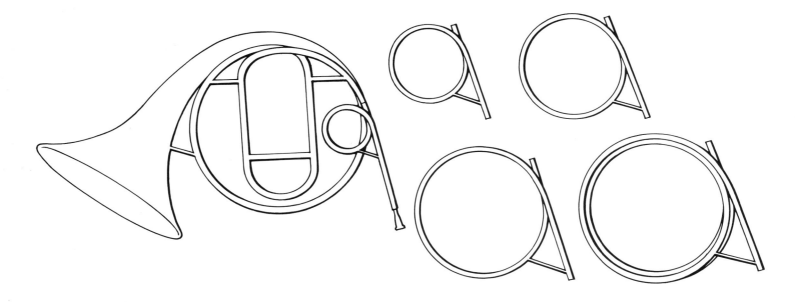

An "Inventionshorn" (crook horn) has tubes of different lengths that can be exchanged to alter its tuning.

Schubert was among the composers who have used the French horn for melody.

"ordinary" horn and the older hunting type, *corno da caccia*.

Thanks to the horn's long, thin tube (3.75-4.5 metres), skilful musicians could produce overtones all the way up to the fifteenth, and thus play extensive melodies in the high register. However, they were still limited to a few particular tonal keys. The Baroque horn was usually tuned in D, but instruments existed in each of the octave's twelve tones.

More keys

One method of changing the key was, of course, to switch between two horns – or pairs of horns – with different tuning. Mozart did so in his symphonies Nos. 25 and 32, calling for four horns which, in large part, were to be played only two at a time. This practice continued throughout the nineteenth century, as an alternative to the more modern technique allowed by the valve system. A clear example is the beginning of Brahms' second symphony.

There were also other ways of increasing the horn's flexibility. Already during Baroque times, extra circular *crooks* of different lengths had begun to be inserted just after the mouthpiece. Instead of switching instruments, one could change such crooks and even couple them in series. But this was a cumbersome method which interrupted the playing.

In the mid-eighteenth century, the technique was rationalized with the *Inventionshorn*. It had U-shaped extra crooks that could be switched while playing in order to provide alternative tunings. Some musicians became virtuosos at doing so in a second or two. Combined with *stopping* (changing the right hand's position inside the bell), this made players better equipped during the

On a double horn, two tunings can be alternated by pressing an extra valve with the thumb.

Repertoire examples

French horn

Orchestral works:
Bach's "Mass in B Minor" and
"Brandenburg Concerto" No.1,
Beethoven symphonies 3 and 9 (3rd
movements), Schubert symphony 9
(intro.), Mendelssohn's music for
"A Midsummer Night's Dream"
(Nocturne), Tchaikovsky symphonies 2
(intro.) and 5 (movement 2),
Bruckner symphony 4 (movements 1
and 3), R. Strauss' "Till Eulenspiegel",
Ravel's "Pavane for a Dead Princess"
and Piano Concerto in G Major,
Prokofiev's "Peter and the Wolf"

Solo works:
Concertos by Telemann,
Haydn, Mozart,
R. Strauss, Hindemith;
Schumann's "Concerto
for Four Horns",
Britten's "Serenade" (with tenor)

Wagner tuba

Orchestral works:
Bruckner symphonies 7
(movement 2)
and 9 (movement 3),
Stravinsky's "Rite
of Spring" (part 1)

Tonal range

Place in orchestra

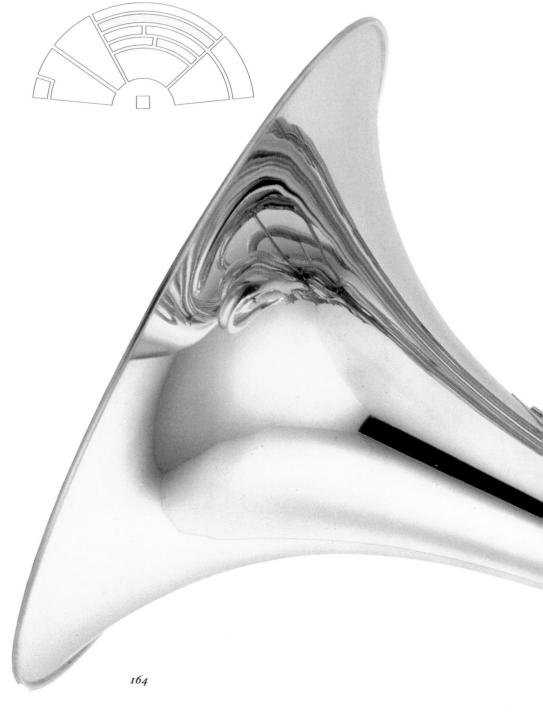

followed by all the "forest Romantics": Schumann, Wagner, Brahms, Bruckner and many others. In that light, amazingly few solo concertos were composed, at any rate by the leading composers.

We have previously mentioned one of the early nineteenth century's modernizations of this instrument – the *key horn*. It became very popular for about fifty years, but primarily in brass bands. All the greater impact was made on symphony orchestras by the highly flexible *valve horn*. Boasting "automatic crook change", the latter proved to be one prerequisite for that century's new ideal of musical aesthetics.

Putting the old natural horns back on the shelf was, however, not an obvious consequence. Certainly the valve system's advantages were soon exploited by far-sighted composers such as Berlioz and Wagner, but others were more attracted to the softer tone of natural instruments. Throughout the nineteenth century, both types were therefore used in parallel. While Schumann wrote for the valve horn at mid-century, his spiritual heir Brahms regarded the natural horn as essential almost until 1900. Yet by that time, composers like Debussy, Mahler and Strauss had rendered the valve instruments quite indispensable.

The French horn has been employed in numerous ways from the nineteenth century onward, often explicitly melodic (as in the beginning of Schubert's symphony No.9 and the slow movement in Tchaikovsky's No.5), or sometimes reminiscent of the hunting-horn background (for example in the scherzo of Bruckner's No.4). Strauss displayed its possibilities of timbre and playing technique to the brink of excess – although never beyond that.

Horns blend well with most other instruments. They frequently take part in festive or ceremonial music along

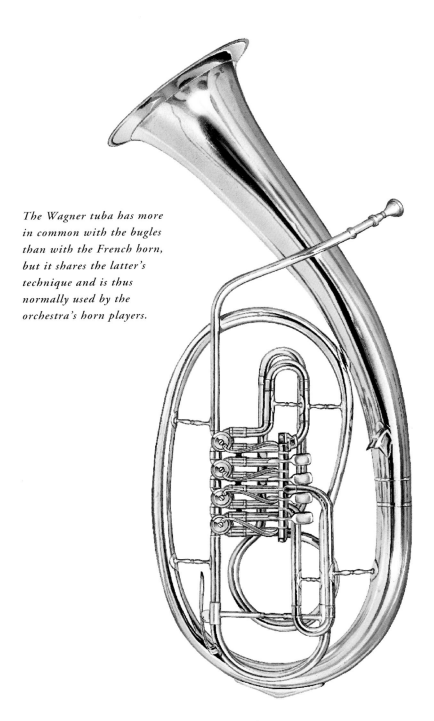

The Wagner tuba has more in common with the bugles than with the French horn, but it shares the latter's technique and is thus normally used by the orchestra's horn players.

late eighteenth century than before. In orchestral music, it was then that composers began to give the horns more independent tasks than filling out the sound and harmony. From Beethoven's third symphony onward, they were used as "full-fledged" members of the orchestra.

The favourite Romantic instrument

If any instrument can be considered typical of the Romantic world of sound, it must be the French horn. Weber employed it for natural settings in his operas, with the trumpet, trombone and tuba. On the other hand, their individual timbre is equally often used by composers to create contrast with those very instruments. In many orchestras, the horn group is consequently placed well apart from the latter. It commonly plays together with the woodwind instruments, able to serve as a bridge between these and other brass instruments.

High and low horns

With an adept player behind it, a horn has a large range of more than four octaves (up to the 17th harmonic). Many horn-players can perform in both the high and low registers, but there is a good deal of specialization in orchestras. This is feasible because composers normally give the high notes to the first and third horns, and the low ones to the second and fourth. Problems may thus arise when a composer neglects that distribution.

The double horn

French horns are still used in several tunings with rather different timbres and characteristics of playing. Most familiar in orchestras are a horn in F and a higher one in B-flat. The only extensive modernization during the past 150 years is the *double horn*, launched at the beginning of our century. It combines both of those tunings and can change between them with a fourth valve, controlled by the thumb. In Vienna classicism and some contemporary music, we occasionally find a small *descant horn* tuned in F, an octave higher than the ordinary one. There are also *triple horns* with this option built into them. Due to the extensive tubing, however, they are fairly heavy and are not appreciated by all horn-players.

The Wagner tuba

While working on his opera tetralogy,

Der Ring des Nibelungen, Wagner needed a new sound in order to depict the heavenly palace of Valhalla. It had to be somewhat distinct from the sound of ordinary brass instruments. Thus, by his commission, the device that later bore his name was built in the late 1860s. It was a further development of a military bugle, some decades older.

The Wagner tuba has four valves and is played with the same mouthpiece as the French horn. As its technique is also identical, it is always handled by the orchestra's horn-players. Although it lacks a comprehensive repertoire, it was used after Wagner in the three last symphonies of Bruckner, as well as by Strauss and Stravinsky among others. Wagner tubas are built with the same tunings as the horn, namely F and B-flat, here called the bass and tenor ranges. Normally two instruments with each range are combined into a tuba quartet. In addition, the tunings are joined to make a *double tuba*.

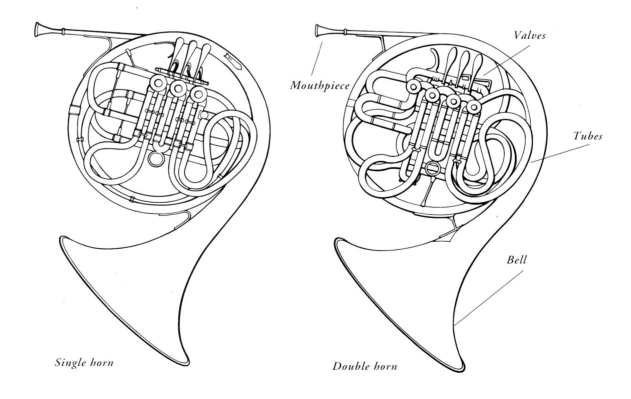

Single horn

Double horn

Mouthpiece

Valves

Tubes

Bell

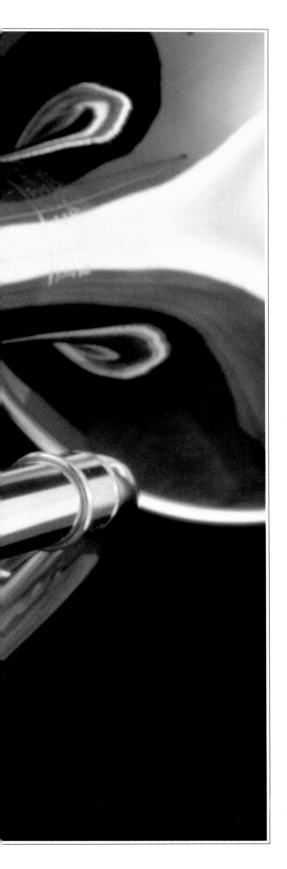

The trumpet

The medieval signal instrument known as a buse, already mentioned, was a long tube that could measure more than two metres (seven feet). It was sometimes bent in a zigzag shape, but the usual form was the extended, rounded one which is familiar today. Most trumpets have kept this basic appearance for more than five hundred years.

Medieval trumpeters, with their natural instruments, played on military occasions and, for example, at knightly tournaments that called for exciting fanfares. From the fifteenth century onward, trumpets were also played in churches. But only around 1600 did they enter the service of concert music and the new art of opera. Their first centre was Italy, especially in Venice where Giovanni Gabrieli – and Claudio Monteverdi, the first great opera composer – reigned supreme.

We have noticed the rise of clarino specialists in the seventeenth and eighteenth centuries, able to control the high register of brass instruments. The clarino range consisted mainly of the eighth to the sixteenth harmonic, including about one octave. Most of the Baroque period's virtuoso trumpet music is within this range. To play it, the musicians used a small shallow mouthpiece. When they wanted to play the triads of the lower register, a mouthpiece with a deeper cup-shape was attached. Those who played only low notes were called *principal blowers*. But a mastery of both the high and low registers was quite unusual.

Development accelerates

In the early eighteenth century, solo concertos became an ever more appreciated musical genre, making the trumpet very popular. This increased the need for playing in several keys. Trumpet manufacturers started a trend of modernization that would take a century to complete. As with the French horn, they began by inserting extra crooks, circular tubes of different lengths, be-

Repertoire examples

Trumpet
Orchestral works:
Handel's "Messiah"
(The trumpet shall sound),
Beethoven's "Leonora Overtures"
2 and 3, Wagner's "Parsifal"
(prelude), Mahler symphony 5
(movement 1),
Mussorgsky/Ravel's "Pictures
from an Exhibition" (intro.),
Lidholm's "Kontakion"

Solo works:
Bach's "Cantata No. 51"
and "Brandenburg Concerto"
No. 2; concertos by Telemann,
Haydn, Hummel, Jolivet,
Arutiunjan; Shostakovich's
Piano Concerto No.1

Cornet
Orchestral works:
Berlioz' "Symphonie
Fantastique" (movement 2,
alternative version),
Tchaikovsky's "Swan Lake",
Prokofiev's "Romeo and Juliet"

Tonal range

Place in orchestra

tween the mouthpiece and the rest of the instrument. Thus the tonic key could be lowered by one or more steps.

However, this required a brief interruption in the playing. It was more practical, as in the slide trombone, to use a stepless sliding U-shaped tube, allowing the tonic key to be changed while playing. Bach and other Baroque composers prescribed such instruments now and then. The *slide trumpet*, in various forms, was a good design and enjoyed long use. It appeared, for example, in British orchestras through almost the whole nineteenth century.

Haydn writes for the keyed trumpet

Another way of expanding the possibilities for playing, and therefore the diversity of trumpet music, emerged around 1770 with the keyed trumpet. Its keys, usually five, provided greater variety especially in the low register, which was previously limited to the triad notes. Some composers of solo music exploited this advantage. Well-known examples are the trumpet concertos of Haydn and Hummel, both written in about 1800 for a keyed instrument that was played by Anton Weidinger in Vienna, a famous virtuoso of the time.

The modern trumpet, with its easily manipulated valves, has set a strong mark on twentieth-century orchestra music.

Yet many people considered the keyed trumpet's sound too feeble, in comparison with older instruments. It did occasionally find use in operas, such as some of Rossini's, but it was not adopted widely in symphony orchestras.

A setback for the orchestral trumpet

The middle decades of the eighteenth century were the heyday of solo trumpet music. Solo concertos were composed then as never before or since. On the other hand, trumpets were not used very independently or imaginatively in orchestras. Haydn, Mozart and even Schubert employed them primarily to reinforce the sound. Beethoven made effective use of one for triad fanfares in a couple of his *Leonora* overtures, but its role is purely soloistic. Not even this in-novator tended to give particularly characteristic tasks to the orchestral trumpet – which would have been perfectly feasible with the various designs that existed.

The valve revolution

Not until the introduction of the valve system did trumpets begin to assert themselves in orchestras. The valve me-

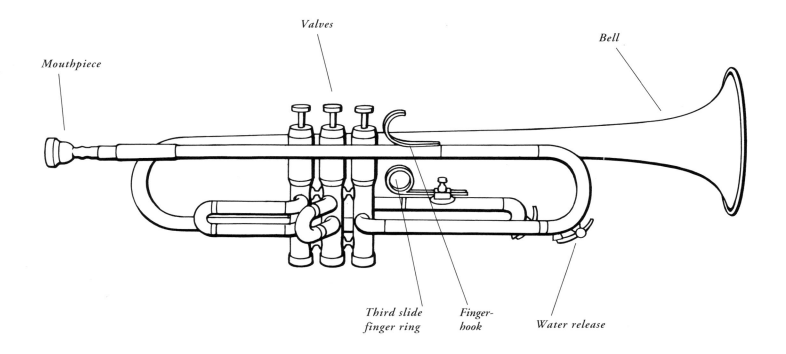

Mouthpiece

Valves

Bell

*Third slide
finger ring*

*Finger-
hook*

Water release

chanism became fully developed during the 1830s, so that composers could use all notes of the octave and shift freely between keys. This novelty was quickly exploited by the most advanced composers, and many orchestras adopted valve trumpets from the early 1840s onward.

Nonetheless, as in the case of valve-equipped French horns, it was quite long before these trumpets won general acceptance. Many composers went on shaping their trumpet parts according to old tradition. It was Wagner who fully recognized the new possibilities. Already in *Tannhäuser* and *Lohengrin*, he gave the trumpets a leading place. Still more sophisticated was his work in the *Ring* and *Parsifal*, where the trumpets make

highly rewarding contributions, both orchestral and soloistic.

Wagner's use of the valve trumpet was to inspire many others, and it became a necessity as music approached the end of the nineteenth century. In Strauss' symphonic poems of this period – such as *A Hero's Life* and *Symphonia Domestica* – as well as in Mahler's symphonies and with Debussy and Ravel, the trumpets make virtuoso contributions. One of the best-known trumpet parts from the early 1900s is found in Stravinsky's *Petrouchka*, and more recent music relies constantly on the trumpet. If the French horn was the most typical sound in the orchestras of the 1800s, the trumpet has become one in our century.

Persistent tunings

There were once trumpets with various tonic keys, D and E-flat being among the commonest. Even since the invention of the valve mechanism, several alternative tunings have continued in use, no doubt partly due to habit. Many contemporary orchestras prefer C and B-flat. But a "double trumpet", analogous to the double horn, has never caught on. Musicians simply choose instruments – or transpose – according to the music that is being played.

Trumpets have a wide range of uses in the orchestra. Their light, penetrating sound is excellent for playing melodies, in soft as well as loud nuances. Good exam-

The cornet

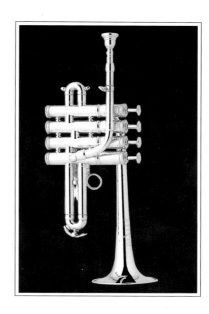

The piccolo trumpet

ples occur in the prelude to Wagner's *Parsifal*, and at the beginning of Mussorgsky's *Pictures from an Exhibition* orchestrated by Ravel. The trumpet's cutting *forte* sound has often been employed for blaring festive music, such as the "Entry of the Guests" in Wagner's *Tannhäuser*.

Trumpets are frequently combined with trombones and the tuba. Their timbre does not mix as naturally with that of French horns, demanding more caution of composers.

The piccolo trumpet

Playing an ordinary trumpet in the high register is difficult and risky: the intended notes may not be reached at all. For very high parts, the musician instead chooses a piccolo trumpet. Like its big brother, it is usually tuned in B-flat or A, although an octave higher. Small trumpets were manufactured already a hundred years ago in order to manage the clarino passages in Baroque music. However, these instruments – known as *Bach trumpets* – are not built in the same way as genuine Baroque trumpets, but are smaller and tuned up to an octave higher, yielding a somewhat different timbre. Nowadays, such music is normally played on a piccolo trumpet in B-flat or A.

During our century, composers like Stravinsky and Ravel have used small D trumpets for the sake of their special sound. In other music, such as Bartók's *Concerto for Orchestra*, piccolo trumpets are often used for the high sections.

The bass trumpet

An instrument that is heard much less often, the bass trumpet, was employed mainly by Wagner in his *Ring*. It also appears in isolated works by, for exam-

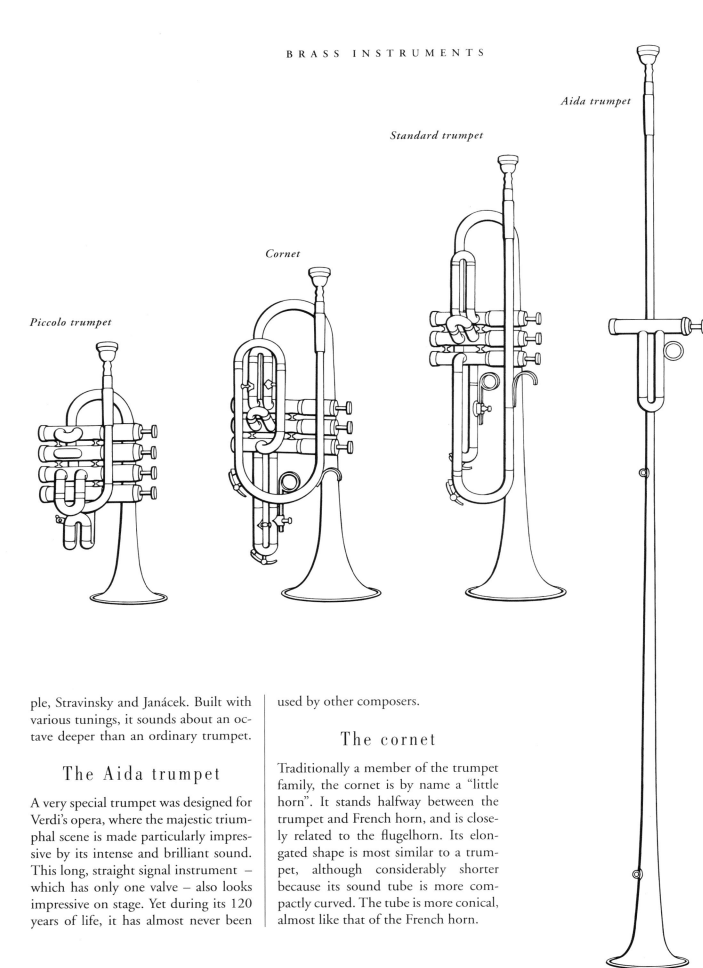

Aida trumpet

Standard trumpet

Cornet

Piccolo trumpet

ple, Stravinsky and Janácek. Built with various tunings, it sounds about an octave deeper than an ordinary trumpet.

The Aida trumpet

A very special trumpet was designed for Verdi's opera, where the majestic triumphal scene is made particularly impressive by its intense and brilliant sound. This long, straight signal instrument – which has only one valve – also looks impressive on stage. Yet during its 120 years of life, it has almost never been

used by other composers.

The cornet

Traditionally a member of the trumpet family, the cornet is by name a "little horn". It stands halfway between the trumpet and French horn, and is closely related to the flugelhorn. Its elongated shape is most similar to a trumpet, although considerably shorter because its sound tube is more compactly curved. The tube is more conical, almost like that of the French horn.

Cornets were invented in France during the early nineteenth century. At first they had interchangeable crooks for different tunings, but they acquired the same kind of piston valves as trumpets when – and even somewhat before – the latter were modernized.

Cornets soon found a place in brass bands, and have kept it down to the present. Still, France has remained the instrument's centre. Its sound, softer than a trumpet's, is a typical timbre in much French music. Rossini included both the cornet and the above-mentioned keyed trumpet in his last opera, *William Tell.* Also a pioneer of the cornet was Berlioz, who prescribed it in several works and added it later to his *Symphonie Fantastique* (a version which, unfortunately, is seldom played, despite the fascinating effect of the cornet sound in the ball scene). A well-known later work with cornets is the symphony by Franck.

Cornets come in a variety of sizes and tunings. The largest sometimes have a bell turned upward. Tunings in B-flat and C are most common in contemporary symphony orchestras. Since the cornet is based on the same playing technique as trumpets, and has a similar mouthpiece, it is wielded by the orchestra's trumpeters.

The trombone

As we have seen, the first brass instrument to receive its final basic form was the slide trombone. Already five hundred years ago, a natural trumpet in the bass range was rebuilt by inserting the ends of an extra U-shaped slide into its sound tube. When this slide was pushed in or out, the air column's length was changed, so that overtones of several fundamental tones could be played. The name "trombone" means simply a big trumpet.

Thus, although trombones and trumpets do not look much alike, they are closely related. Both are built around a sound tube of fairly constant width. They are played with the same type of mouthpiece, normally called a *cup mouthpiece*, which is considerably larger on the trombone. The slight difference between the two instruments is also shown by the fact that *slide trumpets* have been used during long periods, and that *valve trombones* are still common in brass bands.

Repertoire examples

Trombone

<u>Orchestral works:</u>
G. Gabrieli's "Canzoni e Sonate", Mozart's "Requiem" (Tuba Mirum), Berlioz' "Requiem" and "Symphonie Funèbre et Triomphale" (part 2), Wagner's overture for "Tannhäuser", Brahms symphony 4 (movement 4), Mahler symphony 3 (movement 1), Shostakovich symphonies 8 (movement 3) and 15 (last movement)

<u>Solo works:</u>
Concertos by Wagenseil, L. Mozart, Rimsky-Korsakov (with wind orchestra), L. Grøndahl, Holmboe; concertinos by F. David, Milhaud

Tonal range

Place in orchestra

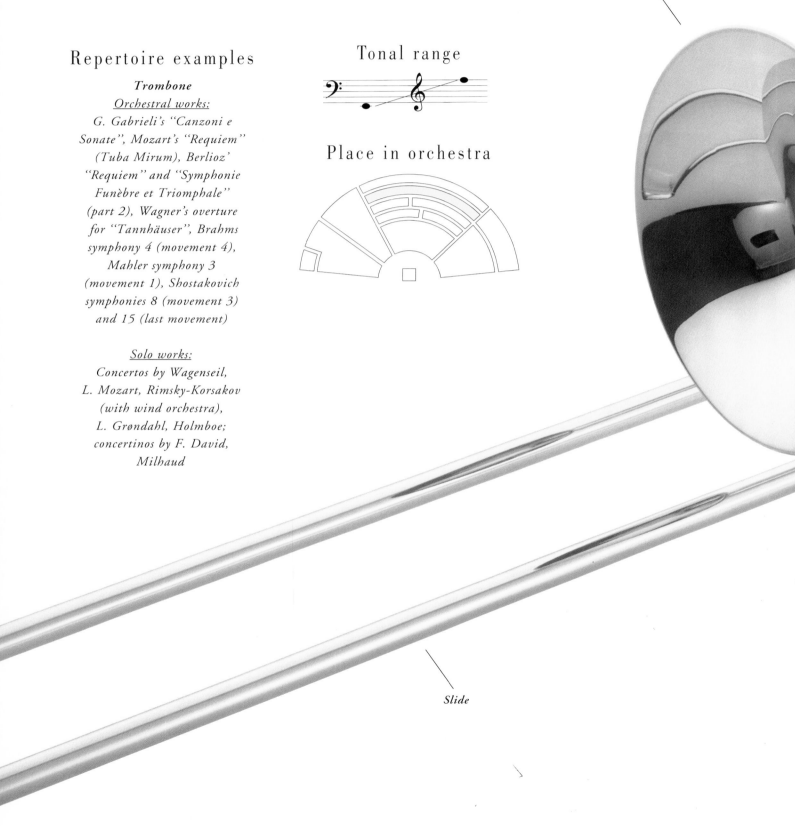

Bell

Slide

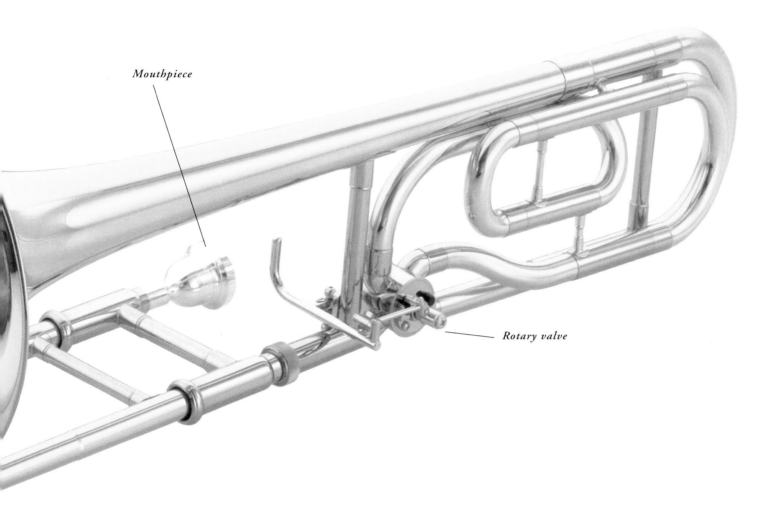

Mouthpiece

Rotary valve

For church and theatre...

Trombones were used in church music from the outset. Their actual repertoire was created towards the end of the sixteenth century in Venice by Giovanni Gabrieli, the master of music for multiple choruses. Baroque trombones were often used as entire quartet families, ranging from soprano to bass. During the next century, the instrument became familiar at theatres; even in the late 1700s, its main employer was the opera. Formal or fateful atmospheres were readily evoked by the sound of trombones. Mozart exploited this quality in *The Magic Flute,* *Don Giovanni* and the *Requiem.* For concert purposes, the trombone was adopted after 1800 with Beethoven's fifth, sixth and ninth symphonies. Once the ice had been broken, trombones were embraced as an indispensable ingredient of the Romantic orchestra.

...and for concerts

Of the trombone's two main forms, with a slide or with valves, only the slide trombone is used in most symphony orchestras. With the U- shaped slide, a player can choose between seven tonic keys at intervals of a semitone. All of the octave's twelve tones are thereby covered.

In earlier days, the trombone existed in a variety of sizes, but the instruments most in use today are *tenor trombones* in B-flat and *tenor-bass trombones* in B-flat/F. With the latter, the tunings are switched by means of a "fourth valve"; some instruments can also be tuned down to D. Finally, there is an even lower *contrabass trombone*, which was once played rarely (as in Wagner's *Ring*) but is sometimes encountered in the music of our time.

One of the orchestra's trombonists normally specializes in the bass range, and shares many tasks with the tuba, while others play in the tenor range. During recent years, trombone sections

Due to its construction, the slide trombone's ability to create a true glissando makes it unique in the orchestra.

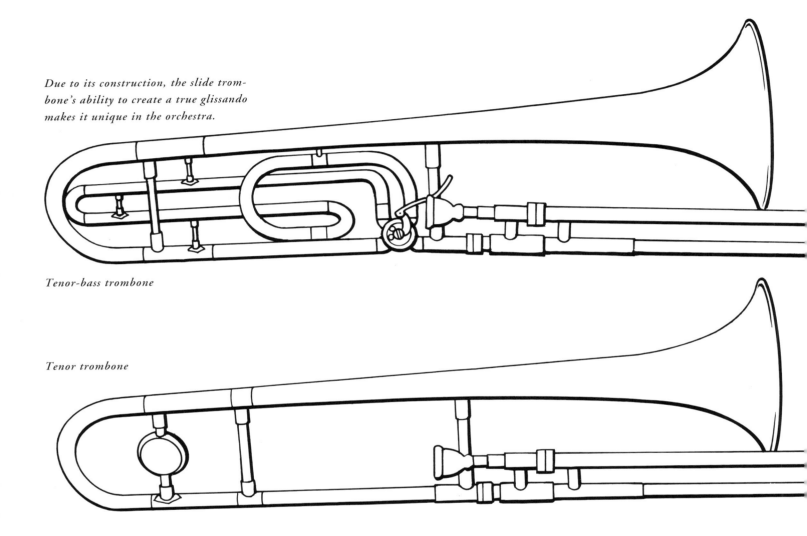

Tenor-bass trombone

Tenor trombone

in many orchestras have become more stylistically minded. The first trombonist once again uses the little *alto trombone* in music by Beethoven, Schumann, Brahms and others.

Specialties of the trombone

The slide trombone has a number of characteristics that are occasionally exploited by composers. It is the orchestra's only brass instrument that can be used for genuine *glissando*, the continuous transition between different pitches. This is most popular in jazz, but contributes regularly to symphonic music, notably from our own century. The same quality is valuable when compensating for the impurity of some overtones.

The fundamentals of the seven slide positions are called *pedal notes*. They sound rather rough and unlovely in comparison with the trombone's normal, sonorous overtone range. Hence they have seldom been used in tradi-tional music, the best-known instance being a couple of movements in Berlioz' *Requiem*. Still 150 years after its composition, these protracted "creaky" pedal notes make a peculiar, though indeed evocative, impression. Today, when composers gladly exploit all possible acoustic media, the pedal notes are used more often.

Blowing down Jericho

Many of us tend to associate the trom-

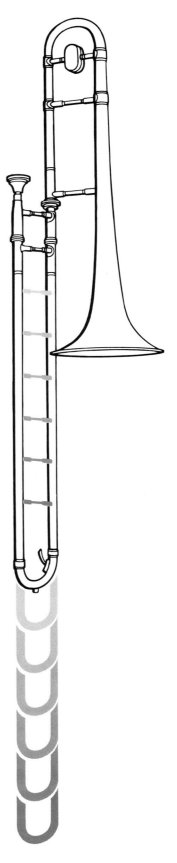

A trombone has seven slide positions. Their fundamental tones, called pedal notes, have a distinctive rough sound.

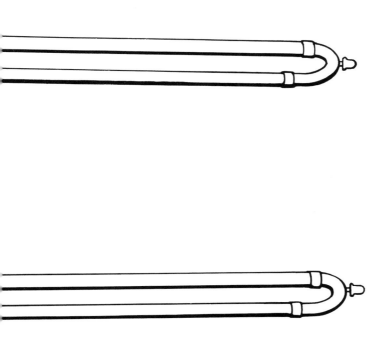

bone's noble sound with majestic music and powerful dynamics, as in Wagner's overture to *Tannhäuser*. The Bible tells how such "trumpets" even caused the walls of Jericho to collapse. However, it is not easy to say what instruments were wielded at that time (more than three thousand years ago); the word in question meant only horns in general. Later trombones may be versatile, but they are certainly not used to demolish buildings!

Power is just one of the trombone's features. We have mentioned how it was used to conjure a lofty atmosphere in the operas of the late eighteenth century, where it is often played in soft nuances. In groups, trombones may sound mysterious and sinister. Yet they can also play quick, blaring passages as in Rossini's *William Tell* overture, and in the third movement of Shostakovich's eighth symphony.

The tuba

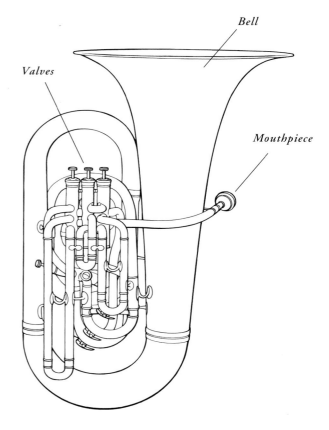

Valves

Bell

Mouthpiece

The instrumental designation *tuba* was introduced by the Romans, as one of the names for signal horns used in the field. Like other such terms, it has changed frequently in meaning through the ages. Even in our day, the word has a wide significance and is not clearly distinguished from instruments such as the French horn and the baritone/euphonium. All these are usually included among the bugles, having a conical sound tube and a wide bore. It is primarily the bass instruments that are called tubas.

Here we shall focus upon the symphony orchestra's most common form of tuba, the *bass tuba*. Younger than many other instruments, it was designed in 1835 by the instrument-makers Moritz and Wieprecht in Berlin. During the preceding decades, orchestras had been using a key-horn in the bass range, known as the *ophicleid*. One famous work that prescribes this device is the overture to *A Midsummer Night's Dream* by Mendelssohn (although its part is now usually played on a tuba). Another ancestor was the *serpent*, used since the sixteenth century, with a conspicuous snake-form which made its

tone-holes easier to reach.

The ophicleid and other bass instruments of the early nineteenth century were not considered very successful, so the tuba's path to triumph was paved beforehand. It first became a member of brass bands, but was soon brought into symphony and opera orchestras.

From crooks to comedians

Wagner must have been delighted to obtain this new tool for melodic playing, as well as for characterizing monsters and villains. He put it to the former use already in 1840, with the introduction to *A Faust Overture*. A good example of the latter purpose is the dragon's music in *Siegfried*. Berlioz was also an early exploiter of tubas.

In addition to being the bass funda-

ment in the brass section, and thus often for the entire orchestra, the bass tuba can perform in many ways. Like the bassoon, it sometimes plays a humorous role, and this is how most children come to know it. In some music, the tuba is mostly given long bottom notes, and may seem to be sluggish. But that is not at all the case: a skilful tubaist can play amazingly fast passages and handle his instrument almost as flexibly as a French horn. It is surprising that so few composers originally took more than occasional advantage of the tuba's possibilities, as has been done during the past few decades all over the world.

The bass tuba is played with a large cup mouthpiece. It may have up to six valves. Orchestral tubas are normally tuned in C and B-flat. Still deeper, but used extremely seldom, is the *contrabass tuba*.

Tonal range

Place in orchestra

Repertoire examples

Tuba
<u>Orchestral works:</u>
Berlioz' "Symphonie
Fantastique", Wagner's
"Faust Overture",
R. Strauss' "Don Quixote",
Mussorgsky/Ravel's "Pictures
from an Exhibition",
Prokofiev symphony 5,
Schnittke symphony 3
<u>Solo works:</u>
Concertos by Vaughan Williams

The percussion section provides greater sound variation than any other part of the orchestra. It is also extremely diverse in contents – although we may tend to think primarily of, for instance, drums and cymbals. In fact almost any object may be used for similar purposes.

Sometimes the equipment contributes to a musical process; in other cases it creates isolated effects. We hear the sound of an anvil in Verdi's *Il Trovatore*, the beats of a hammer in Mahler's sixth symphony, a rattling chain in Schoenberg's *Gurre-Lieder*, a wind machine in Richard Strauss' *Don Quixote*, a typewriter in Satie's *Parade*, and a popping cork in Lumbye's *Champagne Galop*, not to mention the gunshots in Johann Strauss' *Auf der Jagd* and the cannons in Tchaikovsky's *1812 Overture*. All of this is accommodated within the elastic scope of percussion.

For practical reasons, every type of instrument in question is commonly termed percussive. In many cases, however, the playing is done by other means than striking – such as shaking,

Drums

comprises the *membranophones*, also referred to as drum instruments, which are equipped with a stretched membrane that is made to vibrate – for instance a bass drum. Both kinds include devices with indefinite pitch (respective examples are castanets and snare drums) as well as those with definite pitch (for instance, tubular bells and kettledrums respectively). Some idiophones with definite pitch are arranged in chromatic series of tubes or plates for playing melodies.

An ancient heritage

The basic forms of some present-day percussion instruments have been familiar to "primitive" peoples, and were used in ancient civilizations. This is especially true of drums and cymbals, which served for military signalling, religious rites, and to accompany singing or dancing. Composers seldom mentioned any instruments specifically before the seventeenth century, but there are many medieval portraits of musicians playing a drum, cymbal, bell or tambourine. They presumably occurred in Renaissance ensembles, although we can only guess how and when they were used.

During the Baroque period, percussion instruments were certainly more common in folk and dance music than in the new art music. One of the latter's earliest such instruments was the kettledrum (*timpano*), borrowed through Hungary from the Arabs in the late Middle Ages. At first, kettledrums were mostly combined with trumpets in courtly and military music, notably by the cavalry. As the seventeenth century progressed, Louis XIV's master of music, Lully, began to use them in operas, and soon they became permanent components of many orchestras.

Turkish music

Baroque opera also employed cymbals and tambourines for occasional exotic sounds. In the 1700s, some instruments were introduced from Turkey's military *Janissary music*, as a fixed combination of bass drum, cymbals and triangle. Such "Turkish music" won enormous popularity and was composed by Gluck, Haydn (the "Military" symphony), Mozart (*The Abduction from the Seraglio*) and Beethoven (*The Ruins of Athens*, ninth symphony) among others. Consequently, it was this period which gave rise to the orchestra's percussion section.

The Turkish instruments were long played as a constant group for march-like music. Among the first to exploit them individually was Berlioz. Devices such as the tam-tam, bells and tambourine also contributed to his personally coloured orchestration. Together with his new way of treating the wind and string instruments, they make even an early work like the *Symphonie Fantastique* (1830) much more colourful than Beethoven's and Schubert's last symphonies, then only a few years old.

Opera composers, too, stimulated

knocking, scratching or rubbing.

Pitch or no pitch

Two main kinds of instruments are recognized here. One consists of the *idiophones*, whose very material is made to vibrate and thus produce the sound. An example is the triangle. The other kind

Repertoire examples

Kettledrum

Orchestral works:
Beethoven symphony 9 (movement 2),
R. Strauss' "Thus Spoke
Zarathustra" (beginning), Elgar's
"Enigma Variations", Stravinsky's
"Rite of Spring", Nielsen symphony
4, Shostakovich symphonies 1
(movement 4) and 11, Bartók's
"Concerto" for orchestra, Hindemith's
"Symphonic Metamorphoses"
Solo works:
Concertos by W. Kraft,
W. Thärichen

Place in orchestra

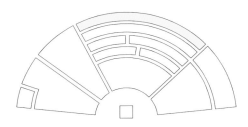

the percussion's growth. A well-known example is Rossini's overture to *The Thieving Magpie*, with its initial rolls on the snare drum.

Wealth in our time

Percussion instruments attracted rather little interest throughout the nineteenth century. As a rule, composers were content with the kettledrums, bass drum and snare drum, cymbals and triangle. Only at the beginning of our century did a great enrichment of the section occur – not least by castanets, wood block, whip, and the xylophone.

A fine illustration is Mahler's sixth symphony (1904) with two pairs of kettledrums, bass drum, snare drum, cymbals, triangle, tam-tam, chimes, cow-bells, deep tubular bells, xylophone, a bundle of rods, and the famous "hammers" (actually clubs). Stravinsky was fascinated by percussion, as in *The Rite of Spring* and *The Wedding*. It also plays prominent parts in several of

Bartók's works.

Between the World Wars, a number of composers started to exploit the percussion group for its own sake, independently of the orchestra. Varèse in France, and John Cage in America, were among the pioneers, followed by Messiaen, Stockhausen, Boulez and others. Permanent percussion groups were formed, and the training of players improved greatly. Due to the past forty years of strong interest in these instruments, they are now handled in many orchestras with a skill that was inconceivable just a couple of generations ago.

The range of instruments has continued to expand, with traditional devices from Africa, Latin America and primarily the Far East (gongs, cymbals, drums and xylophones), as well as with new constructions of all sorts. Often, the latter are not instruments in the usual sense, but other objects that can be used to create sound. In principle, almost anything is usable: clinking bits of glass or stone, tin cans and casks, bicycle and auto components, and much else.

Modern kettledrums

The means of impact

Alongside this avalanche of acoustic tools, a host of equipment with which to strike them has developed. Drumsticks and mallets occur in many versions of size, balance and hardness. The head may be of wood or metal, wrapped in felt, wool, cork, leather, rubber or plastic. Musicians frequently come to a concert armed with several alternatives for varying the character of the touch. A familiar sight is the kettledrummer's collection of three or four pairs of sticks, laid on a high table. It is common to use the same striking device on more than one instrument – drumsticks on cymbals or gongs, vibraphone mallets on drums, and so on – yielding virtually unlimited possibilities of variation.

The experimental urge that typified much music during the postwar period, however, seems to have declined. Many present-day composers display more interest in reviving traditions from earlier centuries.

Multiple duties

From its wide choice of instruments and techniques, we can see that percussion requires a modern player to be very flexible indeed. In principle, he or she must be able to handle any kind of instrument. But there is always some concentration on a particular type – such as the snare drum, the cymbals, or the xylophone together with vibraphone and chimes. A timpanist is the most specialized of all, rarely playing other devices; often the kettledrum is not even counted as part of the percussion section.

The drum instruments

In general, a drum instrument has a frame, usually of wood or metal. Over this is stretched a membrane of animal skin or plastic, which vibrates if struck or influenced in some other way. Its sound is fairly weak, though, and must be amplified by the resonance of, for instance, a tube or kettle.

Kettledrums

The first drum instrument adopted in Western orchestras, the kettledrum has also been the most frequently used. It consists of a metal (often copper-alloy) kettle, with a membrane of calfskin or plastic. Originally the kettle was hemispherical, but nowadays it can also be an inverted cone with its lower end rounded off. At the bottom is a hole that smooths out the vibrations.

Early orchestral kettledrums were tuned by rotating screws around the edge to alter the membrane tension. A tuning key was fitted onto each screw in turn, which took a lot of time. But this was no problem, as the tuning did not yet have to be changed while playing. Towards 1800, the procedure was made easier by giving each screw a knob.

Until then, kettledrums had almost always been played in pairs, tuned a perfect fourth apart for the music's tonic and dominant keys. Here was a survival from the old cavalry kettledrums that

The orchestra's snare drum has a long ancestry, going back to ancient frame drums with attached jingles.

hung on each side of a horse. During the Baroque and Classicistic periods, the kettledrum was struck with hard wooden sticks, giving a distinct sound that especially suited powerful nuances. Throughout the eighteenth century, the custom also continued of playing kettledrums together with the trumpets.

One of the first to recognize the kettledrum's potential was Beethoven. He often wrote dramatic rolls for it, and he used other intervals than the perfect fourth – for instance, an octave in the eighth and ninth symphonies. Sometimes the kettledrums were given solo passages, as in the ninth's scherzo. Weber and Berlioz increased the number of kettledrums, the latter frequently asking for four of them, with at least two musicians so as to play chords. For his *Requiem*, Berlioz prescribed as many as sixteen kettledrums!

Pedal power

By that time, the tuning had become considerably easier. A device was invented in 1812 that transmitted the rotation of a single knob, or crank, to all the screws. Thus the instrument could be retuned during a given movement, and opened new doors to the composers. After the middle of the century, this construction was supplemented with a pedal, which allowed retuning in the midst of playing and even made it possible to produce *glissando* (used subsequently by Bartók and others).

However, tuning remains a kettledrummer's constant problem. A modern pedal kettledrum has an indicator which shows the pitch on a scale, but this is very approximate, so the tuning must be adjusted constantly while the music is being played. Besides, calfskin is sensitive to changes in weather; and the orchestra's pitch is altered by the heat during the course of a concert!

Therefore, even if a player uses the more tolerant plastic skin, we frequently see him bending an ear to the instrument and adjusting it further. His musical ear is his only support – and meanwhile, the rest of the orchestra may go on "roaring"

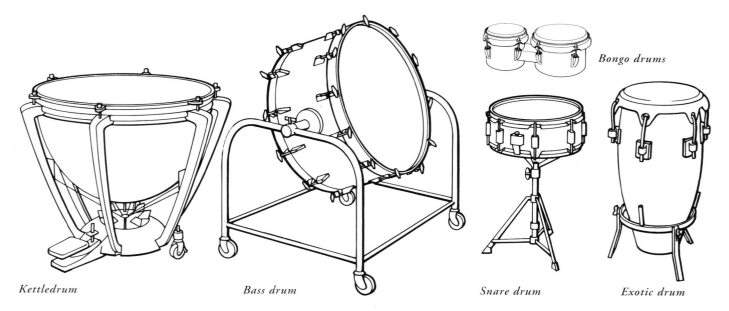

Bongo drums

Kettledrum   *Bass drum*   *Snare drum*   *Exotic drum*

in quite different keys!

Many orchestras own separate sets of kettledrums, respectively equipped with calf-skin (often imported from Ireland) and plastic skin.

Orchestra drums

Numerous other drum instruments belong to the orchestra. Most familiar are the bass (large) drum and snare (side) drum, followed by the tenor (long) drum. Their names are not entirely standardized, and may differ between countries – for example, both the snare and tenor drums are sometimes called *side drums*. All of these instruments are *cylindrical drums*, with a skin at each end. The frame may be of wood (normally on the bass drum), metal (snare drum), or an artificial material, while the skin is again of calf or plastic.

Bass, snare and tenor

The bass drum usually stands upright and is played from the side with a drumstick, often soft-headed. For rolls, two identical sticks are used, or sometimes a double-headed stick to permit rolling with one hand. In size the instrument varies, but a diameter of 60-100 cm (24-40 inches) is common.

The snare drum is mounted horizontally on a stand, and is played from above with a pair of thin wooden sticks. On the bottom, or snare head, are attached removable gut or wire-wound strings, called snares. These shake against the skin when playing, and produce a characteristic rattling sound. A well-known solo with this drum is the rhythm throughout Ravel's *Bolero*.

Playing a part on a snare drum may appear simple, but it is a difficult art that takes years to learn. Normally one does not, as on the kettledrum, strike single beats with the left and right hands alternately. Instead, each hand delivers two, occasionally three, quick beats at a time: RR-LL-RR-LL and so on. Try it yourself, by drumming your fingers sharply and regularly on a table!

The tenor drum is more slender, and usually lacks snares. Its sound is dull and fateful. Romantic opera made use of it when something ominous was afoot. In the present context, it occurs for example in Lutoslawski's *Concerto for Orchestra*.

Exotic drums

An instrument related to the snare and tenor drums, although lacking snares, is the *tom-tom*. Originally from China and Africa, it has been adapted for frequent use in jazz and popular music. Orchestras employ it in sets of up to eight with individual sounds, played with hard or soft drumsticks. We hear it, for instance, in Gershwin's *An American in Paris*.

Drums played by hand are sometimes used too, such as the Latin American *bongos* (small and cylindrical) and *congas* (larger and tapering downward). Their resonance body is wooden, with a skin only on top. Bongos occur in Gershwin's *Cuban Overture*.

The *tambourine*, also called a *Basque drum*, is actually a hybrid of two instruments. It has a drum skin on a low wooden frame, which is cut away at intervals to allow insertion of axles (wires) that hold pairs of movable metal plates. Thus it contains both a membranophone (the skin) and an idiophone (the plates), as if combining a drum with a sistrum. A tambourine can be hit with the hand or shaken, or the skin may be rubbed with a wet finger. It was much used in the Middle Ages for rhythmical dances, and in the Janissary music of Turkey. Berlioz exploited it to brilliant effect in *Roman Carnival*, and since then it has often appeared in orchestras, not least for ballet music.

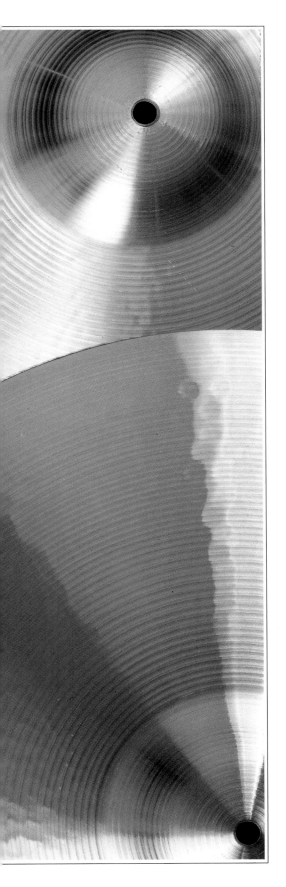

Percussion

The idiophones

The self-sounding instruments which are simplest in structure – although not always easy to construct – are those that consist of one piece of metal or wood. These are frequently of Asiatic origin. They have various forms, but the metallic types are often round plates, more or less cup-shaped, made of brass or bronze alloys.

Cymbals and crotals

In terms of sound and sight alike, the big dishes known as cymbals belong to the most conspicuous devices in an orchestra. They are somewhat curved and have a central dome, to which a leather handle is attached. Their full diameter is usually 35-55 cm (14-22 inches), sometimes more. Orchestral cymbals were originally made by Turkish specialists, but are now manufactured chiefly by their descendants in Switzerland and the United States.

Until the late nineteenth century, cymbals were always played in pairs, whose concave sides were knocked obliquely against each other (a straight-on collision is resisted by air pressure). For soft nuances, the cymbals were made to brush each other's edges. But a genuine *pianissimo* requires such a soft contact around the whole periphery of both cymbals, which is difficult to achieve.

These techniques are still the usual ones, yet others have been added. A cymbal may be hung horizontally on a stand and struck, for example with drumsticks. This also enables one to play rolls and to gradually raise or lower the sound strength. Cymbals reverberate for a long time, but can be damped quickly by hand or against the body.

A related instrument of different character is the *crotal*, an "ancient cymbal" that goes back thousands of years. The version used in orchestras is a small round, fairly thick, metal plate with a

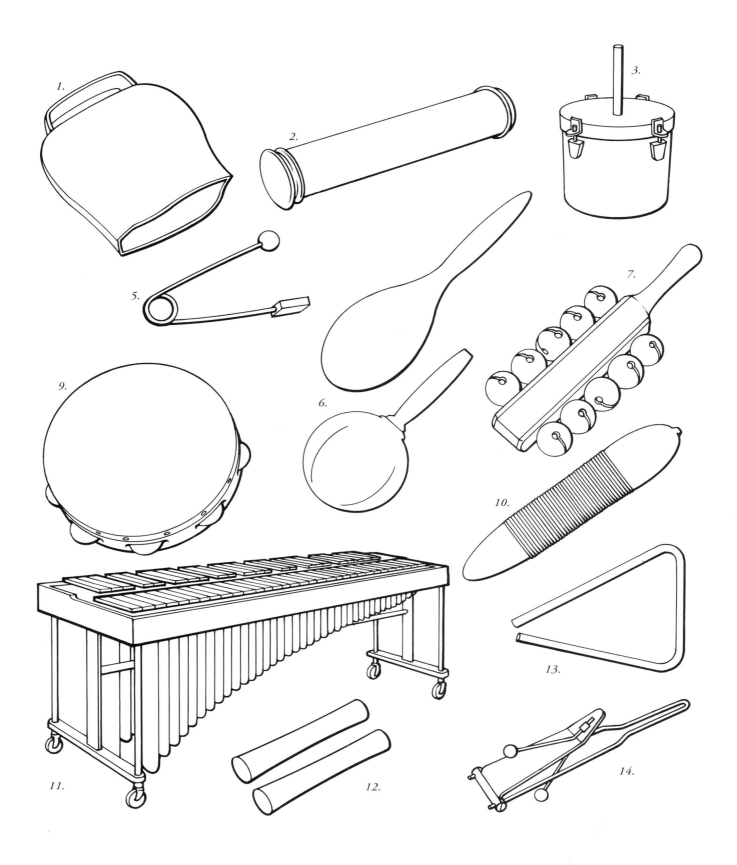

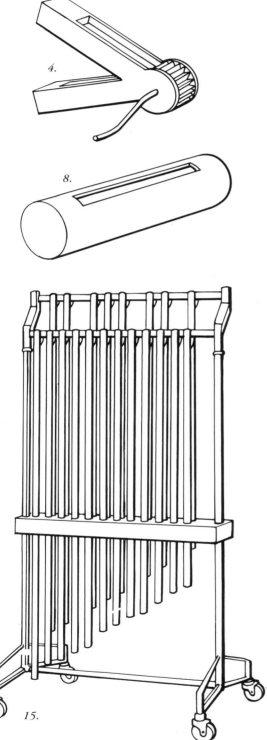

1. *Cow-bell*
2. *Rumba tube*
3. *Friction drum*
4. *Cog rattle*
5. *Vibraflex*
6. *Maraca*
7. *Jingle-bells*
8. *Wood block*
9. *Tambourine*
10. *Guiro*
11. *Xylophone*
12. *Claves*
13. *Triangle*
14. *Flexatone*
15. *Tubular bell*

Position in orchestra

Repertoire examples

Idiophones

Orchestral works:
Orff's "Carmina Burana";
Bartók's piano concertos 1 and 2,
"Music for Strings,
Percussion and Celesta", and
"Concerto for Two Pianos,
Percussion and Orchestra";
Britten's "The Young Person's
Guide to the Orchestra",
Shostakovich symphony 14,
Gershwin's "Cuban Overture"
Soloverk:
Concertos by Milhaud,
Jolivet; Colgrass' "Déjà Vu",
Sallinen's symphony 2

definite pitch. Two can be struck against each other, or a chromatic series of crotals may be mounted with separate axles on a table. Playing is done with steel pins, or little clubs of hard plastic, yielding a light and crisp sound. An early example occurs in Debussy's *Prelude to the Afternoon of a Faun*. Crotals are especially clear at the end of Schnittke's *Ritual*.

Gongs

Among the main traditional instruments of Southeast Asia are gongs. Indonesian *gamelan* orchestras consist of a great number of gongs in different sizes, with a prominent bulge in the middle. The smaller ones nearly produce a distinctive pitch, and are combined in groups for chromatic playing. They are especially useful to create an Oriental atmosphere, as was shown notably by Puccini in *Madame Butterfly* and especially in *Turandot*.

Symphony orchestras have long been content with a single large gong, lacking the central bulge, known as a *tam-tam* (the notion of which, however, is greatly confused and one cannot always be certain as to which type is meant). This object usually has a diameter of 100-150 cm (40-60 inches) and hangs on a stand. Its surface is flat or slightly rounded, and the outer edge is bent backward a bit. It is struck from the front side with a powerful stick, wrapped in felt or leather. During the past 125 years, composers have employed its overwhelming *fortissimo* in shattering climaxes (as in Respighi's *Vetrate di Chiesa* and the finale of Shostakovich's fifth symphony), but also its gloomy *pianissimo* (as in the finale of Tchaikovsky's sixth symphony).

The triangle

A round steel bar, bent in three equal

The plates of a xylophone are chromatically ordered, and are struck with one or more wooden mallets.

parts with one open corner, the triangle comes in many sizes. It is suspended from a stand or from the hand. The player hits it with one or two steel rods – either on the outside or, for *tremolo*, inside near a corner. Its bright, silvery sound was enjoyed in Southern Europe already in medieval times. Opera and symphony orchestras adopted it during the eighteenth century along with

Turkish music. A well-known orchestral example is in Liszt's first piano concerto.

Bells

Early opera music faced a need to imitate church bells. Since the mid-nineteenth century, orchestras have used hanging metal tubes that differ in length and, therefore, in pitch. Eventually

tubes were combined to give all notes of the octave. Modern tubular bells, made of steel, are arranged in two rows (corresponding to the white and black keys on a piano). They are covered at the top, open at the bottom. The tubes are played by being struck at the top with a wooden mallet, sometimes clad in leather. The long reverberation can be damped with a pedal. Good instances of tubular bells are heard in Mussorgsky's *Boris Godunov* (the coronation scene) and in Kodály's *Háry János*.

More forceful bell-sounds are obtainable by striking tuned pieces of thick metal plate, or bells like those in churches. Such equipment is used occasionally in, for example, Berlioz' *Symphonie Fantastique*, Tchaikovsky's *1812 Overture* and Mahler's second symphony. The most imposing bells, as in Wagner's *Parsifal*, are often evoked today by synthetic sounds.

Wooden devices

An orchestra employs few wooden idiophones with any regularity, but these have individual characters. Some are versions of Asiatic *wood blocks*, which may be rectangular and possess a narrow resonance opening along the edge. These occur in *La Création du Monde* by Milhaud, and in *Symphonic Metamorphoses* by Hindemith. Another variant is a round, hollowed-out piece of wood, also with an open slit. Known as a temple block, it appears in *The Syncopated Clock* by Leroy Anderson.

Both types are made with different sizes and tonal qualities. Played chiefly with drumsticks or xylophone mallets, they give a sharp dry sound. Another such idiophone is the Latin American instrument called *claves*, consisting simply of two round, hard wooden sticks that are knocked together. These are used in Gershwin's *Cuban Overture* and Copland's *Appalachian Spring*.

Sets of plates

Wooden rods or plates, too, have long been arranged in sequence of pitch. During the Renaissance, these devices came from Asia to Europe and gained popularity in folk music. They were not introduced in orchestras until the mid-nineteenth century, and at first only for entertainment music. The *xylophone* often added colour to the period's ghost and horror stories, so its first symphonic appearance is not surprising: in Saint-Saëns' *Danse Macabre*. Later examples include Khachaturian's *Sabre Dance* and Shostakovich's fourteenth symphony.

A modern xylophone has wooden bars that are chromatically tuned – with different lengths – and laid in two rows like a keyboard. Each bar rests on a pair of thin wooden strips. Under each bar is a short, vertical metal pipe, tuned to resonate at the given note. Models with an unusually large range are generally called *xylorimbas*. The deepest form of all is the *marimba* (although most directly originating from Central America). A player uses small mallets of varying hardness, once made of wood but now mostly of plastic or rubber. Sometimes two are held in each hand for playing chords.

Of basically similar design are *metallophones* – instruments with series of tuned metal bars. The horizontal *glockenspiel* creates a bright and clear sound, easily heard throughout the orchestra. It is played with little mallets of different hardness. Music for it was written already by Handel, but it first became common in orchestras after the mid-nineteenth century, often in music for the stage. Examples of the glockenspiel are to be found in the *Russian Easter* overture by Rimsky-Korsakov and *The Planets* by Holst.

A larger relative is the *vibraphone* (or vibraharp). It is built rather like the xylophone, but is equipped with tuned, graduated metal bars – made initially of bronze or steel, and nowadays of a special light metal. Under each bar is a resonating tube, atop which a revolving disc is affixed. A motor rotates the discs, causing a vibrato-like sound. The speed can be varied and the bars damped by a pedal. This instrument first appeared in American jazz and popular music during the 1920s, yet soon spread to

Tubular bells ("orchestral chimes"), used since about 1885, are clearer in tone than true bells.

Bronze gong

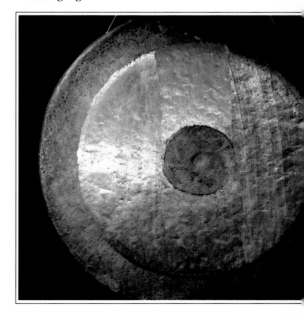

Cow-bells

European art music. Among the early instances is Berg's opera *Lulu*, a later one the Symphonic Dances from Bernstein's *West Side Story*.

Keyboard instruments

The grand piano is the keyboard instrument that occurs most frequently with orchestras. The organ and the harpsichord also play a regular role in this context. To adequately discuss these superb but complex sources of sound would take us far beyond the scope of the present book. Nor, of course, are they primarily designed for orchestral use.

On the podium, however, we often see some devices that look like small upright pianos. In fact, they are normally played by a pianist, but can reasonably be assigned to the percussion section. Both the *keyboard glockenspiel* and the *celesta* are mechanized versions of the horizontal glockenspiel. The former's keys are pushed to activate little hammers that hit steel bars. It is thus easier than with mallets to play fast, and to produce chords or even several parts. A simple example is found already in *The Magic Flute* by Mozart, a more characteristic one in *Mother Goose* by Ravel.

The celesta, by contrast, appeared as late as the 1880s in Paris. Its inventor, Auguste Mustel, padded the hammers with felt, but gave each tone resonance through a wooden pipe. The sound became more subdued than the glockenspiel's, and can perhaps be called "heavenly" as the instrument's name signifies. Tchaikovsky, for the first performance of his ballet *The Nutcracker*, had a celesta shipped home to St. Petersburg, cloaked in utmost secrecy. He reputedly had to guard it during the journey so that no one would be able to present this novelty before him! It proved to be

worth the trouble, and made a great success in the "Dance of the Sugar-Plum Fairy". There is also a conspicuous celesta in Richard Strauss' *Der Rosenkavalier* and in Bartók's *Music for Strings, Percussion and Celesta*.

Scrapers, rattles and clappers

Instruments with grooves, or sometimes teeth, that emit scraping or rasping sounds if stroked with a hard piece of wood, are called *scrapers*. Often the sound is amplified by a cavity. Different versions have existed for thousands of years, and were once used widely in ritual and magic. The scrapers that occasionally appear in orchestras tend to come from Latin American dance music. Best known is the *guiro*, which served Stravinsky as early as 1913 in *The Rite of Spring* and, six years later, Milhaud in *Le Boeuf sur le Toit*.

Rattles are all the instruments that clatter when shaken. These, too, are very old and date back to the pre-Christian era. Some consist of a hard, hollow object (such as a piece of wood, a gourd, coconut shell or tin can) filled with beans, seeds, stones or the like. The "cans" that are shaken in an orchestra may be jingles or rattles, such as the Latin American *maraca*, which is made of an egg-shaped wooden bowl with a handle at one end (used, for example, in Gershwin's *Cuban Overture*). Others have small metal plates on an axle, as is illustrated by the *sistrum* which descends from ancient Egypt. Also assignable to this group is one component of the tambourine.

A well-known instrument with a clapping sound is the pair of *castanets*. Resembling bowls or spoons, they are made of hard wood, joined by a strap. Spanish *flamenco* dancers hold a pair in

Guiro

each hand and clap the bowls together with their fingers. Since this requires a special technique, orchestra players often use a version with the bowls tied to a handle or plate, which is laid on a table. Castanets are naturally employed often to suggest Spain, but they also serve general needs of dance and other rhythmic purposes. Instances occur in Bizet's *Carmen*, and in *The Three-Cornered Hat* by Falla.

Unusual effects

Many devices are employed to create sounds only for particular orchestral purposes. As a rule they belong to the groups surveyed above, but some are worth considering separately. A few wind instruments are occasionally used in this way – such as the *whistle* in Ibert's *Paris*, and the *taxi horns* in Gershwin's *An American in Paris*.

Among the metallic idiophones, we can hear rhythmical hammer-blows on the anvil in Verdi's *Il Trovatore* as well as in Wagner's *Rhinegold* and *Siegfried*, jingle-bells in Mahler's fourth symphony and cow-bells in his sixth. Wooden idi-

ophones include the *whip*, which introduces Ravel's piano concerto in G major (actually a beater made of two long, narrow wooden plates that are clapped together). The cog rattle used in Strauss' *Till Eulenspiegel* has a frame with a pair of stretched wooden tongues, which strike on a gear-wheel as it is rotated.

Most spectacular is the *thunder-plate*, celebrated in Baroque and nineteenth-century dramatic operas. Up to several metres long, it is hung in a stand and "played" with a club, or shaken so

that it thunders. The sound of a *wind machine* also evokes illusions. This is generated by friction when a large cylinder, with parallel wooden bars on its surface, is rotated against a strong piece of cloth. Both of these devices can be heard in the storm scene of Strauss' *An Alpine Symphony*.

Today, a *synthesizer* can reproduce the murmur of wind. Its special effects may also be expected to substitute for other such instruments in time.

Finger-cymbals

The Harp

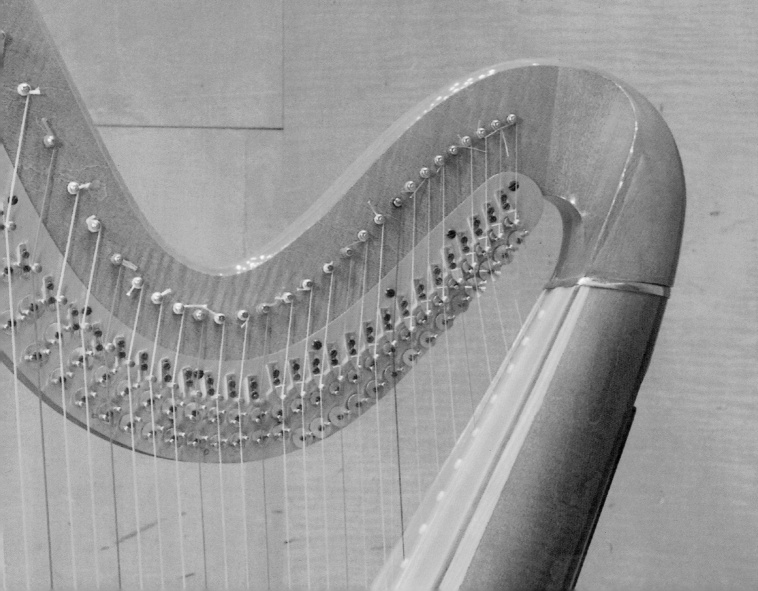

The harp

Plucked instruments, with strings stretched on a resonating body, were used at early dates in many parts of the world. Sumerian and Egyptian paintings, four or five thousand years old, often show lyres and harps of various kinds. Probably the most ancient, and perhaps an imitation of hunting bows, was the *arched harp* with a few strings. The *angular harp* had more strings, and one wonders how it could have been tuned: an open instrument body must have yielded with only slight tension on the strings.

The ancient Greeks and Romans preferred, for festivals and dancing, the lyre and the related *kithara*, which was the instrument of professional musicians. It may have been Plato who persuaded his countrymen to avoid the "all too dreamy" harp. In any case, it is the *kithara* and lyre which we see portrayed with Apollo and Orpheus.

During the early Middle Ages, the harp spread to the British Isles. It was played in Wales and Ireland for hundreds of years by bards, the Celtic poet-singers, and it has been praised down to our time.

In the early twelfth century it became the instrument of wandering troubadours in France and the German countries. Contemporary harps were fairly small and portable. An important difference from their ancient ancestors was that the angular body now acquired a stronger front with a crosspiece, usually somewhat convex. The triangular form of such a *frame harp* has remained basically the same for nearly a thousand years.

Chromatic features

A medieval harp was diatonic, and was tuned purely in only one key. Already during the Renaissance, this proved too restrictive. Elizabethan England, in particular, was more attracted to the chromatic lute´ and to a keyboard instrument, the *virginal*. Making a harp with semitones would occupy designers for several centuries.

The first step was taken before 1600 with the *double harp*. Its strings were mounted in two parallel rows, respectively with diatonic and chromatic tuning (like the white and black keys on a piano). For this instrument, in his opera *Orfeo* of 1608, Monteverdi composed the first significant orchestral part for a harp.

Another variant, the Welsh *triple harp*, had three rows of strings, with the chromatic ones barely accessible in the middle. The problem on a harp, of course, is that the strings should not be so close together that they cannot be plucked individually, yet they must all be within an arm's reach!

At the end of the seventeenth century, builders began to shorten the strings' vibrating length, with a revolving metal hook just under each tuning screw. Any string could now be raised in pitch by a semitone. The next century saw work by Hochbrucker in Germany, and later Cosineau in France, to add a pedal mechanism so that the harp could be retuned without a pause in playing.

The harp is often included in the Romantic orchestral repertoire, but surprisingly little solo music has been composed for it.

There were seven pedals, each influencing a diatonic tone through all octaves. Twice that number was also tried, allowing a further rise of a semitone.

These achievements made the harp popular again. Developed in courtly and noble circles, it became one of the late eighteenth century's fashionable instruments. But even several decades into the nineteenth, it was still rare in orchestras. It is true that music for the harp, during the late Baroque period, had been composed by Handel in various works – to be followed by Gluck in *Orpheus and Eurydice*, as well as by Beethoven in his ballet *Prometheus*. Yet these were exceptions that proved the rule.

Pedals or no pedals

In 1820 a Frenchman, Sébastien Érard, after many years of labour, unveiled his *double-action harp*. A technical breakthrough, it is the kind usually played to

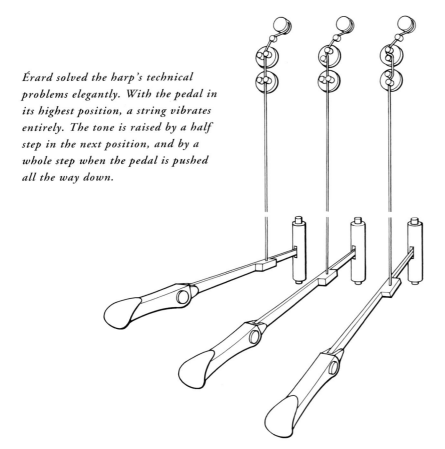

Érard solved the harp's technical problems elegantly. With the pedal in its highest position, a string vibrates entirely. The tone is raised by a half step in the next position, and by a whole step when the pedal is pushed all the way down.

this very day. Instead of the hook, Érard used a round metal disc with two protruding pins, which pressed on the string from opposite directions when the plate was turned. He had a disc for each string at first, and later two in a row for raising the pitch by a half or whole step. By making each pedal movable in two steps, he could limit himself to seven double-action pedals.

Érard's harps were not only technically well-built. They also yielded a stronger sound than previous salon instruments, suitable for urban concert halls. Along with Romantic keyboard masters and violin equilibrists, the harp now had its own travelling virtuosi. Leading innovators of the age adopted the double pedal harp with joy. Berlioz, Meyerbeer, Liszt and Wagner often gave it conspicuous parts, and so did Russians such as Tchaikovsky. Suddenly the harp had become an obvious component of every orchestra.

The decades around 1900 were the true heyday of the harp. Debussy, Ravel and others exploited its mild pastel colours. Better than most, the French realized the harp's potential. Not surprisingly, their works are the favourites of many harp players!

Other constructions are illustrated by the chromatic harp without pedals, from the French piano company *Pleyel*. By arranging the strings on two crossing levels, it created space for all semitones, which could be played with either hand. Debussy's *Sacred and Profane Dances* were commissioned for this instrument. Ironically, they proved easier to play on a pedal harp!

Repertoire examples

Harp

Orchestral works:
Gluck's "Orpheus and Eurydice", Berlioz' "Symphonie Fantastique" (movement 2), Bizet's "Carmen", Rimsky-Korsakov's "Scheherazade", Tchaikovsky's "Swan Lake" and "The Nutcracker" (Waltz of the Flowers), Ravel's "Tzigane"
Solo works:
Concertos by Handel, Mozart (flute and harp), Boieldieu, Glière, Jolivet, Rodrigo, Ginastera; Debussy's "Sacred and Profane Dances", Ravel's "Introduction et Allegro", Hindemith's "Concert Music" Op.49, Martin's "Petite symphonie concertante"

Tonal range

Place in orchestra

Érard's design, soon two centuries old, has kept its dominant status in the symphony orchestra. Such instruments are also made outside France. Especially famous for their high-class harps today are the firms Lyon and Healy in America, Salvi in Italy, and Horngacher in Germany.

The harp's structure

A modern harp has 47 strings, stretched between its *sound board* and the *neck*. Low strings are of metal, high ones of gut or nylon. The front side, or *pillar*, has usually been straight during recent centuries. Inside it run all the connecting rods from the pedals to the neck mechanism, for shortening the strings. The neck's shape, beautifully curved ever since medieval times, has a practical explanation. So that all the strings will have the same tension, the middle ones must be shorter than a straight neck would allow. For this reason, too, grand pianos have a concave form.

The harp has the largest range of the orchestra's standard instruments: just over six and a half octaves. It is tuned in C-flat major (the enharmonic equivalent of B major) and has three positions for each pedal. When all pedals are in the upper position, the strings vibrate throughout their length, giving the diatonic scale of C-flat major. In the intermediate position, the strings are stopped and the pitch is raised a semitone, giving the diatonic scale of C major. In the lower position, the pitch is raised a whole tone, giving the diatonic scale of C-sharp major (the enharmonic equiva-

The harp and the closely related lyre are among the world's oldest instruments. Nowadays the harp is the orchestra's only plucked instrument.

lent of D-flat major). By combining different pedal positions, the harpist can produce any key – as well as many other scales.

Eight fingers

The harp rests against the right shoulder. The right hand is used mainly for treble playing, and the left for the lower register. One plays with the fingertips, using all except the little finger. Thus each chord may consist of up to eight simultaneous notes. A common technique is to "break" the chord, playing

notes *arpeggio* in quick succession.

Effective *glissando* is produced by drawing the fingers across the strings. This can also be done with two or more fingers at the same time, creating parallel movements. By pressing the wrist against a string's centre and simultaneously plucking the string, a damped harmonic results, sounding an octave higher since only half of the string vibrates.

A harpist finds it easier to keep track of the large number of strings because all C-strings (when pedals are in their intermediate position) are coloured red, while the F-strings are blue or black.

String instruments

The heart of the very first orchestras, 400 years ago, was their section of stringed instruments. Some of these were plucked, such as lutes and harps, while others were played with a bow. The latter have remained essential to orchestral music, regardless of other fashions and ways of creating sound.

Bowed instruments in Baroque orchestras were initially of various kinds, but so-called *violin instruments* became standard during the seventeenth century: the violin, viola and (violon)cello. Also the double bass, which has somewhat different origins, won increasing acceptance.

These four instruments are functionally similar. A violin may look fairly simple, with a sound box, a neck and a few accessories. Actually it contains seventy-odd parts, all precisely cut from well-chosen wood. The joints are made with glue and demand equal exactness.

In today's orchestral context, the term "string(ed) instruments" – or just "strings" – is used to mean the bowed instruments. This meaning will be employed in the following.

Components

Most of the parts are externally visible. A violin's resonance or sound box, the *body*, is about 35 cm (13-14 inches) long, consisting of a top – the *belly*, or soundboard – and a back. Both of these are slightly convex, often built of two pieces, and glued lengthwise. Around the body run ribs, about 3 cm high. From there, the *neck* begins at the relatively narrow end, known as the *upper bout*. The neck terminates in a head, or *pegbox*, with four tuning pegs and, at the very tip, a carved *scroll*. One might think that the pegs are threaded screws, but they are slightly conical pins, held in their holes by friction. The body is made more stable by internal blocks at the ends and corners.

The strings are attached at their upper ends to the pegs, and at their lower ends to a *tailpiece* bound to the ribs. They pass over the *fingerboard*, which lies atop the neck and extends onto the belly. Along the way, they run across a *bridge*, which stands upright and is slightly rounded on top, as well as the nut which joins the neck to the pegbox. On the violin, the highest string – and sometimes also the other strings – may be fastened to a small screw device at the tailpiece for fine tuning. But this method is used only for steel strings.

Inside the body, a couple of parts are also decisive for the instrument's performance. Glued to the belly is the *bass bar*, running parallel to the lowest string and under the bridge's left foot. Just under the right (treble) foot sits a little *sound post*, which connects the belly to the back. This pin can be seen if you look through one of the *sound holes* cut in the belly, called "f-holes" because of their shape.

The parts are manufactured from separate materials in order to vibrate differently. The belly is usually of soft pine or spruce, and the belly of harder maple. Spruce also tends to be used for the bass bar and sound post, while maple is pre-

ferred for the ribs, bridge, neck and scroll. For the fingerboard, tailpiece, nut and tuning pegs, the choice is ebony – or, in the last case, sometimes rosewood.

Covering the body, neck, pegbox and scroll is a thin layer of varnish. Everyone agrees that the varnish's quality is of great importance – but there the disagreement begins. Today, opinion holds that the varnish alone does not make the sound any sweeter. Its main value is to protect the instrument, just as one varnishes a wooden boat. But if it is unsuitably hard, or laid on unevenly or too thickly, the tone may be impaired. Now as before, excellent handicraft is needed in order to produce and apply the varnish.

Such varnish was once thought to have almost magical qualities. Legends still circulate about the varnish used by the old Italian masters of the seventeenth and eighteenth centuries. Instrument-makers in Cremona were believed to possess some secret recipe which was inherited and, in time, buried forever. Yet modern methods of analysis have shown that their varnish was not so exceptional, and that the same composition was used in other countries. On the other hand, chemical changes may have occurred in the varnish during its centuries of life on the instruments.

The strings

Strings were long made of sheep tendons, usually referred to as *gut strings*, which gave a round soft tone. In the eighteenth century, when strong sounds were increasingly emphasized, experiments began with strings of metal, or of gut wound with thin silver or copper wire. These, however, were not generally accepted until some decades into the twentieth century. On violins and violas, wound gut is still often used for the lower strings, but solid steel for the highest one. Cellos and double basses frequently have strings made of solid or spun steel. An advantage of metal strings is that they are more durable, as well as less sensitive to variations in climate. Nonetheless, in musical terms, strings of tendon have retained many enthusiasts, especially when playing older music.

Generating the sound

Let us see what happens when the mu-

A Swedish musical gathering in the eighteenth century: a Gustavian interior by Pehr Hilleström.

sician draws his bow across a string. Nothing may be heard at all! First the bow's horsehair must be rubbed in with a specially prepared rosin – either hard natural or synthetic – so that the string feels friction. To obtain different pitches, the string is shortened by pressing it with a finger of the left hand against the fingerboard, allowing only part of the string's length to vibrate. The vibrations are transmitted to the bridge and, primarily through its left foot, to the belly – whence they spread across the surface, partly by way of the bass bar. The bridge's right foot is damped by the sound post under it, but the pin transfers the vibrations to the back, which moves less freely due to its harder material. The sound that we hear, therefore, comes chiefly from the belly and is amplified

by the body's resonance, then emerges from the two sound holes and reaches our ears.

Predecessors

Bowed instruments have existed all over Europe since before the year 1000. A wide range of shapes and sizes developed during the Renaissance. One of them was the *fiddle*, with a perfectly flat belly and back, the merest suggestion of a narrowed waist on its body, and from three to five strings. Another, the *rebec*, had a very bulging back, and resembled a pear sliced down the middle.

Towards the end of the fifteenth century, for example in Italy, the *lira* and *viola* appeared. Each came in two forms that were held, respectively, with the arm

or knees: the *lira da braccio* and *lira da gamba*, the *viola da braccio* and *viola da gamba*. The smallest of them had four or five playing strings, accompanied by some extra *sympathetic strings* that resonated, and the biggest had up to fifteen strings in all. Usually the fingerboard was crossed by a fret for each semitone, as on present-day guitars.

The gamba

Soon the fiddle and *rebec* went out of fashion, and the Renaissance's *da braccio* instruments were replaced by the modern violins. But the *viola da gamba* displayed great vitality and continued in use for several hundred years. It was enjoyed both by solo players and, in varying sizes, by groups or "consorts". The viol's mild, slightly nasal sound was ideal for Baroque polyphonic chamber music, and became popular together with singers and recorders.

In many ways the viol distinguished itself from the violin family. It had a flat back, sloping shoulders, a broad neck with frets, and normally six thin strings that were tuned in perfect fourths with a third in the middle. The sound holes were often C-shaped, and the pegbox usually ended in a carved face. The bridge's upper edge was only faintly arched for easier playing of chords on three or more strings.

There were viols in the treble, alto, tenor, bass and contrabass ranges, the last type being sometimes called a *violone* (large viol). All were held on or between the knees, while the bow was held by underhand (with the palm of the hand turned forward). The low viols were especially loved until the very end of the Baroque period, in the mid-eighteenth century. They occasionally occur in our modern symphony orchestras, for instance in Bach's *Saint Matthew Passion*, which includes an aria with an extensive viol solo.

The violin instruments

The fiddle, rebec and lira proved to be of importance for the early violin family, and the *viol* for the double bass. Both aesthetic and acoustic factors – mainly the latter – have given these instruments their beautiful shape. Until the end of the seventeenth century, experiments were constantly made with new materials, component shapes and the sizes of entire instruments. Almost every detail that we find pleasing to the eye is also of value for the sound or construction. Thus the craftsmen of all ages have striven to combine superb appearance and function.

The form of violin instruments was borrowed most directly from the *lira da braccio*, with its strongly narrowed waist that enabled the bow to be swung more freely. Their characteristics were mostly present from the beginning: a somewhat arched belly and back, nearly straight shoulders, f-shaped sound holes, and a carved scroll above the pegbox. The four strings were tuned in fifths, following the rebec. Ever since then, the violin's normal tuning has been the same. Its music is always written in the treble clef.

A centre in Italy

How these instruments looked when they emerged in the mid-sixteenth century is one thing; but who "invented" them is unknown to us. Treble, alto and baritone versions – the violin, viola and cello – were evidently developed at the same time, perhaps in several parts of Europe. It was not long before northern Italy acquired a particular status. While wind instruments are usually French or German, and percussion instruments from Asia or Latin America, the orchestra's bowed instruments are probably Italian products.

During their first half-century, the violin instruments were used primarily for dance music and song accompaniment. How such music sounded in the sixteenth century is difficult to say. The composers wrote for an unspecified choice of instruments; the same piece could be performed on a violin as on, for example, a viol or lute. The first works to explicitly call for violins were some sonatas by Andrea and Giovanni Gabrieli, for example the latter's famous *Sonata Pian e Forte*. Only from around 1600 can we speak of violin music in the proper sense. Its diverse qualities served the early opera orchestras particularly well.

Instrument-makers

In Brescia during the later sixteenth century, Gasparo da Salò worked on violin instruments; Cremona had its Andrea Amati. As usual in the handicraft professions, their expertise was handed down for generations. Refinements were made early in the next century by Amati's sons, and chiefly by his grandson Nicola, as well as by Gasparo's apprentices. The tone of violins, originally rather subdued, became brighter and more expressive. As a result, composers began to write sonatas

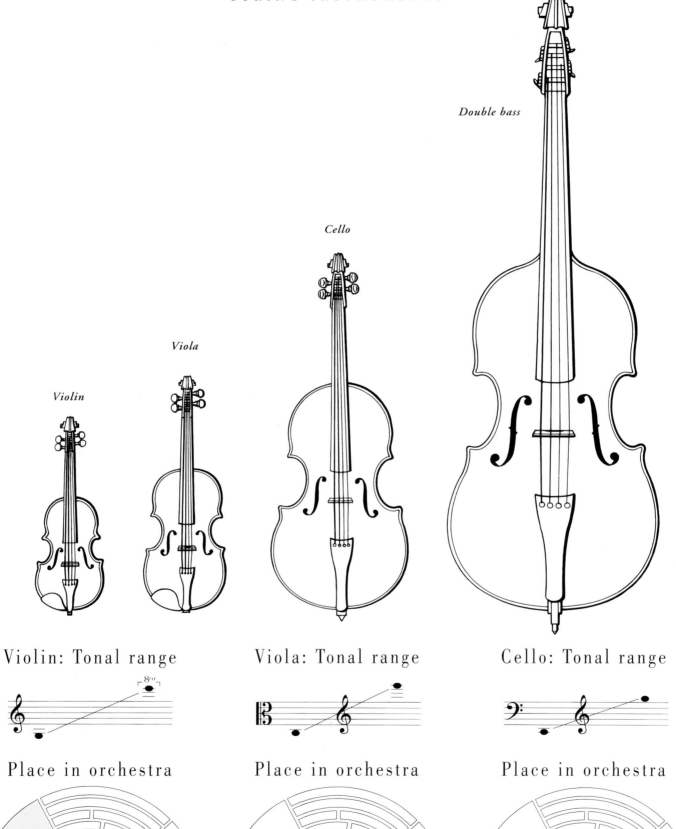

Double bass

Cello

Viola

Violin

Violin: Tonal range

Viola: Tonal range

Cello: Tonal range

Place in orchestra

Place in orchestra

Place in orchestra

Repertoire examples

Violin

Orchestral works: Mozart's "Haffner Serenade", Beethoven's "Missa Solemnis" (Benedictus), Brahms symphony 1 (movement 2), Rimsky-Korsakov's "Scheherazade", Mahler symphony 4 (movement 2); R. Strauss' "Thus Spoke Zarathustra"and "A Hero's Life"

Solo works: concertos by Bach, Albinoni, Vivaldi, Haydn, Mozart, Bruch, Tchaikovsky, Brahms, Dvořák, Saint-Saëns, Sibelius, Glazunov, Elgar, Nielsen, Prokofiev, Szymanowski, Stravinsky, Berg, Schoenberg, Bartók, Hindemith, Walton, Britten, Shostakovich, Schnittke, Penderecki

Viola

Orchestral works: Bach's "Brandenburg Concerto" No.6, Brahms' "Serenade" No.2, Tchaikovsky's "Romeo and Juliet", Sibelius' "A Saga", Mahler symphony 10 (beginning)

Solo works: concertos by Telemann, Vanhal, C. Stamitz, M. Haydn (viola and organ), Walton, Bartók, Schnittke; Mozart's "Sinfonia Concertante" (violin and viola), Berlioz' "Harold in Italy", R. Strauss' "Don Quixote" (viola and cello), Bloch's "Suite", Hindemith's "Der Schwanendreher", Vaughan Williams' "Flos Campi" (with chorus), Berio's "Chemins 3"

Cello

Orchestral works: Beethoven symphony 5 (movement 2), Schubert's "unfinished" symphony (movement 1), Rossini's "William Tell" overture, Glinka's overture to "Ruslan and Lyudmila", Brahms piano concerto 2 (movement 3) and symphony 2 (movement 2), Bruckner symphony 7 (beginning)

Solo works: concertos by Vivaldi, Boccherini, Haydn, Schumann, Saint-Saëns, Dvořák, Elgar, Martinu, Hindemith, Walton, Shostakovich, Dutilleux, Lutoslawski, Penderecki, Schnittke; Beethoven's "Triple Concerto" (piano, violin and cello), Tchaikovsky's "Rococo Variations", Brahms' "Double Concerto" (violin and cello), R. Strauss' "Don Quixote" (cello and viola), Bloch's "Schelomo", Prokofiev's "Sinfonia Concertante", Britten's "Cello Symphony"

Double bass

Orchestral works: Haydn symphony 31, Beethoven symphony 5 (movement 3), Saint-Saëns' "Carnival of Animals" (elephant), Mahler symphony 1 (movement 3), Stravinsky's "Pulcinella", Prokofiev's "Lieutenant Kijé"

Solo works: concertos by Dittersdorf, Dragonetti, Bottesini, Koussevitzky, Tubin, Schuller, Rautavaara

Double bass:Tonal range

Place in orchestra

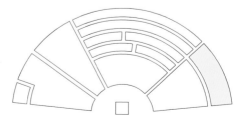

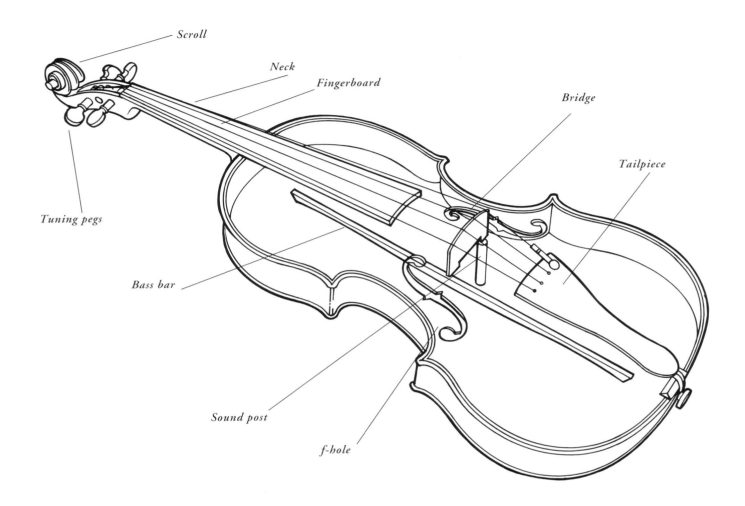

Scroll

Neck

Fingerboard

Bridge

Tailpiece

Tuning pegs

Bass bar

Sound post

f-hole

and other solo music in great quantity. The violin took a position as the leading solo instrument of the 1600s, and had no competitors until the oboe appeared after the middle of that century.

Stradivari

One of Nicola Amati's pupils was to be the very personification of string instruments: Antonio Stradivari (or Stradivarius). During his ninety-year life, he built a vast number of violins, violas and cellos of the highest quality. It was also he who, following the many experiments of the seventeenth century, established the violin body's optimal size of about 35 centimetres (14 inches) – a standard he maintained throughout his last four decades.

Stradivari was not the only master in Cremona. There, the Guarneri family produced a series of violin-makers, the most successful being Giuseppe. As if they were not enough, half a dozen other workshops existed in their immediate neighbourhood! In Venice and other cities, too, high-class manufacture began early. Outside Italy, the best instruments of the late seventeenth century came from Jacob Stainer in Austria. These were regarded as quite equal, and sometimes superior, to the Italian instruments.

The first violin concertos

At that time, the distinction between

composers and other musicians did not yet exist (it arose in the nineteenth century). Thus, early creators of violin music were naturally those who actually played the instrument. During the later seventeenth century, such pioneers in Italy were Giovanni Vitali, Giuseppe Torelli and Archangelo Corelli, all of them outstanding violinists. Torelli composed the first solo concertos, and Corelli some of the finest Baroque solo sonatas, trio sonatas and *concerti grossi*. The most influential was Corelli, who emphasized melodiousness rather than virtuosity. His impact on generations of Italian violinists lasted until Paganini's day, and was felt even in Germany and England, for example through the music of Handel.

Building instruments is a precise craft. The violin well illustrates how beauty and function are combined in orchestral equipment.

In Central Europe, the principal violin composers were then Heinrich Biber and Johann Jakob Walther, both with a virtuoso orientation. In France, the music's primary task was to accompany ballet and other dance; violin instruments were essential to the orchestras, but hardly yet for solo playing.

Late Baroque music

Italy kept its lead during the eighteenth century as a source of superb violin instruments. Members of such families as Gagliano, Grancino and Testore, some of them former apprentices to Stradivari, passed the tradition onward to Naples, Venice and Milan. Up in the Tyrol, Stainer was succeeded by the prominent Mateo Goffriller.

Late Baroque Italian musicians excelled in violin concertos: Torelli, Tommaso Albinoni, Francesco Geminiani, Antonio Vivaldi, and the virtuosi Pietro Locatelli and Giuseppe Tartini. Doing justice to their music called for a powerful and melodious tone. The instruments were given thinner and more tightly stretched strings (a thin string responds better to the bow). Until then, the violin had usually been supported against the player's chest or shoulder, but now it was commonly held under the chin in order to leave the left hand free for playing.

In Germany, Bach wrote several concertos. Still more significant were his six sonatas and partitas for solo violin. Although not rich in effects, they

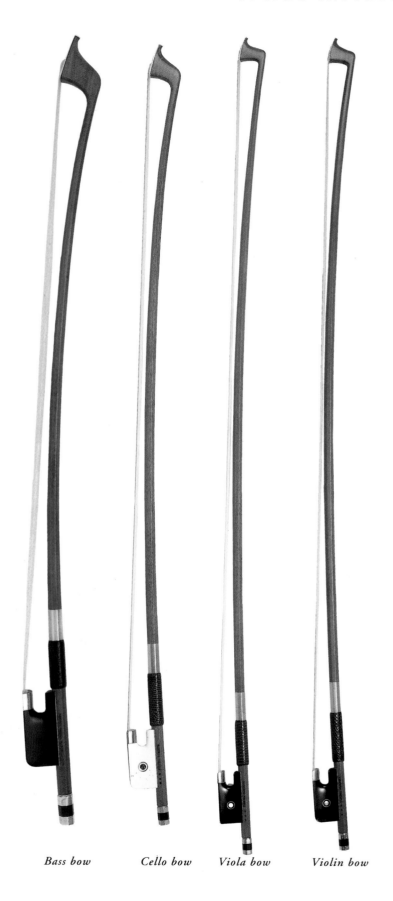

Bass bow   *Cello bow*   *Viola bow*   *Violin bow*

are still very demanding to perform. The French now also began to cultivate violins as solo and chamber instruments, resulting for example in the concertos and sonatas of Jean-Marie Leclair.

The mid-eighteenth century

With the new ideals of the Enlightenment came a period of deep changes in music. The *viol* instruments had nearly lapsed into oblivion, so violin instruments and the double bass were used universally: for chamber music, in orchestras, and by solo players. During the days of "gallant" and "sentimental" music, violins remained indispensable. Among the great solo contributors were two Bohemians working in Germany – Franz Benda and Johann Stamitz.

Italy gives way

Just after 1750 appeared the epoch-making violin schools of Geminiani and Leopold Mozart. Important teaching institutes arose in Paris and later in Brussels, Leipzig and Vienna. The Italian dominance was instantly broken, and several of the leading violin-builders would thenceforth be found in Paris: Nicolas Lupot, Jean-Baptiste Vuillaume, and various members of their families. They were still faithful to Stradivari's models, but France's late start did not prevent it from becoming one of the pioneer violin countries as the eighteenth century drew to a close.

This did not mean that Italy had ceased to yield talent. Pietro Nardini and Giovanni Battista Viotti upheld the tradition as composers and starring violinists. The country's proud heritage ended with one of the greatest virtuosi of all time: Niccolò Paganini.

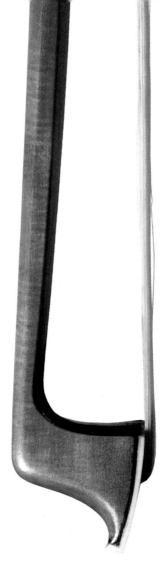

Isaac Stern, one of the greatest violinists of our time

Trend-setting violinists in Central Europe were now Ludwig Spohr and Ferdinand David – followed by Joseph Joachim and Leopold Auer. About 1820, Spohr also introduced the chin rest, which most violinists use; it is fastened around the purfling, and does not touch the belly of the resonance box. The Belgian-French school produced many brilliant musicians, such as Henri Vieuxtemps, Eugène Ysaÿe and Henri Marteau, Henri Wieniawski of Poland, and Pablo de Sarasate from Spain. They were all composers as well.

The combined role of a creative and reproductive musician has become ever more rare during our century. World-famous violinists like Jascha Heifetz, Nathan Milstein, David Oistrach, Yehudi Menuhin, Arthur Grumiaux, Isaac Stern – and currently Itzhak Perlman and Pinchas Zukerman – did not gain recognition with their own music, but by interpreting the works of others.

The bow

A violin bow may seem to be of simple construction, with its bunch of horsehair stretched between the ends of a wooden stick. But its design and properties are crucial for the sound of the music. Some players claim that the bow is even more important than the instrument!

Early violins were played with the bows which had previously rubbed on the fiddle and rebec. Their sticks were thick and curved outward, sometimes almost semicircular. The horsehair was narrow and not very taut, although its tension could be varied with the thumb while playing. Later, bows began to be adapted for the characteristics of new instruments. The seventeenth-century bow acquired a straight, or only slightly convex, shape. Its tip turned inward, and the horsehair was fixed at the grip end to a protruding wooden piece, the *frog*. Bows were usually 45-55 cm (17-22 inches) long.

While the instruments attained their final form around 1700, apart from subsequent reconstructions (see below), the bow continued its evolution for nearly a hundred years more. The technically advanced music of Tartini and his contemporaries led to a search for new qualities in the bow. Manufacturers made the rod longer and more flexible, and increased the horsehair's breadth considerably. Nonetheless, for some time, requirements in different parts of Europe were so distinctive that a universal type of bow was scarcely desirable. The French needed a short, robust bow for their ballet; Central Europe the old type which, occasionally, was a bit convex for clear articulation of polyphony; and Italy a long, flexible bow for a singing tone and the use of new bowing techniques.

Tourte's revolution

Thus, the design of bows took a long time to become more uniform. Experiments were made in several countries, and the best bows proved to be those of François Tourte. Having tested many lengths, shapes, materials, kinds of balance and so on, he presented in about 1780 a new bow that had little in common with its ancestors. This was eighty years after Stradivari had built an ideal violin. Tourte's bows have endured for two hundred years and, today, they rank among the most coveted of all.

Tourte made the stick thinner, and therefore more flexible. It was tapered toward the tip, and curved in a novel way – in towards the horsehair. Its length was increased to about 75 cm (29 inches) for the violin, and somewhat less for the larger instruments. As a material, he chose Brazilian pernambuco wood. Diverse methods of changing the horsehair's tension had been used before. The most recent was a screw mechanism that could slide the frog gradually forward or backward. Tourte adopted this method, and so have all later bows.

The new bows should be viewed in the light of social trends at that time, when music expanded from the aristocracy and the court into public concerts for the middle class. Large concert halls demanded more powerful playing, so that the instruments' sound could reach out and, in solo roles, be heard above the impressive strength of the orchestra.

The viola's size is not standardized like the violin's. It may vary by up to 10 cm (4 inches) between different violas.

Many ways of playing

What made the violin instruments so successful were their tonal beauty and their fabulous many-sidedness. The range of expression is enormous and can be suited to each player's personality. The tone can be varied with subtle shadings, and the means of articulation are numerous indeed. One can, for example, play in parts with *double stops* or *triple stops*, or switch between bowing and a plucked *pizzicato*, and so on.

The bow is handled in many ways, besides the usual *up-stroke* and *down-stroke*. Among other frequent techniques are:

- *legato* (united), a series of notes within one continuous bow movement;
- *staccato*, clearly distinguishing the notes;
- *détaché*, a series of separately bowed notes;
- *tremolo* (trembling), a note's quick repetition with alternate strokes up and down;
- *martellato* (hammering), with emphatic strokes at the point of the bow;
- *spiccato*, with short bouncy strokes at the middle of the bow;
- *ricochet*, when the bow is "thrown" at the string to rebound sharply.

In addition, one can play *sul ponticello* (next to the bridge), which gives a hard but crisp sound – or *col legno*, when the stick instead of the horsehair is pulled, or struck, against the strings. As a special effect, *flageolet* notes are cre-

ated by cautiously pressing a finger against a string at a simple fraction (1/2, 1/3 and so on) of its length. The bow then makes that part resonate, yielding one of the overtones. These have a thin, glassy or flute-like sound (the flageolet was a little flute).

Ever since the seventeenth century, the tone has commonly been damped by fastening a little wooden fork, or mute, onto the bridge. This suppresses the overtones in particular, yielding a softer sound.

Reconstructions

Whereas most other orchestral instruments have a lifetime of a few decades, a first-class string instrument can serve generation after generation of players. Violin instruments and double basses from the seventeenth and eighteenth centuries are the pride of many orchestras. Here and there, treasures of the later sixteenth century are still being used! But all of the old instruments in an orchestra have been rebuilt to meet the ideals of a later age – primarily the need for greater brilliance and tonal range. The neck has grown longer, and the fingerboard is not only longer but also angled slightly backward, so that a larger part of the string can be exploited. The bridge has been raised, while the sound post and bass bar are strengthened to resist the higher string tension.

If Signore Stradivari could see what has happened to the fruits of his genius, he might well be shocked. Yet the million-dollar value of his and Guarneri's instruments is partly due to the fact that they have been able to tolerate such reconstruction without losing their special quality. In their own time, Stainer's Austrian violins were often more expensive, but his and Amati's have not proved as adaptable to Romantic and modern demands for power and shining sound.

The meanings of development

When we speak of changing ideals in instrument-making, we often use terms such as "development" and "improvement". These have no absolute meaning, however, but are related to each period's tastes and ways of expression and composition. A violin, if built or rebuilt according to our preferences today, is naturally suited to playing a work like Sibelius' violin concerto, but not ideal for the concertos of Bach or Mozart. And regardless of how superior in quality, a "Cremonese" in its original condition is as inadequate for Tchaikovsky's and Bartók's concertos as it is perfect for those of Vivaldi.

In the old days, instruments were needed only for works by the player's own contemporaries. A wide spectrum of concert music from different periods, which we take for granted, did not arise before the nineteenth century. That it cannot all be played on the same instruments is hardly surprising. In recent de-

cades, special ensembles for Baroque and Vienna classicism have sprung up, and we are already able to hear Brahms' symphonies played with the kinds of instruments that he heard. The use of gut strings may diminish the sound's glitter, but it adds the warm lustre which was a hallmark of Romantic music.

Similarly, the bows of Tourte and later manufacturers are not objectively superior to earlier types. Everything depends on the aspects of playing and expression that one wants to emphasize. On older bows, the lower tension enables each note to be clearly "rounded in". Tones do not merge together in the seamless *legato* which was cultivated later. Thus, a long Tourte bow can be disadvantageous for playing Baroque music, if clear articulation is desired.

Beyond the violin

Until now, we have concentrated on the violin's birth and growth. Much of its history is shared by the viola and cello – its close relatives – and a fair amount by the double bass as well. Consequently these instruments will be discussed in lesser detail. It should be kept in mind that smaller instruments are generally easier to play, not least because the notes lie closer together on the strings. With greater size, the grip has to be wider, something that affects mobility as well as fingering. But this does not deny us the pleasure of occasionally hearing stupendous virtuoso passages even from a double bass!

The viola

The three upper strings on a viola are tuned like the three lower ones on a violin, whereas the fourth string is tuned a fifth deeper. Music for the viola is usually written in the alto clef, except that the treble clef is employed for the highest notes.

Although violas developed in close association with violins, there are significant differences. First, their size has never been standardized, as was done by Stradivari with violins. Today their length still varies within nearly a decimeter (4 inches). This is because their deep tonal range tends, for acoustic reasons, to require a large body, while a smaller one is urged by the practical need to fit the instrument between the player's chin and hand. Originally the body was made so large at times that few musicians could play on it.

Hence, the viola is a compromise, although self-respecting players hesitate to admit it. In any case, the "shrunken" dimensions result in a sound with less brilliance than either the violin's or the cello's, and the viola has never become a popular solo instrument. Despite this, its dimensions have given it an unmistakable character of profound sonority, reminiscent of a deep contralto voice. Not seldom, other string players say that the viola is actually their secret favourite!

Flagging interest

Enthusiasm for the violin is eternal, but the viola lost many admirers from the mid-1600s until the late 1700s. In orchestras, it often had to be content with doubling other instruments. Ever fewer musicians specialized in it, and the builders received scant orders for new violas. Only a dozen examples by Stradivari survive, in contrast to some fifty cellos and more than 500 violins. The decline spun into a vicious circle, and even the violas which did see light were built so small that they could easily be handled by ordinary violinists.

We should be grateful to those occasional brave musicians who fought for the viola's intrinsic value. They brought forth a number of eighteenth-century compositions which still belong to the instrument's basic repertoire: concertos by Telemann, Jan Vanhal and Carl Stamitz, as well as Mozart's *sinfonia concertante* for violin and viola. The

latter work became a watershed; during the years after it appeared, both Mozart and Haydn began to exploit the viola's individuality in their string quartets. Gluck did the same in orchestral music.

Elsewhere, however, interesting roles for the viola in orchestral music remained rare for the rest of that century. Beethoven sometimes used the viola group more independently, as in certain sections of his third and seventh symphonies.

Reviving the viola

A real change was initiated by Berlioz. In 1834, for a Stradivari viola owned by Paganini, he composed the program symphony *Harold in Italy* with a viola solo throughout. But Paganini never played it, and apparently had no success as a viola soloist. Berlioz continued to lend the viola great importance in both his music and his famous treatise on instrumentation. He also campaigned for better teaching of the viola, and for larger instruments than the usual ones. In his wake followed Wagner, who often used the viola group to advantage in his opera scores.

Brahms excluded all violins from his second orchestra serenade, leaving the violas to bear the melody. His appreciation of the viola's dark tone is shown by several works of chamber music as well. In Mahler's symphonies, the violas are frequently given prominent parts. Even the French impressionists, before World War I, were charmed by the viola. An entirely new awareness of the instrument's benefits and possibilities in the orchestra had arisen, and it was at last taken seriously.

The solo repertoire

On the other hand, significant solo music for the viola was still scarce. Except *Harold in Italy*, a *Gran Sonata* by

Paganini, and Strauss' *Don Quixote* (where the viola has an *obbligato* part), almost no internationally renowned orchestral work of this kind exists from the nineteenth century. Since then, the situation has improved dramatically. Numerous composers of merit have created fine solo works with orchestra. Several of them have been excellent viola players, while others were inspired by leading soloists such as Lionel Tertis and William Primrose, both from Great Britain. This pioneer work is currently being carried

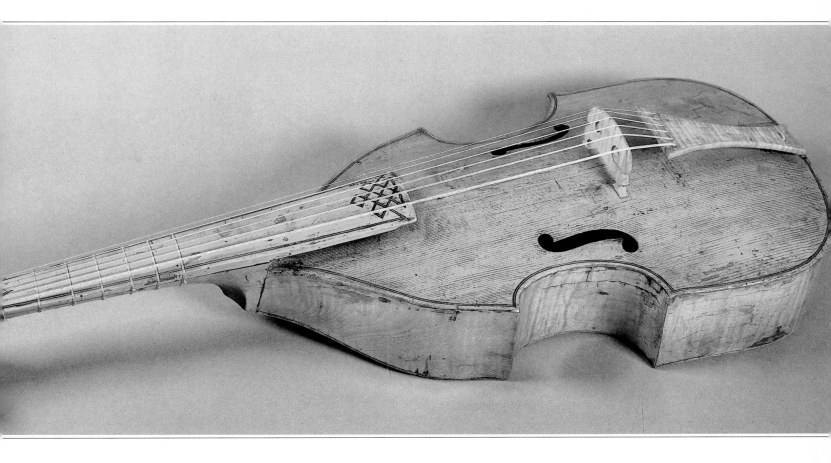

The viola d'amore is one of the violin's many ancestors. This treble version was made by Antonio Ciciliano in Venice around 1600.

on by many excellent musicians.

The viola d'amore

Symphony orchestras seldom include the "love viol". Like the woodwind instruments with similar names, it is characterized by a mild tone. Actually it belongs to the viol family, but it has no frets and, from the beginning, was held against the shoulder or, later, the chin. Normally it has from five to seven strings, and there are additional sym-

pathetic strings under the fingerboard, running through small holes in the bridge.

During the seventeenth and eighteenth centuries, the *viola d'amore* was quite popular and received many compositions, mainly in Italy and Germany, for example by Vivaldi and Bach. After the Baroque period, it virtually disappeared. Yet in the past century it has been revived by, among others, Strauss and Hindemith.

The cello

The four strings on a violoncello are tuned to the same notes as a viola's, but an octave deeper. Its notation is usually in the bass clef, although its range is so great that the tenor or treble clef is used at the very top. Its name means "little *violone*", the latter being an old term for the double bass and signifying "large viol"!

While the viola is, for practical reasons, too small, the cello represents a closer adaptation of the violin's form to

a deeper tonal register. Yet here, too, modifications have occurred. The body is over twice as long and wide as a violin's, but the ribs are no less than four times as high, about 12 cm (4.7 inches). The volume is therefore much more than proportionally larger, giving low tones a lot of resonance, so the instrument acquires a warm and singing quality in both the tenor and baritone ranges.

The cello's bridge is proportionally higher than a violin's, the neck somewhat shorter. Its bow is more robust, but only slightly shorter than that of a violin. In contrast to the *viol*, which is held between the knees, a cello is supported (since the mid-nineteenth century) on the floor by a stand, the *end pin*, extended beneath the lower edge and adjusted to the desired length.

A chequered career

The cello was, in the first place, a successor of the *viola da braccio* in bass form, whose five strings it adopted and kept into the eighteenth century. Its possibilities were not clearly recognized for a long time, doubtless because the *viol* was so widespread and popular. The Baroque *thorough-bass group* gave it a chance during the early 1600s, and throughout that century it was used primarily in the same supportive role.

Towards the year 1700, composers began to write more individual music for the cello. Corelli utilized its melo-diousness in an almost operatic way. His pupil Pietro Locatelli, also a pioneer of string playing, followed suit and – like two other Italians, Alessandro Scarlatti and Antonio Vivaldi – took great advantage of the cello's soloistic qualities. A figure of significance for its further progress was the cello virtuoso known as Franciscello (Francesco Alborea).

At the court of Köthen in Germany, the musical director, Bach, wrote six suites for the solo cello around 1720. Little may he have realized that this music would still be the basis of the instrument's solo repertoire 250 years later. When a present-day cellist has performed a solo concerto and needs an encore, he usually picks a movement from some suite by Bach. A cello concerto by his son Carl Philipp Emanuel is among the best from the middle of that century.

Classicism

During the later 1700s, the most influential cellists were Luigi Boccherini, an Italian working in Paris and Madrid (with at least ten solo concertos), Bernhard Romberg in Germany, and the French brothers Jean Pierre and Jean Louis Duport. Exploiting the clever technique of Franciscello, the latter pair had a notable impact on Central European cello music during their many years in Berlin. Mozart and Beethoven learned much from them about the instrument's possibilities, as can be seen for instance in Beethoven's sonatas.

Another important cellist was Anton Kraft, for whom Beethoven composed the solo part in his triple concerto (with piano and violin). Earlier, Haydn had written the second of his two preserved cello concertos under Kraft's inspiration. However, this work may have been intended for a six-stringed instrument called the *baryton* (related to the bass viol), on which it is considered easier to play.

Romanticism

Thus, the Vienna classicists devoted a good deal of attention to the cello in terms of solo and chamber music. As an orchestral instrument, though, it was only occasionally given a leading role. In this respect it became much more popular during the nineteenth century. Examples of its symphonic use occur, for example, in Beethoven's fifth symphony and Schubert's "unfinished" symphony. We find another method of application in the solo quartet which opens Rossini's *William Tell* overture.

In the mid-1800s, composers such as Schumann, Liszt, Wagner and Brahms, and French opera masters like Gounod, Bizet and Massenet, constantly fueled the cello section with cantilenas and sonorous chords in all sorts of combinations. Travelling virtuosi like François Servais from Belgium, Alfredo Piatti from Italy, and David Popper from Bohemia wrote concertos, but mainly inspired other musicians and composers to devote themselves to the cello.

Solo concerts

One of the best solo works for the cello from the mid-1800s is Schumann's concerto. During that century's last three decades, a number of the most popular repertoire works arose: Saint-Saëns' first concerto, Tchaikovsky's *Rococo Variations*, Brahms' double concerto (for cello and violin), Dvořák's concerto, and Strauss' *Don Quixote* (for cello and viola). These were followed by thin years. After 1910 came Bloch's rhapsody *Schelomo* and Elgar's concerto; in the 1930s, that of Prokofiev (later greatly revised); concertos by Hindemith and Khachaturian during the 1940s, and by Shostakovich and Walton in the 1950s.

Since then, composers have regularly written for the cello, with many excellent solo works. These have often been motivated by leading cellists, who abound in our century. They range from Pablo Casals of Spain, Gregor Piatigorsky and Leonard Rose in the United States, Pierre Fournier and Paul Tortelier in France, Mstislav Rostropovich from Russia, and Jacqueline Du Pré in England, to younger stars such as Lynn Harrell in America and Yo-Yo Ma.

The double bass

The double bass is the violin family's least typical member. Its most conspicuous features are perhaps the tapering "shoulders" and distinctive tuning pegs.

As its background differs somewhat from that of other string instruments in the orchestra, the double bass cannot be unreservedly called a violin instrument. Its very appearance shows some divergent features. The body's upper part does not end in straight "shoulders", but tapers off and merges into the neck. The bottom is less arched than the cello's and, on some instruments, is flat with an upper beveling into the neck. We may recognize certain details from the *viol* family, which in fact was an ancestor of the double bass. However, there are no frets, the sound holes are f-shaped, the pegbox terminates in a carved scroll, and the strings are usually four in number – all of which characterize the violin family.

The thick strings are given extreme tension, which makes the normal type of conical tuning pegs inadequate. Instead, the pegbox is equipped with worm-gear tuning devices. The instrument is supported on the floor by an adjustable peg.

Notes for the double bass are written an octave higher than they sound. Thus, it is a transposing instrument. The notation is done chiefly in the bass clef, but the higher register calls for the tenor or even the treble clef.

Double bassists in concert

Form, tuning, and bows

The shape of the double bass has never become uniform. During its first centuries, many forms and sizes were experimented with, ranging from miniature to enormous. The number of strings varied from three to six, although four have been normal since the 1700s. Even today, it can be found in forms resembling that of the violin – which are preferred in Italy, the violin's heartland – as well as in versions resembling the viol.

The tuning, too, was long diverse. Just two hundred years ago, a unified tuning was decided upon, but it did not imitate the fifths of other string instruments. The notes being much farther apart on its strings, these were instead tuned in fourths. The lowest note is an E, although this has sometimes proved impractical: the double bass group in an orchestra often plays together with the cellos (an octave below), which go down to C. Therefore, since the later nineteenth century, double basses are also made with a low fifth string, tuned in C (or B). In many present-day orchestras, half of the bass players use five-stringed instruments. The alternative in some places is to use a mechanism for lengthening the usual E string. A well-known orchestral example with these extra low notes is the introduction to Stravinsky's *The Firebird*.

The bow used on a double bass is another sign of its dual origin. In Central and Eastern Europe, the bow is held obliquely underhand, as on the *viol*. This is called "German bowing". Yet in most other countries, an overhand bow-hold, known as "French bowing", is employed – as on violin instruments. How the bow is held is largely a matter of tradition. Formerly each orchestra cultivated its own style, but nowadays the different techniques are increasingly coexistent.

The double bass in orchestras

It was in the early eighteenth century that double basses became established for orchestral music. Bach still called the instrument a *violone* (large viol), although this meant various types of very low string instruments. Until the early 1800s, there was little independent use of double basses. Normally the bass player had to be content with doubling the cello an octave lower – often playing from the same part, as the double bass is a transposing instrument and sounds an octave lower than written. This accompaniment is still frequent in Beethoven's works. On the other hand, he realized that both of these instruments had greater potential, as can be heard in the trio section of the scherzo in his fifth

symphony, and in the great recitative in the finale of his ninth.

The double bass has never matched the cello in melodic independence. Nonetheless, its lower register plays a vital role in nearly all orchestral music of the past two centuries. It lays a solid foundation for the string section and for the orchestra as a whole. Just as a piccolo can give the strings or brass extra brilliance, the double basses colour and deepen the timbre in the lower register, when combined with either individual or grouped instruments. Sometimes they join forces with the tuba, bass clarinet or bassoons; with equal grace, they can accompany lighter-sounding instruments. Especially enjoyable is the double bass's sonorous *pizzicato*, which can lend a rhythmical profile to otherwise static music.

All ways of playing and types of bowing that have been mentioned for violin instruments are also possible on the double bass. However, since the span – the distance between notes on strings – is so wide, it is difficult to perform them as quickly and fluently on a double bass.

Solo music

There are more solo concertos for double bass than the average listener may be aware of. Unfortunately, they tend to be written by leading bass players rather than important composers. As a result, they are designed to display virtuosity and a vast range of playing techniques, seldom with real artistic content. It is a

curious fact, though, that Mozart composed a concert aria during his last year – entitled *Per questa bella mano* – for bass singer, double bass and orchestra!

Among the principal solo works from older times are the concertos by Karl Dittersdorf, Domenico Dragonetti, and Giovanni Bottesini (who was also an important conductor and presented the world première of Verdi's *Aida* in Cairo). There are, in addition, double concertos by Dittersdorf (for viola and bass) and Bottesini (violin and bass). Otherwise, bass players may perform arrangements of viola and cello concertos. Even such a work as Dvořák's cello concerto has been set for the double bass!

Perhaps the best-known of all concertos was written in 1902 by Serge Koussevitzky, the Russian who later became world-famous as a conductor and was himself a practising double bass player. Since World War II, this instrument – like others on the fringe in solo contexts – has seen a steadily growing repertoire. Concertos well worth playing have come, for example, from Eduard Tubin and Einojuhani Rautavaara in Sweden and Finland respectively, and from Gunther Schuller in America.

Tonal ranges of the commonest orchestral instruments

The lowest tone is generally standard, although most woodwind instruments can be played with short extra tubes to go a half or whole tone lower than shown here. But the highest tone (except from a harp or kettledrum) depends on the musician's skill, so the table shows only very rough limits. For the alto saxophone and double bass, the highest octaves (marked with lines) are used almost exclusively for solo playing.

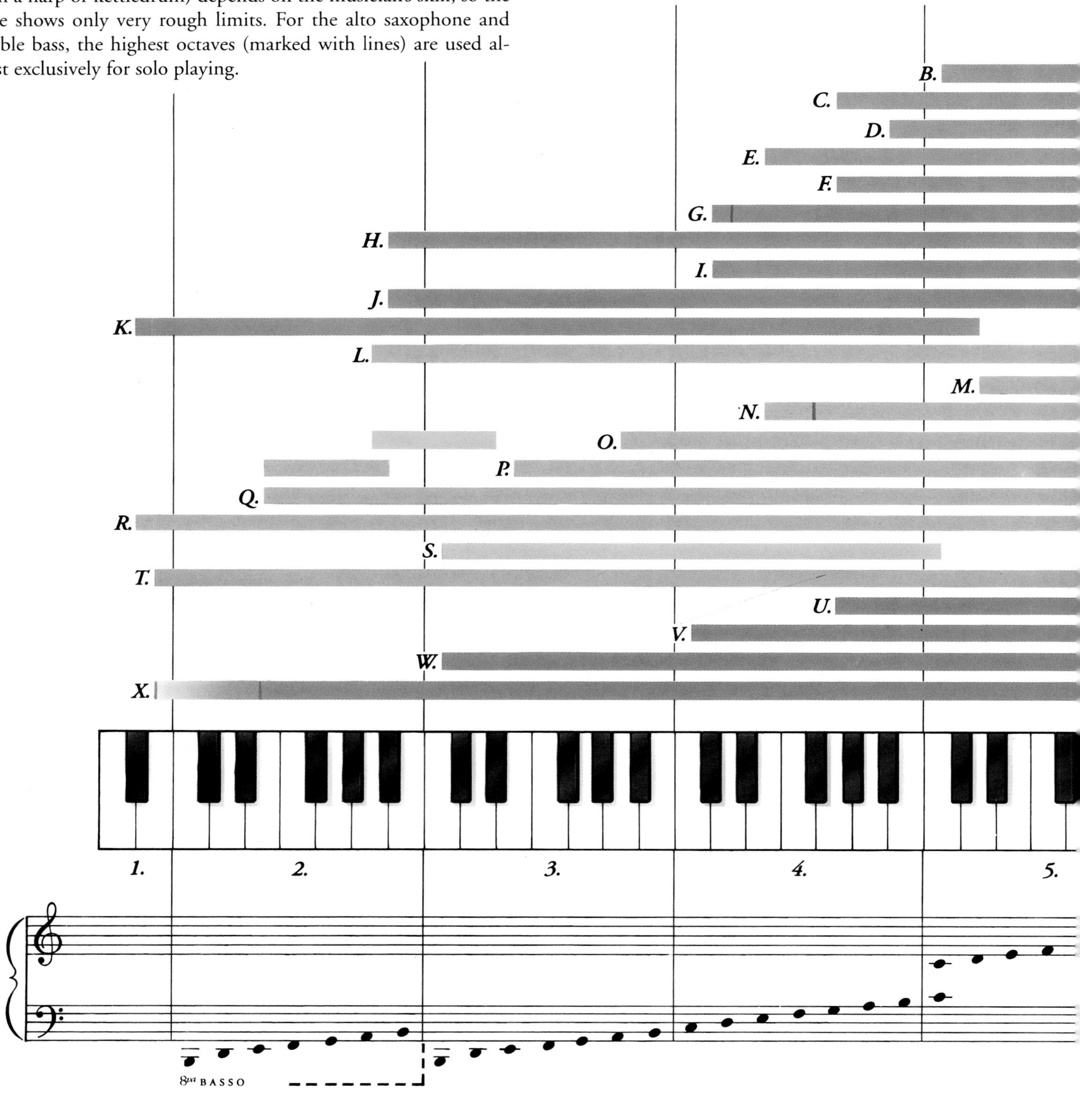

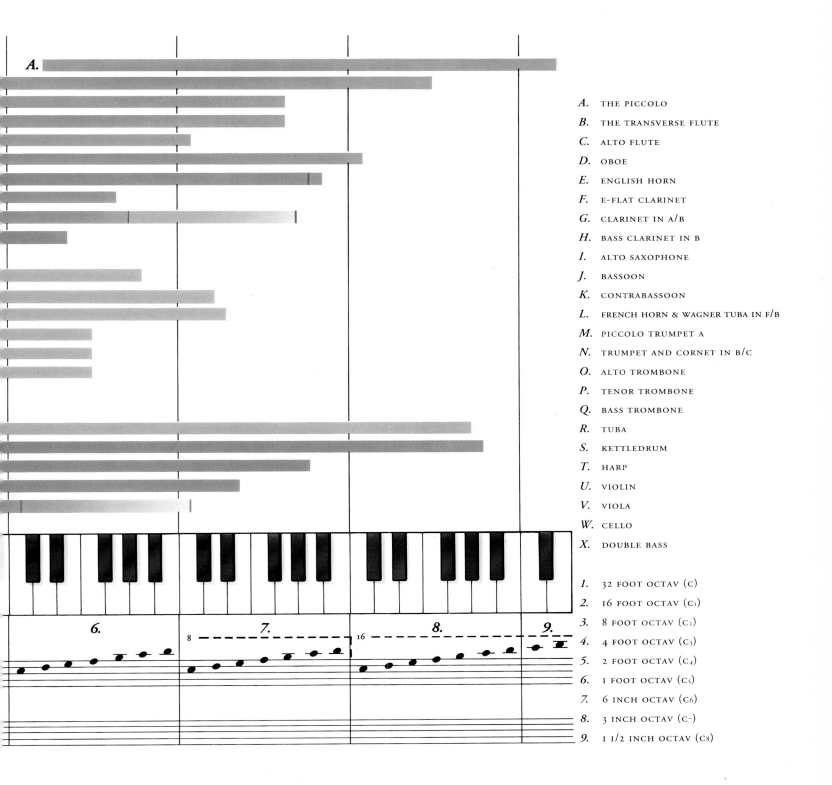

A. THE PICCOLO

B. THE TRANSVERSE FLUTE

C. ALTO FLUTE

D. OBOE

E. ENGLISH HORN

F. E-FLAT CLARINET

G. CLARINET IN A/B

H. BASS CLARINET IN B

I. ALTO SAXOPHONE

J. BASSOON

K. CONTRABASSOON

L. FRENCH HORN & WAGNER TUBA IN F/B

M. PICCOLO TRUMPET A

N. TRUMPET AND CORNET IN B/C

O. ALTO TROMBONE

P. TENOR TROMBONE

Q. BASS TROMBONE

R. TUBA

S. KETTLEDRUM

T. HARP

U. VIOLIN

V. VIOLA

W. CELLO

X. DOUBLE BASS

1. 32 FOOT OCTAV (C)

2. 16 FOOT OCTAV (C₁)

3. 8 FOOT OCTAV (C₂)

4. 4 FOOT OCTAV (C₃)

5. 2 FOOT OCTAV (C₄)

6. 1 FOOT OCTAV (C₅)

7. 6 INCH OCTAV (C₆)

8. 3 INCH OCTAV (C-)

9. 1 1/2 INCH OCTAV (C₈)

INDEX OF SUBJECTS

234

Illustration sources

ALBERT HALL, LONDON:
77

BOOSEY & HAWKES, LONDON:
134, 135, 138, 146, 147, 213, 215, 216, 226-227

ENAR MERKEL RYDBERG, STOCKHOLM:
83

ET ARCHIVE, LONDON:
16-17, 18-19, 22-23, 24-25, 26, 27 bottom, 30, 31, 32-33, 36-37, 43, 44-45, 46, 47, 48, 50, 52, 54-55, 56 bottom,
57 bottom, 58-59, 60-61, 62-63, 64, 66 right, 68, 70, 71 bottom, 75, 91, 92, 94, 95, 96 right, 97, 98, 123, 162, 205

GOTHENBURG CONCERT HALL:
100, 114-115, 186, 217, 218, 220, 228

HÅKAN BERG, GOTHENBURG:
87, 125, 133, 140, 142 centre, 144, 154-155, 158, 160-161, 168-169, 170-171, 173, 190,
192-193, 196, 198, 199, 206-207, 210, 217

HULTON DEUTSCH COLLECTION, LONDON:
80-81

IBL BILDBYRÅ, LJUNGBYHED (SWEDEN):
42, 49, 73, 78-79, 82, 120, 222-223

INGEMAR JERNBERG, GOTHENBURG:
121, 130, 136-137, 145, 146, 151, 152, 163, 174, 178-179, 185, 197, 200-201, 202, 221

JAN ALM, GOTHENBURG:
14, 35

KARI JANTZÉN, GOTHENBURG:
109

KONGELIGE BIBLIOTEK, COPENHAGEN:
40-41, 99 (EMIL HARTMAN: SYMPHONY NO.4, OP. 49)

MUSIKHISTORISK MUSEUM, COPENHAGEN:
21

MUSIKMUSEET (STATENS MUSIKSAMLINGAR), STOCKHOLM:
67, 69, 71 top, 72, 82, 84, 142 bottom

SIEGFRIED LAUTERWASSER, ÜBERLINGEN(GERMANY):
12-13, 15, 74-75, 88-89, 92-93, 101, 102 , 103, 105, 106, 107, 110-111 top, 224-225

STATENS KONSTMUSEER, STOCKHOLM:
28-29, 208-209

TEKNISKA MUSEET, STOCKHOLM:
99

ULF SÖDERQVIST, GOTHENBURG:
20, 24, 27 top, 29, 34, 39, 40, 51, 53, 56 top, 57 top, 62, 65, 66 left and middle, 76, 90, 93, 96 left, 104, 108,
110-111 bottom, 117, 118, 122, 124, 127 bottom, 129, 132, 136, 137, 139, 141, 142 top, 143, 149,
152, 156, 157 top, 159 bottom, 160, 162, 166, 167, 172, 176, 182, 183, 184, 191, 194-195, 203, 204, 212, 214

YAMAHA (SCANDINAVIA, GOTHENBURG/HAMAMATSU, JAPAN):
113, 119, 126-127, 128, 131, 148, 150, 152, 153, 157 bottom, 159, 164, 177, 180, 185, 188-189

INSTRUMENTS PHOTOGRAPHED BY HÅKAN BERG WERE LOANED BY
BULLER & BÅNG, PROCURA, WAIDELE MUSIK, AND YAMAHA (ALL IN GOTHENBURG).